NEWSLETTER SOURCEBOOK

second edition

mark beach *and* **elaine floyd**

WRITER'S DIGEST BOOKS
CINCINNATI, OHIO

acknowledgments

Gallery-style books like this are only possible with the cooperation of hundreds of people. Mark would like to thank the many editors across the world who've contributed newsletters for this and previous editions. Elaine would like to thank many of her colleagues who provided not only examples, but detailed explanations of why they designed their newsletters the way they did.

Both Mark and Elaine would like to thank Dawn Korth, our fearless editor at Writer's Digest Books. In addition, many of the newsletters shown in this book are winners of a design contest from The Newsletter Clearinghouse. Sincere gratitude goes to Paul Swift and Howard Penn Hudson of The Newsletter Clearinghouse for supplying back issues of their publication featuring contest winners, *Newsletter Design.*

Mark and Elaine also want to recognize and celebrate the design influence of expert newsletter design trainer, Polly Pattison. Polly's design principles, along with the work of her thousands of students, touch every page of this book.

And finally, tremendous appreciation goes to Susan Todd, Elaine's left brain, and Kathleen Ryan, Mark's right brain, for doing much of the real work on this book. Even with all of this wonderful help, we have decided to keep our own names on the cover. Authors will be authors.

Mark Beach
Manzanita, Oregon

Elaine Floyd
St. Louis, Missouri

Newsletter Sourcebook. Copyright © 1998 by Mark Beach and Elaine Floyd. Manufactured in China. All rights reserved. No part of this book may be reproduced in any form or by any electronic or mechanical means including information storage and retrieval systems without permission in writing from the publisher, except by a reviewer, who may quote brief passages in a review. Published by Writer's Digest Books, an imprint of F&W Publications, Inc., 1507 Dana Avenue, Cincinnati, Ohio, 45207. (800) 289-0963. Second edition.

Visit our Web site at www.writersdigest.com for information on more resources for writers.

To receive a free weekly E-mail newsletter delivering tips and updates about writing and about Writer's Digest products, send an E-mail with the message "Subscribe Newsletter" to newsletter-request@writersdigest.com, or register directly at our Web site at www.writersdigest.com.

03 02 01 00 99   6 5 4 3 2

Library of Congress Cataloging-in-Publication Data

Beach, Mark.
    Newsletter sourcebook / Mark Beach and Elaine Floyd. — 2nd ed.
       p.   cm.
    Includes index.
    ISBN 0-89879-869-8 (pbk. : alk. paper)
    1. Graphic design (Typography) —United States.   2. Newsletters—United States—Design.
I. Floyd, Elaine, 1961– . II. Title.
Z246.B42 1998
686.2'252—dc21   97-42969
                                                               CIP

Content edited by Dawn Korth
Production edited by Patrick Souhan
Designed by Brian Roeth

In addition to *Newsletter Sourcebook*, Mark Beach is author of *Editing Your Newsletter, Getting It Printed, Papers for Printing* and *Graphically Speaking*, guides to graphic arts production that are used throughout North America for corporate training and classroom instruction. Mark can be reached at his e-mail address: mbeach@pdx.oneworld.com

Elaine Floyd is president of St. Louis-based Newsletter Resources. She helps businesses, associations and nonprofit organizations implement new technology for print, e-mail and website communications, including computer templates and preprinted newsletter papers. In addition to *Newsletter Sourcebook*, Elaine is author of the books *Marketing with Newsletters, Advertising From the Desktop* and *Making Money Writing Newsletters*. She publishes a newsletter website (www.newsletterinfo.com) and can be reached at her e-mail address: nlthatsell@aol.com

table of contents

YOUR GRAPHIC LOOK

Establish a look that suits your organization and your mission. Help readers identify your publication at a glance. Make reading easy and information memorable.

NAMEPLATES

Create a nameplate that grabs attention and invites readers. Tell who you are and why people need the information you provide. Identify your organization and purpose. Evoke a strong image.

BUILDING PAGES

Follow a few simple guidelines to make your newsletter content easy to read and remember. Put your most important information in the places readers see first. Make visuals and captions count.

TYPE

Promote efficient reading on screen or on paper. Build interest and create emphasis by using type wisely. Use the results of readability research to boost the impact of your text.

ESSENTIALS

Use four visual elements to make your publication effective and distinctive: mailing panel, masthead, calendar and contents box. Anticipate reader questions and give them instant information. Identify and include the essentials.

YOUR GRAPHIC LOOK

Information is a buyer's market. Your newsletter competes for attention with television, the Internet and the Web, newspapers, magazines and other newsletters.

Effective newsletters hit the recycle bin in days—instead of in seconds. To command attention, they must deserve respect. In other words, effective newsletters:

- look suited to their publisher
- are easy to identify and remember
- make reading easy

Whether you produce a newsletter for employees, customers or members, the way your publication looks tells readers about you. Type, colors, paper and other design elements work together to convey your image, whether it's conservative, friendly or authoritative.

Readers judge your organization not only by the information you present, but also by how you present that information. Trendy clip art may not suit a newsletter from a bank. Primary colors work well for a day care publication. Large typography serves readers of a retirement newsletter. Make sure that your graphic look fits your organization.

In addition to shaping readers' judgment, your graphic look helps readers identify your publication at a glance. Keep your nameplate, format and especially the colors you use the same, issue after issue, to ensure instant recognition. Also make sure that your newsletter design harmonizes with business forms, letterhead and other documents produced by your organization. Consistent design builds instant recognition and dependable recall.

Design consistency has the added benefit of saving you time and money. After developing your graphic look, stick with it until you have strong reasons to change it. Solve design problems once every few years, and then concentrate on the content of each issue.

Good design makes reading easy. The most important information appears in locations that readers see first. Words and pictures are carefully blended. Type and content match readers' abilities.

The following five pages show how several designers developed successful graphic looks. By putting the interests of their readers first, they produced newsletters that contribute to their organizations' missions.

New PRODUCTS

Ergonomically Correct Products from Copytek

Copytek Office Products continues to research ergonomic products to enhance productivity and reduce injury in the workplace. With multiple manufacturers in the marketplace making claims to be the "best" ergonomic solution, we feel it's important to align ourselves with products that truly are of high quality and meet the needs of today's workplace. One such company is MESA, producer of ergonomic computer/workspace accessories. MESA keyboard supports, palm rests, mouse trays, foot rests and other products meet current ergonomic

criteria (ANSI/BIFMA) and carry a lifetime warranty. Multiple product combinations and a local stocking program combined with exceptional pricing have made MESA a brand that Copytek is pleased to recommend to our customers. MESA products will provide you with the flexibility to create an ergonomic standards program that your organization can be proud of. MESA products available through Copytek include: keyboard supports; palm rests; mouse trays; and, foot rests. ■

Featured product: "The Professional" package (#M6180)

Package includes:

#M6130 fully articulating arm with all necessary functions including ball bearing slides for ease of movement, 25 degree positive/negative keyboard tilt, single knob control, 360 degree rotation and 6" height adjustment, lock out for keyboard.

#M6255 keyboard clamp that will accommodate up to 22" wide keyboards of any shape or depth securely.

#M6263 palm rest with the perfect density of foam support.

#M6300 adjustable mouse tray that can mount on clamp or under work surface.

#M6180 .... $229.00

Contact Copytek for more information on MESA products.

"Studio RTA" is a new line of value-priced highly flexible workstations for computer users.

Featured product: Studio RTA's Symmetrix Series 100

Our featured product this quarter is Studio RTA's "Symmetrix 100." This resourceful workstation is ideal for your multimedia needs. It's a highly flexible unit which offers many options to the user. Shelving, sliding keyboard shelf, and CPU holders can each be repositioned to either the left or the right of the station. It has a 30" x 60" surface, a 15" x 33" laser printer shelf and a slide-out keyboard shelf. The surface is reversible for choice of finish — in color combinations of pearwood/cherrywood reversible or black/granite reversible. The finish is a durable laminate, and the unit is supported by an all-steel base with a powder coated black finish. Laminated

privacy panel and integrated cord management system are included.

#10100 .... $275.99

③

Now available at Copytek: a CD that records

CD-Recordable technology (CDR) is more affordable and easier to use than before. With more CDR drive prices tions around the corner (there are many models under $1,000 – Copytek not carry the drives) CDR technology becoming more accessible to everyone.

The advantages to CDR are single disk can hold up to 650 that can be read by any CD ROM makes it a great medium for backup or archiving. However, many companies forms, graphic and photographic can all be recorded on CDR. In format lends itself to almost any application and can be a great scale sales and training presentation.

Unlike regular CD ROM store data using pits and lands physically carved into the CD by pressing, CDR drives create pits by ing the organic dyes that coat the face. It is "burned" into the disk so it will no longer reflect light. done, you can not erase or

CDR disks are available in (550MB) and 74 minute (650M and use a variety of dye layers and have a life rating of ten to ...

"The advantages to CDR are ... disk can hold up to 650 MB ... be read by any CD ROM player ..."

#15337 (650mb) 74 min ...

Repeat logo in nameplate

Copytek links the newsletter to the store by printing its company color (purple) as the newsletter's spot color. The Copytek logo forms part of the *Tek Files* nameplate design. The headline typestyle for all of the inside articles, including the reader survey on page 4, mimics the nameplate design. The survey further connects the newsletter to the business.

NAME *Tek Files*

PUBLISHER Copytek Office Products, Williston, Vermont

PURPOSE/AUDIENCE Service and marketing to customers

PRODUCTION/PRINTING Two-color on white 60# offset

FORMAT 8½" x 11"; four pages

DESIGN Copytek Office Products

NEW PRODUCTS AND OFFICE INFORMATION FROM COPYTEK

TEK files

VOLUME 1, NUMBER 1
JANUARY 1997

Introducing TEKfiles

Copytek Office Products is pleased to present you with our very first issue of "TEKfiles." This quarterly publication has been designed to inform you on the latest advancements and new products in the office products industry, and to show you all the great services that Copytek has to offer (eg. did you know that we offer free delivery of office supplies?). "TEKfiles" also acts as our SALE FLYER, highlighting for you what's on sale right now at Copytek. It's full of products designed to make life in your workplace easier. As always, we welcome feedback on our company and the services we provide – please see our "reader survey" for the chance to win a "Brownie Gram" from Joan & Annie's just by responding to our questionnaire.

Copytek Office Products Merges with Boise Cascade Office Products

On November 1, 1996, Copytek merged with Boise Cascade Office Products. Boise Cascade is a national office supply company that provides supplies to businesses nationwide, and is noted for their excellent customer service. The Vermont division of Boise Cascade will consist of the staff that was formerly McAuliffe (which became Boise Cascade one year ago), and Copytek. The staff at Copytek is excited about this change and looks forward to serving you under the new Boise name. The best part is that the people who you've come to know and trust at Copytek and McAuliffe are still here. Tim Williams, who was president of Copytek, has become General Manager of the Vermont Division of Boise. This arrangement will allow Tim to run things locally while having strong national backing. This all transcends into more customer benefits. To our customers both old and new, we offer you our sincerest thanks for your past and continued support.

Highlights to note about the merger:

1. The Xerox Division of Copytek has been spun off and formed a new company called Vermont Document Company. They are a full-service Xerox Agency located at 4049 Williston Road. Phone (802) 658-8225, Fax (802) 658-6917.
2. The former McAuliffe staff and the former Copytek staff have teamed up to offer service as Boise Cascade Office Products.
3. Beemer's Office Innovators of Plattsburgh, NY is the entire state of Vermont.
4. The Copytek retail stores in Williston, VT and Plattsburgh, NY will remain OPEN FOR BUSINESS! ■

Boise Cascade Office Products

COPYTEK Office Products • Taft Corners Commercial Park • Williston, Vermont 05495 • 1-800-639-3375 • FAX (802) 879-0438
BEEMER'S Office Innovators • 79 Hammond Lane • Plattsburgh, New York 12901 • 1-800-233-6487 • FAX (518) 563-2329

Vermont's ...

Since 1989, Copytek's 18,000 square foot retail store in Williston has been one of Vermont's best kept secrets. For one reason or another, many of our customers who do business with us by phone are unaware that we have such a spectacular facility. Tucked away in the one time "pastures" of Taft Corners, we are conveniently located just off Interstate 89 in Williston and offer a shopping environment that is truly unique.

Quality products and superior service are Copytek's hallmark. We have two floors devoted entirely to quality products such as: Vermont's largest selection of writing instruments, office supplies (from the basics to the hard-to-find), computer accessories, fine stationery, executive briefcases & leather accessories, greeting cards, gifts, and the largest and most complete selection of office furniture in the entire state – including computer furniture and home office furniture.

So whether you're seeking basic office supply or the most advanced ergonomic workspace, we have it all with a professional, friendly staff ready to provide you with solutions.

Copytek is open from 7:30am to 7:00pm Monday through Friday and 9am to 5pm Saturday. We are located in Taft Corners Commercial Park, where we have recently been joined by some other retailing legends including Toys R Us, Hannaford's, WalMart and Home Depot in January. Come shop or browse in an environment that is comfortable and interesting, and the service is exceptional. "Copytek...office products and a whole lot more!" ■

Community EVENTS

Holiday Spirit Shines at Copytek

Each year at holiday time, the employees at Copytek do their part to try to help those less fortunate. Here's what "holiday magic" was in store this year.

For Thanksgiving at the Sara Holbrook Community Center, a center for children and families in need, the employees of Copytek provided food for a Thanksgiving meal for a large family. For Christmas, employees were even more giving–providing holiday gifts for two entire families. For Women Helping Battered Women, Copytek employees provided holiday gifts for a family of six. And lastly, Copytek hosted

a Burlington Housing Authority "Giving Tree" in the retail store. Both Copytek employees and customers participated in this tree and bought gifts for several low income children and elderly people. A special thanks to our customers who took part in the "Giving Tree" and also to the South Burlington Lion's Club, whose generous donation helped us purchase many of the gifts.

And let's not overlook year-round giving. This year's Copytek United Way campaign employee participation was up 40%.

Happy New Year to all! ■

④

... and that the help and ... is tops!"

... staff is very customer ... oriented."

Just for thought...

"If you believe that you can, or if you believe you cannot, you are probably right."

-Mark Twain, American author

Reader SURVEY

We want to provide you with the best service available. To do that, we need to hear from you. Please take a moment to jot down any comments or ideas you may have that would improve our service to you. (Compliments are accepted too!)

Please return this by fax, mail, or with your next invoice to the attention of Linda Covelli. Responses received by February 14 will be entered into a drawing for a delicious Joan and Annie's "Brownie Gram".

GKTW News
Summer 1996

American Airlines, AMR Corp. Employee Ideas Generate Funding For "Park of Dreams"

Employees of American Airlines and its parent company, AMR Corp., will create even more magic at the Give Kids The World Village. A portion of the savings generated by employee ideas will go to build and maintain "The Park of Dreams," a completely wheelchair-accessible playground for children at the Village.

Robert L. Crandall, chairman and chief executive officer of American Airlines and AMR Corp. announced the $1 million commitment to the campaign on Feb. 1 to a crowd of almost 200 in front of the Castle of Miracles. The Park of Dreams, which is scheduled to open in mid-1997, will include an interactive water area, an animated miniature golf course and an outdoor amphitheater.

As part of the project, American will also fund trips for 50 families to stay at the Village through the Make-A-Wish Foundation. In May, 20 families from Texas,

American Airlines and AMR Corp. Chairman and CEO Robert L. Crandall enlisted the help of GKTW wish children Medley Wollenmann and Matthew Swinton along with Mickey and Minnie Mouse to unveil the rendering of the "Park of Dreams".

Oklahoma and Louisiana arrived at the Village from a special American Airlines "Dream Flight." The families participated in a special groundbreaking ceremony for the park.

"Give Kids The World touches more than 4,000 families a year, and we hope this new park can add a measure of joy to their lives," said Crandall, making the announcement.

"While the Village has lots of wonderful things, it will be more special with a playground that is fully accessible to all children, particularly those with physical

(continued on page 9)

Managing Director of IdeAAs in Action Bob Stoltz, AA Vice President of Operations Bob Baker, GKTW Vice Chairman Pam Landwirth and AA Senior Vice President of Corporate Services Tom Kiernan get ready to break ground for the Park of Dreams with Seaver Sewell (center, front) and his family on May 11.

Inside...
Perkins Family Restaurants corral support for GKTW with the "Round Up for Kids" with an enthusiastic campaign in April. Details on Page 2

BellSouth Mobility provides GKTW families free phones to stay in touch as they explore the vacation capital of the world. Story on Page 3

WDW Marathon and Fun Run Participants run! Recap on Page

Central Florida Village - photos

Children Delight at Daily Treasures Delivered By Gift-Giving Volunteers

a daily trek around the Village to leave
the children in the villas as well as ensur-
tors are stocked with snacks.

d sodas provided by Coca-Cola, milk and
by Publix Super Markets, lunchables pro-
yer, orange juice provided by Citrus
n from Albertson's. The volunteers also
s provided by Procter & Gamble and
Mars Corp.

dance for this program, please contact
Amy Jacobsen at (407) 396-1114.

GKTW Welcomes Robert Crandall, Ken Blanchard to Executive Advisory Board; Orlando Magic Coach Brian Hill, American Airlines VP Jaynne Allison to Board of Directors

Give Kids The World is pleased and proud to welcome Robert L. Crandall, chairman and chief executive officer of AMR Corporation and American Airlines, and Ken Blanchard, co-author of The One Minute Manager and noted speaker and consultant, to the executive advisory board of the organization. In addition, Brian Hill, head coach of the Orlando Magic basketball team, and Jaynne Allison, vice president of human resources for American Airlines, have accepted seats on the Give Kids The World Board of Directors.

Joining American Airlines in 1973, Crandall became the chairman and chief executive officer in 1985. He has been recognized in the marketing and aviation industry as a leader and innovator for accomplishments which include successful programs in both customer service and satisfaction and participative employee relations policies.

Blanchard includes among his clients a multitude of Fortune 500 companies for his unique approach to managing and developing people. His One Minute Manager Library has sold more than nine million copies and has been translated into more than 20 languages. Blanchard is chairman of Blanchard Training and Development,

Inc., a full-service management consulting and training company which he founded in 1979 with his wife Marjorie.

In his second and third seasons as head coach of the Orlando Magic, Brian Hill guided the team to consecutive division championships and a trip to the 1995 Finals. Hill joined the team during the 1990-91 season from the Atlanta Hawks. His extensive coaching career spans 24 years over a variety of levels, including high school, college, and professional teams.

As vice president of human resources for American Airlines, Allison oversees the actions of a 300 member department which devises, implements, tracks and evaluates policies affecting all 80,000 American Airlines employees worldwide. Allison first joined American in 1985 as an attorney in the Legal Department. Prior to her current position, Allison served as vice president of corporate real estate for American Airlines.

"We are extremely fortunate to have these talented, accomplished and respected individuals join us in our mission," said Pam Landwirth. "Their contributions to Give Kids The World can allow us to continue to bring hope and joy to families from around the world."

American Airlines To Build Wheelchair-Accessible "Park of Dreams"

(continued from page 1)
limitations," said Crandall.

"Through the caring efforts of American Airlines and its 120,000 em-

ployees, families will have a special place at the Village where children who are in wheelchairs or have other limitations can play right alongside

their brothers and sisters," said Landwirth. "Families will spend even more special moments together because of the love and commitment of the American Airlines family," said Landwirth.

The Park of Dreams design team is being led by Kaleidoscope Magic, Inc. of Orlando, and will also include IDEAs, Inc. of Orlando, and the Atlanta office of Water Technologies, which is based in Beaver Dam, Wisconsin.

Funding for the entire project will come from savings generated by the American Airlines and AMR Corp. IdeAAs In Action program, which encourages employees to save the company money in return for incentive awards. The program has been recognized as a leader in the suggestion systems and employee involvement arena since its inception in 1987.

American Airlines and AMR Corp. broke ground for "The Park of Dreams" on May 11. The park, to be completed in early 1997, will feature a wheelchair-accessible miniature golf course, interactive water area and amphitheater.

Design with mission in mind

This redesigned newsletter from Give Kids the World (GKTW) shows a striking sense of purpose. This was achieved by enlarging the logo, changing the name and its typography, and adding the mission statement to the nameplate. The two-column grid was changed to a more flexible three-column grid. A similar page template is used for two other newsletters published by GKTW: *Angel Advisor* is published for volunteers; *Clayton's Corner* is published for supporters and foundations and features the GKTW rabbit mascot.

NAME *Miracles & Memories*

PUBLISHER Give Kids the World, Kissimmee, Florida

PURPOSE/AUDIENCE Service to supporters

PRODUCTION/PRINTING Two-color on white 70# offset

FORMAT 8½" x 11"; eight pages

DESIGN Christine Magness, GKTW

Miracles & Memories
give kids the world.®
News for those whose compassion and support has touched the lives of terminally ill children and their families

December • 1996

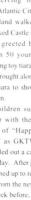

GKTW

Inside this issue . . .

World's largest car wash 2
New train station 3
Golf tourney recaps 4
American Express shares 5
Bozo grants wish 6
Letters from families 7

210 S. Bass Rd.
Kissimmee,
Florida 34746
(407) 396-1114
Fax (407) 396-1207

Give Kids The World® is a nonprofit organization that provides a memorable six-day, Central Florida vacation experience for children with terminal illnesses and their families, at no cost to them. It serves qualified children from around the world whose last wish is to meet Mickey Mouse and visit the Walt Disney World Resort® and Central Florida attractions.

Children delight in visits from celebrities
Miss America and Harlem Globetrotters spend time at Village

Surprise celebrity visits highlighted the stay of children visiting the Village recently. Tara Dawn Holland, the newly crowned Miss America 1997, and the world-famous Harlem Globetrotters each spent a morning with the children during their respective visits.

Less than two weeks after receiving her crown in Atlantic City, Miss Holland walked into a packed Castle of Miracles greeted by more than 50 young girls wearing toy tiaras. Tara had brought along her own tiara to show the children.

The children surprised her with their rendition of "Happy Birthday" as GKTW staff wheeled out a cake to celebrate her 24th birthday. After group photographs, children lined up to receive hugs and autographs from the new Miss America.

One week before, the Avenue of Angels turned into a basketball court for the

world-famous Harlem Globetrotters. Performing their well-known "Magic Circle" act, the Globetrotters amazed families with their basketball talents and tricks. A few children (and some GKTW volunteers) tried their hand at some hoop tricks. After, cameras and autograph books appeared in abundance as children visited with the players and captured special memories.

Both Miss America and the Harlem Globetrotters took time out of their visit to Walt Disney World Resort to visit the Village. We thank our Disney friends who made this possible.

New train station

Toy trains and talking animals are just two of the many surprises awaiting children in the Amberville Train Station, planned to begin construction next year at the Give

(Continued on page 3)

Giving Kids The World

We would like to thank the following groups for "Giving Kids The World" through their fund-raising efforts on our behalf.

Disneyana
Disneyana artists auctioned off several art pieces to benefit GKTW. $40,850 was the total with $14,000 coming just from two live auction items, one being a Glenn Close Cruella De Vil Doll.

Mystery Fun House
During weekends in October, $1 from all tickets sold at the Mystery Fun House was given to GKTW totaling over $1000.

LBV Factory Outlet
LBV Factory Outlet raised $1200 for GKTW through "digging for dollars" at their grand opening.

Davidson Hotel
A wine tasting and auction at the Tampa Airport Hilton raised over $500 for the children.

Gayfers Great Benefit
Gayfers sold tickets for their Holiday sale which was from 6 a.m. to 10 a.m. ... Proceeds from tickets wil ...

Huggie ...
Ten cents ... diapers b ... 31 will b ... 88 stores ...

American Express makes a difference

American Express card holders made a difference in the lives of children with terminal illnesses this fall. From Sept. 15 to Oct. 31, American Express donated two cents to GKTW for every transaction in the Central Florida area, up to $25,000 dollars. "Make a Difference with American Express" is patterned after the highly successful Charge Against Hunger Promotion.

In addition to the donation, American Express partnered with Gayfers Department Stores. The Peabody Orlando, WCPX-TV, Orlando Magazine and two Paxson Communications stations, SHE 100.3 and Magic 107.7 for a marketing campaign blanketing the entire region with information about GKTW.

"The success of Charge Against Hunger has proven that our Cardmembers and service establishments do care and can make a difference," said Carlos Viera, vice president and general manager of the southern region for American Express. "Now, starting with Give Kids The World and our Cardmembers and service establishments in the greater Orlando market, we hope to make an important difference for worthy causes on a regional level."

Two tournaments raise $105,000 for kids

The greens at Walt Disney World's Bonnet Creek Golf Club were filled with GKTW supporters on two different occasions during September.

Albertson's sponsored a golf tournament on Sept. 6, raising more than $51,000 for GKTW. Many of the supermarket chain's vendors and clients played in the event through a hot morning, retiring later to a buffet lunch served at Planet Hollywood.

The fifth annual GKTW Golf Classic, with premier sponsor American Automobile Association (AAA), was held on Sept. 16. The day kicked off with a clinic conducted by U.S. Open Champion Ken Venturi. After a round of golf, players had dinner, followed by an auction, hosted by WCPX sportscaster Mike Storms. After the last item was sold, the event raised $54,000 to fulfill the dreams of children with life-threatening illnesses.

At the Albertson's Golf Classic, foursome Jim Upchurch (Marketing Specialists VP GM), Tammy Bowman (Bonnet Golf Course GM), Pam Landwirth (GKTW Presidents), and Ron ...

Happy Anniversary GKTW supporters

Last May, many corporations, organizations and individuals joined to celebrate the tenth anniversary of Give Kids The World. This fall, GKTW used the occasion of two companies' anniversaries to recognize their commitment to help children's dreams come true.

Mayor Clayton the Rabbit presented a banner to Walt Disney World College Program students who volunteer at the Village to commemorate their 25th anniversary. WDW supports GKTW in every way imaginable from attraction tickets and character visits to landscaping and preventive maintenance at the Village.

The Peabody Orlando is celebrating their 10th anniversary. The premiere convention hotel hosts the annual GKTW Black and White Gala, raising more than $2 million since 1989. In addition, the Peabody provided rooms for families before the Village opened in 1989.

GKTW congratulates both companies on their special occasions, as well as sharing the deepest gratitude for their commitment and compassion for the children visiting Give Kids The World.

World's largest charity car wash

Budget Car and Truck Rental employees from across the globe grabbed a sponge and created suds galore as part of the World's Largest Car Wash on August 17.

At more than 300 locations from Tokyo to Orlando to Chicago to Honolulu, employees washed cars to raise money to support their commitment to GKTW. The project netted more than $66,000 to provide transportation for families staying at the Village.

Since Budget began its commitment to GKTW, the car and truck rental company has provided more than 150,000 complimentary rental days to families.

Budget provides rentals for each family during their stay. The use of a rental car, truck or van creates flexibility in their trip, allowing them to create memorable moments to stay with the families for a lifetime.

Dave Rapier, Vice President/General Manager of Florida Region for Budget Car and Truck Rental, helps an employee's daughter wash cars in Orlando, just one of the 300 Budget locations participating in Budget's World's Largest Car Wash. The $66,000 raised will be used toward rentals for GKTW families.

Renee Cline (GKTW Manager of Development), Stephanie Jones (Special Events Representative), and Mayor Clayton present congratulations banner signed by children staying at the Village to Winn DuLagos and Alan Villaverde of the Peabody Orlando which hosts the Black and White Gala every May.

Clayton's Corner

News for wish-granting foundations which partner with Give Kids The World

October • 1996

Inside this issue ...

210 South Bass Rd.
Kissimmee,
Florida 34746
(407) 396-1114
Fax (407) 396-1207

Give Kids The World is a non-profit organization that provides a memorable six-day, all expenses paid Central Florida vacation for children with life-threatening illnesses and their families. It serves qualified children from around the world whose last wish is to meet Mickey Mouse and visit the Walt Disney World Resort and Central Florida attractions.

GKTW Celebrates Tenth Anniversary
More than 25,000 families visit village since 1986

Ten years ago, the tragedy of an eight-year-old girl whose dream was to meet Mickey Mouse touched one man to reach out to more than 25,000 families from around the world. When hotelier Henri Landwirth learned that more than 50 percent of children with life-threatening illnesses wished to visit Walt Disney World and Central Florida, but time proved to be an enemy in arranging the trips, he called upon friends and colleagues in the hospitality industry to join his mission to help these children.

Setting up operations in a hotel room, Henri and a small staff began to coordinate all aspects of the vacations for families referred from wish-granting foundations and hospitals around the world, including complimentary accommodations, attractions tickets and local transportation.

"Because of the close partnership with the wish granting foundations... we have been able to touch the lives of more than 100,000 people."

In the beginning, logistics of these vacations required as much as six weeks of planning, but through the support of many organizations and businesses, Give Kids ...

The World was soon able to welcome a child with less than 24 hours notice. It was soon apparent that there ... a need for a special facility just for these families. Give Kids The World Vill... opened, offering accommodations for families in 56 two-bedroom, two bath villas, fully accessible to guests w... disabilities. The organization quickly gre... serving nearly 4,0... families in 1995. Tod... this magical resort enc... passes 35 acres and f... tures a Gingerbread House restaura... a fantasy-themed activity center cal... the Castle of Miracles, swimming po... ice cream parlor caboose and fu... stocked fishing pond. Construct... plans are underway this fall for t... new additions to the Village. (S... Amberville and Park of Dreams, pg ...

Pam Landwirth, vice chairman ... Give Kids The World, shares apprec... tion for those who have helped ma... the past ten years possible. "Beca... of the close partnership with w... granting foundations, we have be... able to touch the lives of more th... 100,000 people. We are so thankful ... share in this partnership with ot... who have the same mission: to ma... wishes come true for children."

Angel ADVISOR

Newsletter for the "Angels" who volunteer at Give Kids The World

February • 1997

Inside this issue ...

210 South Bass Rd.
Kissimmee,
Florida 34746
(407) 396-1114
Fax (407) 396-1207

Give Kids The World is a nonprofit organization that provides a memorable six-day, all expense paid Central Florida vacation for terminally children and their families. It serves qualified children from around the world whose last wish is to meet Mickey Mouse and visit the Walt Disney World Resort and Central Florida attractions.

Park of Dreams construction underway
Dedication set for Gala weekend

Park of Dreams construction is now in progress. This new facility will surround the existing pool at the Give Kids The World Village.

Outdoor Amphitheater — Pool — Interactive Water Area — Mayor Clayton's Bunny Hut

Channel six broadcasts live from Village

The holiday spirit came alive at the Village when Walt Disney World and the Central Florida Chefs' Association collaborated on a special celebration that catered to more than 300 guests.

Excitement filled the air as WCPX-TV, the Orlando CBS affiliate, broadcasted live to the evening news the pinnacle of the evening, the lighting of the Christmas tree rising in front of the Castle of Miracles. WCPX-TV, Anchor Grace Rabold served as emcee.

Featuring music from the Walt Disney World Executive Band, holiday magic filled the air while each child received a gift from their favorite Disney characters and then enjoyed an incredible feast with their family.

Pam Landwirth (GKTW President), Grace Rabold (Channel Six) and Disney friends excite the crowd just moments before the tree lighting. Kalani Pors, young guest of the Village, wishes everyone at the party and watching the broadcast a special "Merry Christmas."

CAMPUS FACILITIES

HIGHLIGHTS

APRIL 1996

Special thank you card sent to CF staff

One hundred and ninety-eight little feet every day. One child development lab. Open from 6:30 a.m. to 6:00 p.m. Toys, cookie crumbs, and lots of interactive activities. What does this have to do with Campus Facilities?

"We're always calling the Service Desk needing something extra," says Kathy Thornburg, director of the Child Development Lab. "I think we've used every service that Campus Facilities offers," she says.

Thornburg describes the lab as a very high use area with kids, college students, and staff coming in and out all day. "I have the sense that we need services more frequently than other departments," she says. She describes Campus Facilities staff as always responding pleasantly and promptly to their requests.

The lab also must be safe and clean at all times. In a recent incident, the glass in a door was broken. "Dave [McReynolds] was here within 20 minutes," she says, "He put a board up and made sure there was no possibility of kids getting hurt. The teacher hadn't even finished putting tape on the door."

The heavy use of the lab area creates considerable work for the custodians to keep bathrooms and floors clean, trash emptied, and any activity spills cleaned up.

Thornburg says that "the idea came up at a meeting that we should do some-

thing to thank Campus Facilities for how much they do for us."

For the thank you project, the CDL staff decided to make the most of the resources at hand: the children. The children went to work painting, drawing, and writing a supersized thank you card for the maintenance and building services staff.

Hearts, handprints and snowmen decorated the card along with a long list of thank yous. The thank yous covered a wide range of activities from "getting big hornets away from the playground" to "unclogging toilets when small toys are flushed."

In all, there were 25 thank yous including "thank you for smiling when you come out to help us."

On February 15, five of the children—Christopher, Cyrus, Myriam, Eesha and Alan—and two CDL staff members brought the card to the Conley Avenue maintenance shop along with trays of goodies and soda.

Howard Patrick, Patricia Neef, Danny Johnson, Mabel Mitchell and Raeann Akers are the building services staff who clean the Child Development Lab.

David McReyn[...] Dennis and Pe[...] thank you card[...] Child Develop[...] maintenance d[...]

Maintenar[...] ployees w[...] shop on th[...] freshment[...]

Thornbur[...] children a[...] know mat[...] ees by na[...] here to of[...] them," sh[...]

NAME *Facilities Focus*

PUBLISHER University of Missouri—Columbia, Columbia, Missouri

PURPOSE/AUDIENCE Service to the university community

PRODUCTION/PRINTING Two-color on white 60# offset

FORMAT 11" x 17"; four pages

DESIGN Marcia K. Lindberg, University of Missouri

Pinpointing your audience

Serving both internal and external audiences with one newsletter often slights both groups. To solve this problem, editor Marcia Lindberg split *Campus Facilities Highlights* into two separate publications: *Facilities Focus* and *Highlights*. For *Facilities Focus*, she created a professional and well-organized look to appeal to the deans, directors and faculty who need a quick read. A larger page size stands out in the recipient's in-box. The green second ink reinforces the publisher's role in creating an attractive campus with grass and trees. The newsletter is divided into sections to make it easy for busy readers to find information in the same place each issue.

News about MU facilities for faculty, students and staff

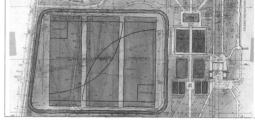

Facilities
FOCUS

Published by Campus Facilities

Spring 1996

Stankowski Field offers sports in all weather

Do you want to play basketball at ten o'clock at night? How about a softball game after a rainy day?

If so, you'll want to check out Stankowski Field when it's finished in August. You'll be able to play basketball, soccer, softball, volleyball and run the track in any weather at any time of day.

"We'll be able to play out there year round," says Phil Erwin, MU student. "You won't have to worry about mud destroying the grass, and the snow won't be on there long in the winter."

The synthetic turf used on the field absorbs rain and snow. "Students will be able to play after a thunderstorm," says Candy Whittet, director of Recreational Services. "This field will expand our programming intramurally."

Once improvements to the field are complete, students, faculty and staff will be able to enjoy three synthetic-turf football/soccer playing fields, two softball diamonds, a 1/3-mile running track, basketball courts, and sand volleyball courts.

Bright lights will illuminate the area throughout the evening hours.

All-weather athletic facility was student idea

The idea for an all-weather outdoor athletic facility was generated from students, Whittet says.

An intramurals supervisor as well as a student, Phil Erwin has a personal interest in seeing this project completed. "Intramural fields are scattered around the campus," he says.

Stankowski Field will include three synthetic-turf football/soccer playing fields, two softball diamonds, a 1/3-mile running track, basketball courts, and sand volleyball courts.

> "Stankowski Field is central to all the facilities and is easily accessible from Greektown, the dorms, and off-campus housing."
>
> Phil Erwin, MU student

Intramural sports participants often ride their bikes or drive to the existing intramural fields: Epple, Hinkson, Reactor and East Park fields.

"Stankowski Field will bring it all together to one site. Stankowski Field is central to all the facilities and is easily accessible from Greektown, the dorms, and off-campus housing," Erwin says.

He served as the student representative on the Recreational Services and Campus Facilities committee that evaluated design and construction of the field.

Funding was team effort

The $4.3 million project was funded from different sources. One million dollars came from student fees, and the remaining funds came from Recreational Services, Residential Life, Campus Dining, and the University Bookstore.

"It was a team effort to get it done," Whittet says. "We didn't want to overtax the students. This was a different concept since other departments were contributing. I see this as a positive move within the university to benefit the students."

"I think students will get their money's worth out of it," adds Erwin.

Whittet says the construction phase is progressing well. "The construction project manager and contractor are just excellent. Everything has fallen into place."

Larry Hubbard is the facilities project manager; Larry Elliott and Tom Wieck are the construction project managers for the Stankowski project.

Welcome to Facilities Focus

Campus Facilities welcomes you to the first issue of Facilities Focus. This quarterly newsletter has been developed to keep you up-to-date on our activities across the MU campus.

The newsletter will include articles and information about how our operation works and how you can receive the best, most efficient service possible.

If you have any comments on our first issue or suggestions for topics of interest, please contact our editor, Marcia Lindberg, at 882-3552.

For those who previously received the Highlights newsletter, you will now receive Facilities Focus.

We hope you enjoy this new publication and find the information helpful.

FASTFACT

Statistics about MU facilities, activities, and people

26,352 pieces — Chalk used at MU every year

57,000 square feet — Chalkboard erased by custodians every day

Source: Building Services, University of Missouri-Columbia

The design approach to the employee publication *Highlights* was quite different. The design team switched from cream paper to bright white, but kept a lighter version of the blue ink to appeal to the mostly male audience. The casual font, clip art and photos were all selected to loosen up the look. Note how the Q&A section allows the editor to deal with topics that do not deserve full stories.

NAME *Highlights*

PUBLISHER University of Missouri—Columbia, Columbia, Missouri

PURPOSE/AUDIENCE Service to the university community

PRODUCTION/PRINTING Two-color on white 60# offset

FORMAT 8½" × 11"; four pages

DESIGN Marcia K. Lindberg, University of Missouri

New Faces

Yuping Zou
programmer analyst II, systems development

Jim Henley
construction project manager, construction mgmt.

Kevin Kuretich
facilities project manager, project management

Ken Frye
construction project manager, construction mgmt.

Harriet Smalley
interior designer, design services

Jan Russell
office support staff III, campus construction

Jack Beard
MTS / refrigeration, campus construction

Robert Laswell
MTS / pipefitter, maintenance

Transfers and promotions

Curt Adams from groundskeeper to groundskeeper II in grounds

Harvey Brown from planner/estimator to construction estimator in campus construction

Ken Dothage from maintenance service attendant to MTS/controls in energy management

Lisa Erickson from office support staff III to administrative assistant in construction management

Gary George from trades helper to temporary maintenance service [...] management

[...]m student [...]ctural assistant

[...]m office sup[...]r secretary in [...]t

[...]r in campus

[...] trades helper [...]ction

[...]an

Chris Foote, trades helper in maintenance

Chris Gehlken, trades helper in maintenance

Twyla Key, custodian

Larry Lawrence, custodian

Eddie Martin, construction project manager

Glen Pipes, Jr., custodian

Elicia Senor, custodian

Foster Sisson, construction project manager

Matt Thornton, trades helper in maintenance

Students

Ian Bedell in building services

Elaine Kelly in building services

Kim Lancaster in building services

Changku Park in building services

Cathryn Sanstra in building services

Lucretia Sheard in personnel

Jennifer Spauhorst in campus construction

Q&A

Question:
I've heard that the General Services Building will be demolished to build the new basketball arena. Is this true?

Answer:
The General Services Building is one of two sites under consideration for the new arena. The other site is south of Memorial Stadium. However, you shouldn't start packing your boxes yet. The athletic department still needs to raise approximately $40 million (the Laurie family donated $10 million).

If the arena is built on the site of GSB, the athletic department's funds for the project would have to pay to relocate Campus Facilities, General Stores, Procurement and the MU Police into other facilities.

Question:
The clips on our I.D. badges make it difficult to run them through security card readers such as the one at Clydesdale Hall. Can anything be done?

Answer:
We tried to accomplish a lot when we designed the new badge, but it does have a few limitations such as the one you describe. CF Personnel will issue you a second I.D. card with no clip if you use these readers on a regular basis. Contact Personnel at 882-7111.

About Q&A
Do you have a question about Campus Facilities or MU activities? Call or e-mail Marcia Lindberg with your questions (882-3552 or Lindberg on Groupwise).

3

Sharing news and taking pride in Campus Facilities   October 1996

Building services recognizes staff with outstanding team member awards

It's a confidential ballot. Your work group is voting to select one employee who displays high quality work and is a good team player. Who would you vote for in your work group? Would you be chosen?

Ten people were chosen in just such a vote during the annual Building Services Employee Appreciation Week held September 23-27.

The vote for "outstanding team member awards" was a new addition to the recognition ceremonies this year.

Employees who received the award were: Rubyn Key, Kevin

Key, Reno Jackman, Lou Frances Maxwell, Raymond Leaton, Byron Smith, Jeff Chandler, Bessie Mikel, Carolyn Woody, and Norlan Hackman.

top10
Employees chosen by peers to receive outstanding team member awards

Rubyn Key	Byron Smith
Kevin Key	Jeff Chandler
Reno Jackman	Bessie Mikel
Lou Frances Maxwell	Carolyn Woody
Raymond Leaton	Norlan Hackman

The purpose of Building Services Employee Recognition Week is to recognize the excellent work performed by building services employees in the past year. All employees attend a banquet and awards ceremony.

In addition to outstanding team member awards, employees were recognized for top building awards. Top building awards are given to employees whose buildings receive top quality ratings in customer surveys and building inspections.

Employees with exemplary attendance and those with an injury-free year also were acknowledged. Twenty-three building services employees had a 98% attendance rate, and 119 employees had an injury-free year.

A special "Year in Review" edition of *Gatekeepers Gazette*, building services' newsletter, also was distributed to all employees at the banquets. ■

Grounds employees take a horticulture field day

Adults don't get field trips from work, but grounds employees had the next best thing: a horticulture field day at the Agroforestry & Horticulture Research Center in New Franklin, MO.

The one-day event, sponsored by the Missouri Landscape and Nurseryman Association and the MU horticulture department, allowed grounds employees to learn different techniques and aspects of horticulture.

All regular, full-time grounds employees attended the field day

on September 25. Topics included: tree digging and planting, constructing decorative block walls, and field growing and holding nursery plants and trees.

Grounds employees Brad Mann and Scott Keith also were involved in presenting information. "They gave a tree climbing and tree pruning demonstration," says Tom Flood, superintendent of grounds.

As part of the event, grounds employees toured the center's greenhouse and growing facility. ■

Inside ➡

chapter one

NAMEPLATES

Imagine your newsletter on a table or desk covered with newspapers, magazines, reports, memos and other newsletters. Competition for attention starts with your nameplate. Use your nameplate to help readers identify your newsletter in the pile and to invite them to reach for it first.

Except for date and issue number, keep your nameplate the same issue after issue. Consistent design trains readers to identify your publication. More important, consistency lets you focus exclusively on content for each issue.

To get maximum value from your nameplate, design it to follow these simple guidelines:

IDENTITY. Let your name and subtitle tell who you are and why readers should pay attention. Make sure that readers can immediately identify your organization and purpose.

INFORMATION. Include the required information—name of newsletter, subtitle and date—and optional information such as logo, issue number and publisher or editor.

IMPACT. Ensure that your nameplate design helps readers focus on your message. Use boldface type, color, placement and other graphic techniques to highlight your most important words.

SIMPLICITY. Verify that you have an uncluttered design that readers can understand at a glance. Delete every word and image that doesn't contribute to your message. Avoid using the word "newsletter" in your nameplate: Use a more precise communication term.

IMAGE. Evaluate whether your design fits the image of your organization. Is it too formal or too informal? Too classical or too modern? If typefaces or colors don't feel right, change them.

Graphic designers created the nameplates on the following pages to evoke strong images for their publications. You can give your newsletter strong visual impact by using some of the same design techniques.

Tea Leaves

for prescient readers

VOL I   NO I

Tea Leaves

for prescient readers

VOL 1   NO 1

Tea Leaves

VOL 1
NO 1

for prescient readers

Tea Leaves

for prescient readers

VOL 1   NO 1

Design with personality

Experiment with various type-styles and logo treatments before deciding on the look of your newsletter.

VOLUME 1 • NUMBER 1　　　　　　　　　　SUMMER 1995

SPECTRUM

THE NEWSLETTER FOR MEMBERS OF PR NEWSWIRE

Retirement Today

Financial strategies for retired Canadians　　　　Vol. 1, No. 1

A newsletter that seeks to connect the LSU Medical Community with all who care about the genetic health of our families

Vol. 1 Issue 2
Fall 1995

Communicating with color, type and design

Broad type shows off the graduated rainbow screen of *Spectrum*. Soft shadows adorn *Retirement Today* in a nameplate using the gentle colors teal and blue. *Linkage* uses the colors of the teaching institution that pays for its publication. The flamboyant swash *L* in the *Creative* *Secretary's Letter* definitely says this publication is for creative people. *Sales MasterMind*, with its use of tight three-dimensional block letters, appears bold and confident. The background pattern of a universal symbol adds just the right touch to the *copyRights* nameplate.

CREATIVE

SECRETARY'S Letter

OCTOBER 30, 1995

Today's Newest & Best Success Ideas for Secretaries

The Economics Press

SALESMASTERMIND

Real-world selling strategies and techniques from great salespeople

Issue 106 • December 1996

January/February 1997
Vol. 2, No. 1

copyRights ©

The Newsletter on Rights and Permissions

Issue Number/Date

Issue Number / Date

Issue Number/Date

Date/Issue Number

Information at a glance

The type and elements chosen to create a nameplate leave an impression on the reader. Note how the subtitles of these newsletters form part of the design. Design works with the subtitle to reflect your newsletter's purpose.

All nameplates in this spread are designed by J Hondorp Graphic Design, Manzanita, Oregon.

West Hills Wildlife Alert

Monitoring flora and fauna in Fairfield western ecosystems

Issue Number/Date

Issue Number/Date

LastCall

Trends in Square Dancing from Anchorage to Miami

Issue Number/Date

HoodviewHorizons

Recreational opportunities throughout the Mt. Hood National Forest

Tracking the
hottest bands
in the hippest clubs
Issue Number/Date

HEADLINER
HIGHLIGHTS

The Leadership Journey
Forming Alliances and Overcoming Obstacles
Presented by Malaika Horne, Ph.D., M.P.E.
Thursday, March 6, 1997 11:30 Networking   Noon Luncheon
Lenoir Community Center   Cost: $10.00 members, $12.00 guests

The mission of Women's Network is simple: "to encourage personal and professional growth through networking and to support and develop leadership roles of members at the local, state and national levels." However, achieving this mission is not so simple.

Dr. Malaika Horne, University of Missouri Board of Curators President, will share her experiences and suggestions for reaching leadership positions. She will discuss the issues of access and how networking contributes to board appointment at the local, state and national levels.

Horne received a bachelor's degree in sociology from UM-St. Louis, a master's in urban affairs and a doctorate in public policy analysis and administration from St. Louis University, as well as a degree in psychiatric epidemiology from the Washington University School of Medicine.

Horne is chief operations officer at Haley Travel Service. Since 1991 she has served as an adjunct professor at Webster University, teaching classes on cultural pluralism. She also writes for the *St. Louis Argus* newspaper and *The Crisis* magazine, as well as other publications.

Married to William Haley, the son of author Alex Haley, Horne resides in St. Louis, Missouri.

Women's Network is pleased to welcome Greater Missouri representatives as special guests to this luncheon. Greater Missouri is a program of the Missouri Foundation for Women's Resources, Inc., and serves to enhance the personal, economic, political and professional status of women in Missouri.

Please send your reservation and payment to the Columbia Chamber of Commerce by Tuesday, March 4, 1997. A $5.00 late fee will be assessed to registrations received after March 4.

Inside

Repeat your theme

The impact of the three-dimensional nameplate for *Women's Network Newsletter* is repeated through the other elements: the table of contents, calendar, standard columns and masthead. This technique coordinates the pages of the twelve-page newsletter.

NAME *Women's Network Newsletter*

PUBLISHER Women's Network of the Chamber of Commerce, Columbia, Missouri

PURPOSE/AUDIENCE Service to members

PRODUCTION/PRINTING Two-color on 70# linen text

FORMAT 8½" × 11"; twelve pages

DESIGN Visionwork Graphic Design

new members & announcements

Prema Khanna
Marketing & Promotions
Assistant
University of Missouri -
Athletics
375 Hearnes, 65211
882-0745; 882-4720 fax

Marchea Klang
Standards Engineer
Toastmaster Inc.
1801 Stadium Blvd., 65202
446-5634; 446-5676 fax

Alyce McNeil
Public Affairs Communications
Specialist
State Farm Insurance
4700 S. Providence, 65217
499-2699; 499-2001 fax

Sandi Odor
Customer Service Manager
United States Cellular
2909 Falling Leaf Lane, 65201
881-8329; 474-4985 fax

Toni Sutherland
Personnel Consultant
Deck & Decker Personnel
1900 N. Providence, Suite 319;
65202
449-0876; 449-0878 fax

March 1997 Calendar

Sunday	Monday	Tuesday	Wednesday	Thursday	Friday	Saturday
2	3 Chamber Week Business Owners 5:30PM	4 Chamber Week	5 Chamber Week Special Activities 12:00PM	6 Chamber Week MONTHLY MEETING 11:30AM	7 Chamber Week	8
9	10	11 Mentor 7:30AM Membership 12:00PM	12 Program 12:00PM Newsletter 12:00PM	13 Committee Chairs 8:00AM Registration 12:00PM	14	15
16	17 St. Patrick's Day	18 Public Relations 12:00PM	19 Mentor Program 7:00PM	20 First Day of Spring	21	22
23 Palm Sunday	24 Business Managers 11:45AM	25	26	27 Steering 7:30AM	28 Good Friday	29
30 Easter Sunday SportsFest 10AM–6PM	31					

National Nutrition Month
National Women's History Month
Poison Prevention Awareness Month
Chamber Week March 3–7

member profile

Carolyn Coley
Stabilization

"Stabilization." I squinted at her a little bit, not immediately understanding what she meant by that. "Well, the frivolous part of me says 'travel,' but money should allow you to be comfortable, stable. I'm not really into materialism, but just to be able to do the things I want to do. What's the use of going on vacation if you're worried about your bills?"

Up to that point, I'd been trying to figure out what spin I wanted to put on this article about Carolyn, and I reali[zed] that moment that I'd just [...]

For two years, Carolyn worked as the Administrative Coordinator of Women's Network and in this position quickly learned about the business community of Columbia, as well as the value of Women's Network. In 1994, she became a Sales Forecasting Analyst for Toastmaster Inc., but remained interested in Women's Network and currently holds the position of Membership Committee chair.

"I enjoy working with people. I enjoy [commu]nication and working in a [environ]ment. I also enjoy working [...] and putting my degree to [...]

Carolyn also enjoys gardening, reading, working out and movies, especially those with lots of subplots. (She's a big fan of Robert Altman films.) She caught the travel bug when she was 14 and toured Europe while she was in college. She hopes to return soon and spend at least a month in Ireland, a place she has never seen, but whose romantic notions fascinate her.

"I want to go for at least a month, because I want to go in and experience the culture. The best times that I've had [travelling] were meeting the local [...]

Openings for City/County Commissions

To apply for **Boone County Commission** openings, contact the Commission office at **886-4305** for more information. Obtain applications at Boone County Government Center, 801 E. Walnut, Room 245. The following committees are seeking involvement:

- **Building Code Board of Appeals** (Rocky Fork township)
- **Mental Health Board of Trustees**
- **Senior Board** (one opening, Rocky Fork township)

City of Columbia board openings: Contact Sherry at **874-7208** if you are inter[ested] ... serving. Sherry can estimate timing of future openings in your field of interest.

newsletter committee

Newsletter Committee members: Angela Haun: chair, Columbia Daily Tribune, 815-1806/815-1801 fax; Cynthia Baker, Thom Baker Sound & Video, 445-9955; Cynthia Barnes, University Club, 882-1347; Szasz Benedict, Norman Robert & Associates, 443-4388; Leigh Burkhalter, Missouri Pork Producers Assoc., 445-8375; Leanna Hafften, Parry Publishing, 499-1830; Rose Lloyd, Legend Automotive Group, 875-5000; Pam Pearn, Freelance, 449-5289; Holly Smith-Berry, Toastmaster Inc., 446-5645; Roberta Uhrig, American Express Financial Services, 499-4945; Cathleen Veach, Pearson/Veach Shelter Insurance Agency, 443-1588; Becky Wall, Job Finders/Temp Finders, 446-4256; Craig J. Weiland, Visionworks, 449-8567; Sherry Wohlgemuth. **Newsletter design & layout** by Visionworks. **Printing** by Media Graphics. **The views expressed** in this newsletter are not necessarily those of the Newsletter Committee, Women's Network or the Columbia Chamber of Commerce. Submissions are welcome; the deadline is the first Wednesday of each month for the following month's issue.

GETTING WIRED *cont. from p.1*

The industry needs an HTML equivalent for learning development. The good news is that it's coming. Developments from major software publishers, such as Or___ are fo___ ing on a set of standar___ development. And, ou___ Learning Council will ___ propose a first round ___

2. Piloting and Exp___ We need to test our ass___ the next 12 months, or ___ invest tens of millions ___ development of intran___ ing delivery. However, ___ research on the compo___ tiveness. It is critical th___ departments take time ___ evaluate the impact of ___ We need graduate ___ focus on these issues ___ so we can build a kno___ what works, under w___ stances, for which top___ which types of learne___ hear that, colleges?

3. New Images an___ The view of online le___ cally different in busi___ training departments ___ online learning as an ___ the classroom. Their f___ classes, instructors, le___ modules. Business un___ more performance-ba___ They are interested in ___ learning, support for ___ and access to expertis___ faculty and lesson pla___ Trainers should liste___ ness unit mantra. The f___ learning will blur disti___ training programs, kno___ bases, and performanc___

4. New Skills. We n___ develop a new set of s___ ing and deploying onl___ our organizations. Trai___ will use new criteria to___ intranet-delivered lear___ and developers will ha___ new models for seque___ bridging elements with___ programs. Classroom t___

have to integrate online learning into their curricula.

5. Technology. There are several aspects of intranet delivery that must mature before we will have the full capacity that is needed.

The Lakewood Report On
TECHNOLOGY for LEARNING

GETTING WIRED

Taking the High Road to Widespread Online Learning

By Elliott Masie, contributing editor

In late 1996, while in Scotland, I was preparing to give an after-dinner speech when an executive of a large European company asked me a simple question: "What is standing in the way of delivering learning to employees at their desktops? We bought the computers. We have an intranet and browsers. Why can't we just put our training online?"

I wanted to give a simple answer to this perfect question for two reasons. First, I was wearing a kilt and the breeze from the doorway was blowing right up it. Second, I wanted to honor the enthusiasm for universal online learning with an encouraging reply.

Unfortunately I had to tell them that it was a long answer and I'd get back to them after organizing my thoughts. The end result of that question was an e-mail reply to conference attendees, and it turns out, this column:

7 Requirements of Online Training

1. Standards. There are no standards for online learning development. Organizations are building significant learning projects in closed and proprietary systems, which means their course development investment may not be leveragable to other authoring or distribution systems.

GETTING WIRED *cont. on p.2*

How 3M's Centralized Support Staff Got Employees Interested in Training

In 1994, the 3M facility in Austin, TX, gave its training and support teams the power to completely reorganize the way the two separate groups functioned. They formed a unified training and PC support team for the plant's 1,500 clients, and implemented dramatic changes that prompted employees to appreciate how valuable technical support really is.

Each Department Has an IT Expert

Originally each of the seven departments had its own PC expert, says Kathy Macchi (512.984.6575), IT manager. In some cases it was a network specialist, in others a secretary or someone else who just knew a lot about PCs. So when Macchi began the reorganization process,

3M TRAINING *cont. on p. 3*

FEBRUARY 1997 • VOLUME 3 NUMBER 2

INSIDE THIS ISSUE

4 INTERNET-BASED TRAINING
3 Web-based training programs you can test drive right now

5 WEB RESOURCES
How to choose the right search engine for your research needs

6 PERFORMANCE ASSESSMENT
A model for evaluating your distance learning program (part 2)

7 INTERNET SUPPORT
3 reasons why a training Web site will save you time, stress

8 INTERNET-BASED TRAINING
Why IBM and NYU joined forces to offer business training online

9 IDEAS FROM EXPERTS
Learn why creative navigation tools are crucial for successful CBT

10 PRODUCT NEWS
Video Express Mail sends audio/graphics e-mail without downloads

11 OFF-THE-SHELF MULTIMEDIA
New rating system judges design, media, and interface

12 NEWS DIGEST
Intel and Microsoft introduce video phone software for the Internet

Lakewood Publications
www.lakewoodpub.com, 800.328.4329
SFister@aol.com

Giving print the Web look

The nameplate of *Technology for Learning* is the same used in the web page (opposite), where the shine effect really shows up. Web-style buttons list the contents. The masthead includes e-mail addresses for staff members who deal with the public. But in the final analysis, it is easier to read paper than a screen, so an eye-catching subscription form is included to entice the reader to access the information both ways.

NAME *Technology for Learning*

PUBLISHER Lakewood Publications, Minneapolis, Minnesota

PURPOSE/AUDIENCE Service to subscribers

PRODUCTION/PRINTING Two-color on white 60# offset

FORMAT 8½" × 11"; twelve pages

DESIGN Sarah Fister, Lakewood Publications

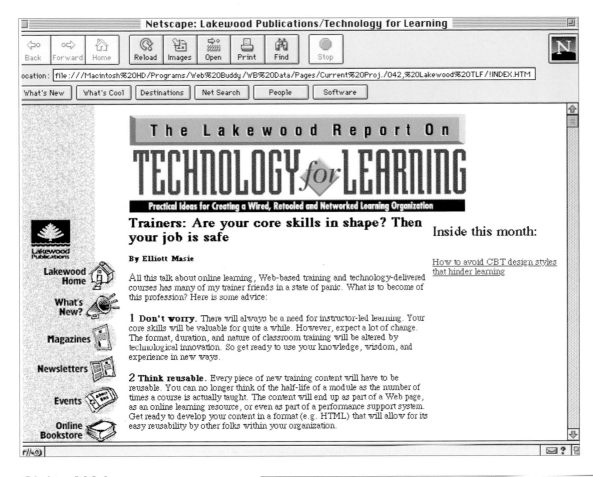

Giving Web pages the print look

The website for *Technology for Learning* includes the same nameplate as the print version. The page also includes a link to an offer for a free trial subscription.

NAME www.lakewoodpub.com/newslett/tfl/index.htm

PUBLISHER Lakewood Publications, Minneapolis, Minnesota

PURPOSE/AUDIENCE Service to subscribers

PRODUCTION/PRINTING Web

FORMAT Web

DESIGN Sarah Fister, Lakewood Publications

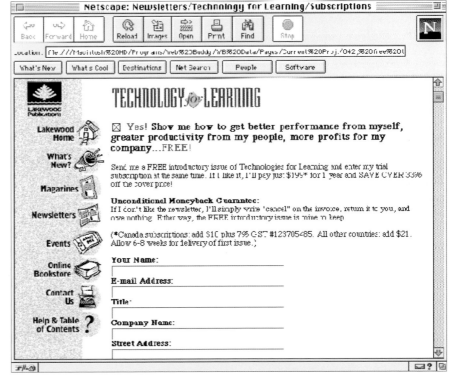

chapter two

BUILDING PAGES

You can create newsletters with content that readers read and remember by following a few simple guidelines. We based these guidelines on extensive research about graphic design.

Research identifies the places that readers see first. Common sense says to put your most important information in those places. Readers look at your newsletter in the following order: the front page, the back page and, finally, the inside pages. Put your most important information on page one.

When readers look at inside pages, they see the right hand pages first, and then the left hand pages. Readers start reading at the upper left of a spread, but they glance at the right page first. Use the upper half of the recto page for your calendar or important visual elements such as graphs or illustrations.

When readers look at a page, they see, in order: photos and illustrations; captions; headlines; kickers and decks; pull quotes; subheads; and text. Use photos and illustrations to tell your story, not just as decoration or as filler. And make those captions count. Put the essense of the story in the caption that readers see even before headlines.

Does your graphic design put your most important messages where readers look first?

Vol 1. No.1/1996

CHATHAM BUSINESS ASSOCIATES, LTD., INC.
Tel: 908-464-8002
Fax: 908-464-8002
(Note new fax number)

New Fax # 908-464-8143

FYI

INFORMATION AND IDEAS FOR YOUR BUSINESS

Disability Coverage Broadens

For many people under 50, there is a general disbelief that they will ever be sick long enough to need disability insurance. For others, the high cost of disability premiums, 2% to 4% of annual earnings for a typical policy, has been a barrier. In fact, most people spend more to insure their houses and cars than they do to protect their earnings. But changes in the industry have made insurers offer broader policies, putting coverage within the reach of more people.

might have shrugged off are now filing claims against their policies and calling an end to their careers.

So insurers have expanded their policies to broader markets, typically small business owners and people with salaries from $30,000 to $80,000. The policies offer less generous coverage in exchange for more economical rates. Instead of lifetime benefits, most policies run to age 65. Fewer insurers offer same occupation coverage, which provides benefits if a person is unable to work in the same occupation. Instead they

Vol 1. No.1/1996

GlobeTrends Inc.
Exclusive Importer of
Taylors of Harrogate Teas
Tel: 1-800-416-TEAS
Fax: 201-984-7422

Tea Trends

Interest Brewing in Gourmet Tea

Americans are drinking more tea. The market for gourmet tea is particularly strong, with industry sources reporting a growth rate of 25% per year that is expected to continue for the next five years.

Several trends are fueling this growth. As the 76 million baby boomers age, many of them are substituting tea for coffee. Tea fits in

As consumers begin to understand teas, they realize they have many more choices in loose tea. In fact, our finest single estate teas are available in loose tea only. But since many U.S. consumers appreciate the convenience of tea bags, we import

Cronin & Company
Tel: 201-460-7543
Fax: 201-460-7916
E-mail: 71334.3160
@compuserve.com

Vol 2. No.5/19

pointers

marketing ideas for growing businesses

Seven Trends to Watch in '97

Ever wonder what the big companies are up to? Here are some of the strategies the major business-to-business (b-to-b) marketers will be adopting in 1997:

1. One-to-one marketing. Direct marketing continues to be a fast-growing area for b-to-b marketing. One-to-one marketing, also referred to as feedback marketing or relationship marketing, takes direct marketing a step further by using databases to create very specific lists that anticipate what customers need. Small, targeted campaigns then deliver the right information at the right time using tools like E-mail, mailings, targeted print or broadcast, faxes or CD-ROMs.

2. Consumerization. Just as three-piece suits are giving way to khaki trousers, business marketing is taking on a more relaxed, personalized approach. This is especially true for companies marketing to the small office, home office (SOHO) groups.

3. Web marketing. It's estimated that two-thirds of companies with $10 million or more in sales have a presence on the Web. That number is expected to be 100% by mid-1997. So far, most sites are just extensions of the companies' printed material.

Time to Add E-ma

After several years of making logo professionally designed. A ink was dry on my new stati business cards, it looked like I mi reprint them when New Jersey's codes went into effect. Luckily, R was spared.

If you're getting a new area c have until May before it takes eff not take advantage of the time to set mail account if you don't already h and add the number to your station business cards? More and more bus are using E-mail, and the newer pr are easy to learn–even for the technol ly challenged. Who knows, your kid even think you're cool.

–Judy Cro

Spring 1996

Micro DataNet, Inc.
Tel: 908-931-0666
Fax: 908-931-0965

Micro DataNews

Improving Warehouse Management

A warehouse management system (WMS) can improve your existing procedures and reduce your costs. The best way to decide on the specifications for your system is to map your material flow and information flow and compare them.

Typically, material follows one path while information follows another. This often creates time lags between where the material is actually moved to, and where people think the material is. These time lags affect the efficiency of your entire operation.

To get an accurate picture, look at the

You should consider:
- How many people handle the item
- The kind of paperwork generated
- Who completes and processes the paperwork on the floor and in the office
- How storage locations are selected
- How long it takes an operator to store an item once it has been received
- The view of inventory available to customer service to fill orders
- How orders are released and transmitted to the warehouse for picking
- Whether picked items are staged or loaded directly for shipment
- The orders lost because inventory can

continued

n a Tent

entory Management, ns the hasty selection of m to the fellow living out s a tent. It's better than ter, but if he had looked ve seen the cottage down the same price.

"Gesundheit!"

Tree-Free Papers

If you're interested in green marketing, two great looking papers can help your communications standout. Crane & Company works with the Federal Reserve to convert a portion of the worn and unfit currency into its Old Money® papers. A palette of green shades is achieved by blending the currency with recovered cotton fibers. The process involves no deinking and hence no sludge or residuals.

A collaboration between Crane, Levi Strauss and Cottrell Paper converts denim scraps into a paper and corrugated board. Denim Paper® and Denim Blues® are stronger than their wood-based counterparts and have been put to a variety of uses. For the local distributors, call Crane & Company at 413-684-2600.

continued from front

2. Simple graphics are most effective. Graphics take the most time to transmit, and you don't want to keep people waiting to get to your content.
3. Frequent updates encourage repeat visits. Multiple visits reinforce awareness of your products and services. Keep your site fresh with new information, stories, contests or games and let people know you'll be making these changes.
4. An E-mail link lets visitors contact you immediately, while their interest is highest. Answer their inquiries within 24 hours.
5. Direct people to your Website by registering with the major search engines. Put your Web address on all your literature and mention it in your promotions.

Keep in mind that it may take several months before you see the results from your site. As with your other marketing efforts, it takes repetition and consistency.

CRONIN & COMPANY
Small Business Marketing
P.O. Box 253
Rutherford, NJ 07070

Newsletters on postcards

Even for professional writers such as Judy Cronin, finding time to produce a newsletter can seem overwhelming. Inspired by Bob Westenberg's famous postcard newsletter, *Imp,* Judy developed *Pointers,* an oversize postcard that is fast to create and arrives "already open." The red lines and logo are preprinted on shells to further accelerate production. Any organization or business can use this type of marketing-style newsletter postcard.

NAME *Pointers, Tea Trends, FYI, Micro Data News*

PUBLISHER Cronin & Company, Rutherford, New Jersey

PURPOSE/AUDIENCE Service and marketing to customers

PRODUCTION/PRINTING Red preprinted on 8½" × 11" shells; black overprinted

FORMAT Trimmed 5½" × 8½" oversized postcards, two-sided

DESIGN Judy Cronin, Cronin & Company

What you see is not what they get

When you design an e-mail newsletter and send it online, what your readers see on their screens isn't always what you see on yours. These sample documents illustrate the challenges of e-mail. Note the differences in the footers, headers, distribution lists, typefaces, type sizes and page breaks.

Examples A and B have the same headers and footers, but the typefaces, type sizes and page breaks are differ-ent. Newsletter C printed out with large, sans serif type and the distribution list included at the beginning. Newsletter D contains much smaller type than C, and a footer different than any of the others.

The test newsletter in this example contained fifty characters per line, as well as hard returns to avoid awk-ward line lengths and line wraps. Also note the separation of each article by using the ~, -, < and > keystrokes.

C

```
Subj:   newsletter design test
Date:   Mon, Apr 14, 1997 10:54 PM EDT
From:   mbeach@pdx.oneworld.com
X-From: mbeach@pdx.oneworld.com (MARK BEACH)
To: NL@mrin39.mail.aol.com
CC: Mershon@mrin39.mail.aol.com,  Ronnie@mrin39.mail.aol.com,
Bill@mrin39.mail.aol.com,  Fred@mrin39.mail.aol.com,  friend2546@aol.com,
Kathy@mrin39.mail.aol.com,  Polly@mrin39.mail.aol.com


M A R K'S  N E W S L E T T E R  D E S I G N  T E S T
April  1997

<><><><><><><><><><><><><><><><><>
PLEASE READ QUESTIONS AND THEIR 'ARTICLES'

> What is good design for email newsletters?
> Will your screen look like my screen?
> Will your printout look like my printout?
> Does anyone receive an email newsletter that they
consider has especially good design?
> Why do this test?
<><><><><><><><><><><><><><><><><>


~~~~~~~~~~~~~~~~~~~~
WHAT IS GOOD DESIGN?
I think that some line such as ~~~~ or ____
the headline, not below it, to connect it vis
story.

~~~~~~~~~~~~~~~~~~~~~~~~~~~~~~~~~~~
WILL YOUR SCREEN LOOK LIKE MY SCREEN?

I am typing in courier with my default set a
per line. Do you see courier and 50 characte
  Line length is more readable at 40 charact
but 40 seems visually too narrow. What do

      4/15/97        America Online: N
```

D

```
Subj:   newsletter design test
Date:   97-04-15 11:51:59 EDT
From:   mbeach@pdx.oneworld.com (MARK BEACH)
To: fhgerlach@aol.com

M A R K'S  N E W S L E T T E R  D E S I G N  T E S T
April 1997

<><><><><><><><><><><><><><><><><><><><><>
PLEASE READ QUESTIONS AND THEIR 'ARTICLES'

> What is good design for email newsletters?
> Will your screen look like my screen?
> Will your printout look like my printout?
> Does anyone receive an email newsletter that they
consider has especially good design?
> Why do this test?
<><><><><><><><><><><><><><><><><><><><><>


~~~~~~~~~~~~~~~~~~~~
WHAT IS GOOD DESIGN?
I think that some line such as ~~~~ or ____ should go above
the headline, not below it, to connect it visually with the
story.

~~~~~~~~~~~~~~~~~~~~~~~~~~~~~~~~~~~
WILL YOUR SCREEN LOOK LIKE MY SCREEN?

I am typing in courier with my default set at 50 characters
per line. Do you see courier and 50 characters?
  Line length is more readable at 40 characters than 50, but
40 seems visually too narrow. What do you think?


_____
WILL YOUR PRINTOUT LOOK LIKE MY PRINTOUT?
I type in courier, but my DeskJet 820 printer works in
helvetica, so my lines seem narrow and the rules don't run
to the full width of the headlines. Doubtless I could train
my printer to work in courier, but, as an average reader,
would I?
  And is printout even relevant? Do readers print anything
from email newsletters or only read them on screen?


_____
OTHER EXAMPLES OF GOOD DESIGN

Newsletter writing often calls for bullet lists that might
look like the following list of wishes:
  * to use bolds in my email.
  * to find the option key on my keyboard.
  * to know where is the end of this page.
  My final wish is that I receive a printout back from each
of you. _____ WHY DO THIS TEST?

I am working with Elaine to revise my book about
outstanding newsletter design. We want to learn whether or
```

working SOLO.

Reaching
independent
entrepreneurs

- It is estimated that by 2010 all existing knowledge will double approximately every 90 days.

- Women-owned U.S. companies employ more people than the Fortune 500 does worldwide.

N E W S L E T T E R

Contents

SECOND QUARTER 1996

NUMBER 7

The Working Solo Newsletter (ISSN 1086-6027) is published quarterly by Portico Press, PO Box 190, New Paltz, NY 12561; 914/255-7165 (voice); 914/255-2116 (fax); terri@workingsolo.com (internet). Subscriptions are $24/year. Editor: Terri Lonier. All material is ©1996 Portico Press, all rights reserved. Photo credit, this page: Arthur L. Cohen. For reprint permission, just give us a call. WORKING SOLO is a registered trademark of Terri Lonier.

Working with Power Partners

Successful independent entrepreneurs understand that working solo is *not* working alone. The goal is to maintain your independence, but not focus on doing every aspect of your business on your own.

The partnerships you make with others can have a significant impact on the success of your own business. Let's consider a few of these relationships:

Business Advisors

No matter what size your company is, or at what level of development, consider putting together a board of advisors. This may be comprised of fee-based professionals who offer business services such as accounting or legal counsel. Or, it may consist of a group of colleagues who share insights as a peer-to-peer relationship.

This group of individuals can become a powerful extended cheerleading squad for your company. They can steer you clear of business pitfalls, and give you valuable insights from their cumulative experience.

Marketing Alliances

It's smart to partner with companies that are targeting similar customers, but are not direct competitors to you. This can be a win/win arrangement with great payoffs for each party. Consider doing joint direct mail campaigns by combining your mailing lists to reach a larger audience. Another option is to cross-market each other's products or services, or

include literature or coupons in mailings. Swap lists of names or referrals. The possibilities are endless, and so are the opportunities for stretching your valuable marketing dollars.

Terri Lonier

Think Virtual

While "virtual company" may seem to be the latest business buzzwords, the concept has been around for years—highly specialized individuals working together on a project basis. Hollywood has been using this business model for decades, and even Mick Jagger has spoken about the "virtual corporation" the Rolling Stones created for their world tour last summer.

Solo entrepreneurs in all fields are creating alliances with other peer professionals as a way to extend their business, stretch their abilities, increase their profits, and combat a sense of loneliness. The goal is to focus on what you do best and find others whose skills are complementary to your own.

Where can you find power partners? Begin by developing an awareness that you may find a partner anywhere—from a local business meeting to a national conference. It may be through a referral, or even an online connection. The world is brimming with partnership possibilities—waiting for your discovery.

Expertise shines

The scholar margin—the area used in this newsletter to place pull quotes—the *Working Solo* logo, a masthead and a table of contents frame the simple and effective black-only page design. Note the balanced design on the front page, with the logo in the upper left corner forming a visual diagonal with the body of the page. Both the information on the address panel and the skimmable briefs on the back page get readers involved from the moment the newsletter arrives.

NAME *Working Solo Newsletter* (now offered e-mail only from: info@workingsolo.com)

PUBLISHER Working Solo, Inc., New Paltz, New York

PURPOSE/AUDIENCE Service and marketing to customers and subscribers

PRODUCTION/PRINTING One-color on gray 60# recycled offset

FORMAT 8½" x 11"; eight pages

DESIGN Newman Design/Illustration, Seattle, Washington

ASK AN EXPERT

Network Your Way to Success

by Constance Hallinan Lagan

When I ask new entrepreneurs to define *networking*, they most often respond, "Networking is using others to advance one's own interests." I advise them that they've only captured half of the equation. If you network only to improve your own bottom line, you'll never truly enjoy the benefits of professional networking. The other half—and the more significant part of the networking equation—is *giving*. When entrepreneurs network in the spirit of giving, they will reap rewards far greater than when they network with an attitude of "What's in it for me?"

When one networks only to *take*, the street becomes a one-way dead end for that individual. When one's primary focus is to *give*, the street becomes an active thoroughfare for everyone in the network pool.

To network effectively, introduce yourself to others in a manner that indicates you are willing, even eager, to help them reach their goals. Be prepared to offer a brief description of who you are and what you do, while shaking hands. Ask what the other person does for a living. Discover his or her concerns, and offer information that you feel might help him or her to address those concerns.

Be sure to exchange business cards, and jot notes on the card to help refresh your memory when you're back in your office. The notes may concern what you suggested, what he or she offered, or how you foresee this relationship developing. Follow up with a phone call, letter, or e-mail within a few days, stating you enjoyed your encounter and offering additional assistance in the future.

When others realize you are willing to aid them, most will likewise be interested in assisting you to reach your goals. Mutuality, not reciprocity, is the key to networking suc

Looking out for others' interests may be the best thing you can do to advance your own business.

The advantages to successful networking are numerous. You're able to reach more potential clients, suppliers, sponsors, financial backers, and others through your ever-expanding number of contacts. You can ride the "coat tails" of those who have gone before you and who have established themselves in a positive light. In exchange, you reap the rewards of knowing you have helped others, too.

There is, on occasion, a downside to networking. You may find yourself associated with someone who has less than a favorable standing in the business community. From your brief initial encounter, you may not realize this.

When you network, you also risk being "used" by someone who has no intention of reciprocating. There are networkers who only take. Fortunately, these individuals don't survive very long in the network pool, because their selfish style becomes known and others avoid them.

Networking is rarely an if-you-do-this-for-me-then-I'll-do-that-for-you situation. Although there is a structure to making the introduction, feeling out the needs of others, ascertaining how they can help you, exchanging business cards, and following up, networking is still a loose arrangement. Each network encounter has the potential for increasing the success of both participants.

Treat your network contacts with tender care, nurturing each one with respect, and you will be amazed at how much will come back to you in terms of expanded market share, increased market penetration, and enhanced profit figures.

Author and speaker Constance Hallinan Lagan is director of The Entrepreneurial Center for Small Business Development. She can be contacted at (516) 661-5181 (phone); (516) 321-0615 (fax); or at 35 Claremont Ave., North Babylon, NY 11703.
© 1996 Constance Hallinan Lagan

Working Solo Newsletter #7 ©1996 Portico Press

SOLO MANAGING

The Art of Selecting a Successful Partner

by Edwin Richard Rigsbee

Partnering, like anything else, has its pitfalls and unexpected land minds. The benefits of an alliance relationship, however, usually outweigh the drawbacks if care is taken to develop the alliance correctly. Knowledge must precede action. Here are 9 key qualities to keep in mind when selecting a successful partner.

1. Wants to win.
There is no reason to partner with a loser. This type of relationship will only drag you down. You, and any partner, must have a like desire to win, to want to do better, and create synergy with another.

2. Knows that they are ultimately responsible for their own success.
Partners, like you, enter into an alliance because they understand the value of developing synergy. Knowing when not to partner is also important. Accountability is a double-edged sword. Partners are human and will not always act in their partner's best interest.

3. Is an active listener.
To keep in touch with the heartbeat of an alliance, active listening is crucial. Alliance members must know when their partners need some extra energy for various reasons. Without highly tuned listening skills, offering assistance when needed becomes impossible.

4. Understands and cares about what drives their partner's business.
Since successful partnering is about creating synergy, partners must consistently *give* to the relationship. The giving must be value added in a method that serves in all directions. This is what I call making "Relationship Bank Deposits."

5. Responds well to feedback.
This means receiving in an unprotected manner and then acting on the feedback. Forward and mutually beneficial movement is only possible when all involved are willing to accept counsel.

6. Is flexible in all situations.
This is especially important when unexpected events occur. The ability to change direction is paramount in today's business environment. Knowing when to stand firm and when to accept the flow is a quality that brings great value to a relationship. Flexibility is absolutely necessary, since things often do not happen as expected.

7. Is trustworthy and has integrity.
If your partners respect all with whom they come in contact, they will respect you. Watching potential partners' actions may be more of a clue about their integrity in this area than listening to their words.

8. Seeks win/win solutions.
While it seems as a given that a potential partner would seek win/win, this is not always the case. Some only look to enter a partnering alliance to shore up their own weaknesses. Being in a relationship with this type of person or company will not benefit you in the long run.

9. Understands that partnering is a relationship of interdependence.
It is crucial to understand the distinction between dependence, independence, and interdependence. Dependence implies weakness, while independence can be an oxymoron to alliance relationships. The interconnection is key. You must understand how your actions affect others.

Partnering is a life-long attitude towards business. Adopt the belief that all concerned parties can win, and you'll prosper abundantly over time.

Choose your partners well and the benefits to your business will pay off abundantly over time.

Edwin Richard Rigsbee is the author of The Art of Partnering (Kendall/Hunt, $24.95) and president of Rigsbee Enterprises, Inc., a strategic management and marketing consulting firm. Rigsbee is also a speaker and sales trainer, and can be contacted at (805) 371-4636 (phone); (805) 371-4631(fax); at edrigsbee@aol.com (e-mail); or at PO Box 6425, Westlake Village, CA 91359.
© 1996 Edwin Richard Rigsbee

Working Solo Newsletter #7 ©1996 Portico Press

Reaching independent entrepreneurs

Working Solo, Inc.
PO Box 190
New Paltz, NY 12561

ADDRESS CORRECTION REQUESTED

Want more information on our full line of Working Solo books, audios, newsletters, seminars, and site on the Web? Send an e-mail to: info@workingsolo.com, and our computer will instantly zip back to you complete details.

Your Working Solo Newsletter has arrived!

OCF manages charitable funds which have been established by individuals, families, and other organizations. Distributions from these funds support a variety of Oregon's humanitarian, educational, and cultural programs.

CORNERSTONE
NEWSLETTER

OREGON COMMUNITY FOUNDATION

A Tradition of Community Caring

Alex Byler

Annual Meeting Highlights

At its November 6 Annual Meeting, the OCF Board of Directors elected Alex Byler of Pendleton to a second, one-year term as Chair. Other officers elected were: Donna Woolley of Eugene and C. Morton Bishop, Jr. of Portland as Vice Chairs; David Rhoten of Salem as Secretary; and John Hampton of Portland as Treasurer.

The board also approved grants to nonprofit organizations serving communities throughout the state that totaled $2,773,926. The grants fell into the following categories: Children and Families $1,485,000 (53%); Education and Culture $960,496 (35%); and Citizen Involvement $328,404 (12%).

Foundation President Greg Chaillé reported that OCF's assets had reached $150 million at the year-end of June 30. A record level of $14.5 million was awarded in the last fiscal year in grants and scholarships.

Sauer family creates a charitable fund.
See page 2.

Annual OCF Luncheon Draws Capacity Crowd

Peggy Cushman Speaks on Building the Tradition of Family Philanthropy

Peggy Cushman of Bend addressed a capacity audience of over 500 guests at OCF's November 6 annual luncheon on the topic of developing a family tradition of philanthropy and community caring. Peggy is the daughter of the late Oregon newspaperman, civic leader and philanthropist Bob Chandler.

"In our family, philanthropy was a lifestyle. It was not spoken, but lived by dad, mom, and when mom passed away, by our step-mother Marge. We saw them being active and generous citizens of Bend and of Oregon and we assumed it was the way to be."

Peggy discussed specific examples of how her parents seized opportunities to teach her and her siblings the benefits of giving to others. The full text of Peggy's address is on pages 8-10 of this newsletter.

Peggy challenged other Oregon families to develop their own tradition of community caring, just as her family follows the giving tradition set by her parents and grandparents. She believes she has been given a legacy that she wants to pass on to her children. In Peggy's own words, "We must display a sense of leadership and selflessness with our time and money to ensure that Oregon continues to be a place where our children and grandchildren can have that quality of life with which we have been so blessed."

"We must display a sense of leadership and selflessness with our time and money to ensure that Oregon continues to be a place where our children and grandchildren can have that quality of life with which we have been so blessed."

Peggy Cushman

Winter 1997

1

Picture perfect

In *Cornerstone*, scholar margins on either side of the page provide the perfect spots for photographs and icons. Note the effective use of three ink colors and the bleed of the marbleized folio on each page. A reply envelope stitched in the center spread (the only reason ever to use staples in a newsletter) solicits contributions.

NAME *Cornerstone*

PUBLISHER The Oregon Community Foundation, Portland, Oregon

PURPOSE/AUDIENCE Service to members and the community

PRODUCTION/PRINTING Three-color on white 70# offset

FORMAT 8½" x 11"; twelve pages

DESIGN The Oregon Community Foundation

GRANTS AROUND THE STATE

STATEWIDE

SOLV—
Stop Oregon Litter & Vandalism

$20,000 to expand SOLV's statewide volunteer base

"While SOLV is best known for cleaning up illegal dump sites, organizing massive beach clean-ups, and implementing the innovative river adoption program, our organization felt we needed to bolster the people part of SOLV. We wanted to give a greater number of individuals, families and companies across the state the chance to work together. An increased SOLV volunteer base

provides a conduit for people to produce win-win results without any political or social agendas," says Jack McGowen, SOLV's Executive Director.

Currently, SOLV boasts 40,000 volunteers throughout Oregon. The OCF grant will be used to increase that number by 10,000 volunteers and foster a greater sense of pride and ownership in the state's future.

"I can't begin to tell you what the impact of this grant will have on our organization and the people of Oregon. By increasing our volunteer base, we expand awareness for the need to work together to preserve this treasure called Oregon. Our goal is to be inclusive in every corner of the state so anyone who wants to share in preserving Oregon's beauty can participate."

Emerald Kidsports of Eugene/Springfield

$25,000 to prepare a plan to create four regional sports complexes serving children and youth

For over 40 years, Emerald Kidsports has made a positive impact on the lives of thousands of kids in the Eugene/Springfield area. This innovative organization's commitment is to ensure universal sports access to children and youth regardless of skills or ability to pay. Everyone plays at Kidsports. And, the organization guarantees every child a minimum of playing time

"OCF's grant is helping take Kidsports to another level. It is allowing us to seek matching, local contributions of $25,000 from businesses and individuals to help us develop a new strategic sports plan. This plan will call on design professionals and local sports authorities to look into the future and decide how best to meet the needs of our kids and how to fund those needs," says Bob Josephson, Executive Director. "Basically, the money will allow us to conceptualize the dream so others can share and help plan its reality."

The demand for sports activities has just exploded in the Eugene/Springfield metro area in the past 20 years and aging facilities have not kept up with the demand. "If we are to adequately service our youth with the goal of keeping them interested and out of trouble, we need to provide satisfactory playing sites to serve these youths. The OCF-funded plan will provide for that," Josephson said.

WILLAMETTE VALLEY

GRANTS AROUND THE STATE

NORTHERN OREGON

Interfaith Caregivers of East Multnomah County

$5,000 to organize volunteers to provide services for seniors and the disabled which encourage self sufficiency

Dr. John Milbrath, who is the Executive Director of the Interfaith Caregivers of East Multnomah County, loves people and that feeling just naturally spills into this program. "Our motto is: 'Kindness is the language that helps the blind to see; the deaf to hear.' I feel this is true of the over 70 volunteer caregivers who participate in our program. Our main thrust is to use the power of an organized interfaith volunteer effort to effect positive change in our local community. And, it's working."

In just the last month, the Interfaith's small office received over 650 calls from senior citizens and disabled residents. These neighbors were requesting everything from help with transportation, to assistance with home repairs, yard work, and light housekeeping. With the recent ice storm and flooding in East Portland, the Interfaith Caregivers were available to immediately offer assistance.

"Our goal is to keep people independent and living in their own homes by offering a bit of needed assistance. With this incredible grant from OCF, we can do a more effective job by reaching and expanding our volunteer base to service the hundreds of requests we receive each month," ends Dr. Milbrath.

Medford Community Health Center

$6,000 to provide medical services for children from working poor families

The Medford Community Health Center has operated for 25 years. This year the center, which operates clinics out of Medford and Ashland, recorded over 10,000 patient visits—with 1/3 of those visits from patients under 17 years of age.

The $6000 OCF grant provides funding to enhance primary and preventive care for these children from working poor families. Peg Crowley, Executive Director, explains, "For many of Jackson County's low-income families, our clinic represents the first line of medical defense. We provide diagnosis, treatment, and treatment management. Our medical services assure them an opportunity to access physicals, immunizations, and follow-up care. We are not a free clinic; we ask all participating families to pay a nominal fee for our services."

The clinic's primary focus is to maintain the health of local, low-income children and families. Staff members have recently begun concentrating on increased community outreach efforts to educate families on the importance of preventive care for children—such as immunizations and regular physicals. The OCF grant will provide for these efforts.

SOUTHERN OREGON

communication briefings™

ideas that work

A monthly idea source for decision makers

ISSN 0730-7799 Volume 8, Number 5

Tips of the Month

■ **The next** time you update your telephone and membership directories, be sure to list fax numbers along with regular telephone numbers. Keeping fax numbers in a separate directory wastes time.

Source: Marina Johnson, NRECA, 1800 Massachusetts Ave. NW, Washington, DC 20009.

■ **Always include** the date above your signature when you approve an invoice for payment. This can help identify bottlenecks in your organization's accounts-payable process when a bill is not paid.

Source: Kim K. Ross, 4554 Mill Village Road, Raleigh, NC 27612.

■ **Keep a travel** card in your wallet for out-of-town trips. List your office telephone and fax numbers, frequent-flyer club membership numbers, travel-agency and airline numbers, credit-card numbers and any other information you might need quickly while traveling.

Source: P. Nash, AACC, 2029 K St. NW, Washington, DC 20006.

■ **Keep a copy** of the final proofs you return to a printer. Have the printer initial your copy. If something goes wrong with the printing, it's always better to have written proof of who authorized what.

Source: Frank McGeough, 600 Front St., Box 848, Lynden, WA 98264.

■ **Write an executive** summary of a report before writing the report itself. This provides a road map for the report and discourages you from going off on tangents.

■ **If you** have to address a noisy gathering, try playing music as the crowd gathers before the speech begins. When music stops abruptly, groups usually stop talking and turn to see what happened.

Source: Thomas J. O'Grady Jr., Whitesell Co., 1 Executive Campus, Route 70, Cherry Hill, NJ 08002.

Writing

Apply the Conversational Test

If you want to avoid stilted writing, apply the Conversational Test developed by John Louis DiGaetani of Hofstra University. *How:*

Ask yourself if you would ever *say* to your reader what you are writing.

For example, would you say, "Enclosed please find the price lists you requested"?

You would probably say, "Here are the price lists you requested."

The Conversational Test helps you get rid of business jargon and impersonal writing. It forces you to write in human terms and adds color and interest to your writing.

Caution: Don't assume that the Conversational Test gives you a mandate to use slang. You still have to assume a proper business tone.

Some things to note:

● **Jargon, wordy** expressions and puffy sentences *don't* make you appear more polished. They impress only the naive.

● **Business** writing *isn't* supposed to seem stuffy and impersonal.

● **Trying to** hide bad news in a fog of wordiness just doesn't work.

Source: The Wall Street Journal on Management, Mentor, NAL Penguin Inc., 1633 Broadway, New York, NY 10019.

Persuasion

How to Convince Your Boss

If your boss is the type who doesn't usually react favorably to new ideas, consider these approaches:

● **Shape your** idea so that it can be approved by your immediate boss. If the boss has to go upstairs for approval, it might never happen.

● **Discuss the** idea with your peers and others who might be affected. If the boss says, "The others won't like it," note that you have obtained support of the people who would be involved in the change.

● **Find something** in the company guidelines or policies that will support what you want to do. Bureaucrats, especially, love to follow manuals.

● **Explain how** the change will help

the organization get where it wants to go faster, easier and perhaps cheaper.

● **Show how** the change will make the boss look good and the organization more reputable.

● **Use company** jargon and terms that are hot buttons in your organization. If possible, relate the change to something that is one of the organization's key goals or objectives.

● **Use illustrations** and examples to persuade.

● **Offer three** reasons why your idea should be accepted. Two may not seem like enough and four may be too many.

Source: The George Odiorne Letter, MBO Inc., 5531 9th St. N., St. Petersburg, FL 33703.

What's Inside

Don't miss next month's issue. Subscribe now. Call 800-888-4402. Carole Rennie, Subscription Manager

Just what the readers ordered

The publishers created this classic three-column news-letter after hours of focus groups with targeted readers. Writers and communicators wanted condensed, short articles filled with useful tips, and valued graphic aids to help them access information quickly. Rounded corners add an element of softness and decoration. Clip art and other embellishments are rarely used in this newsletter. The subscription form is always included on page 7 and printed directly behind the address label on page 8, a good device for tracking which subscriber's copy is being used.

NAME *communication briefings*

PUBLISHER Encoders, Inc., Blackwood, New Jersey

PURPOSE/AUDIENCE Service to subscribers

PRODUCTION/PRINTING Two-color on cream 60# linen text

FORMAT 8½" × 11"; eight pages

DESIGN The editors of *communication briefings*

Ships & Shipwrecks

The Newsletter of Nautical History and Discovery

Vol. 2 No. 1   January/February 1991

The Search For Columbus's *Gallega*

By Denise C. Lakey

In 1982, a group of graduate students in nautical archaeology at Texas A & M University launched a project to look for the lost ships of Columbus. In 1989, having received our degrees, we incorporated our own research institute—Ships of Discovery. Today the group consists of Donald Keith, Toni Carrell, Jerry Goodale, Joe Simmons, and me. We are hot on the trail of the caravel, *Gallega*. If we find it, the *Gallega* will be the first ship discovered that is known to have sailed under Columbus.

We started looking for the *Gallega* as a result of our work on the Molasses Reef wreck in the Turks and Caicos Islands in 1982. We knew the shipwreck we were excavating was very early. It had a lot of artifacts, but time, weather, and the marine life had destroyed most of the hull. And, studying only one site raised more questions than it answered. We wanted

to find a similar shipwreck that had good hull remains. We looked at the Highborn Cay wreck, discovered in the 1960s, but it had been heavily salvaged.

We wanted to find a wreck that definitely tied into history. We knew that the Molasses Reef and Highborn Cay wrecks dated from the early Spanish exploration, but there were no details about these ships in the historical record, so it was difficult to identify them. We decided to look for a shipwreck that could be documented.

It was natural for two reasons to look for a Columbus ship. First, so much historical research had already been done on Columbus (well-documented studies of original sources), that it gave our work a head start. Second, the public is interested in Columbus's ships. It would be more exciting for everyone if we found one of his ships, rather than one of a lesser known explorer.

In 1503, this idyllic bay at the mouth of the Rio Belen river, Panama, became a trap for Christopher Columbus. One of his caravels remains here, entombed in the bottom mud.

All photos: Ships of Discovery

In This Issue

Smooth sailing

A simple three-column format, with its flexibility of illustration and photo arrangement, moves the news along. The floating rules help the eye stay within the columns for the long articles with few subheads. Note how the watery blue second color and flecked recycled paper of *Ships & Shipwrecks* enhances the newsletter's theme of ancient treasures under the seas. The blue also appears as a screen tint representing water in the inside illustration. *Syvamonitor* lets bold art break out of the careful rules containing text.

NAME *Ships & Shipwrecks*

PUBLISHER Nautical History and Discovery, Riderwood, Maryland

PURPOSE/AUDIENCE Service to subscribers

PRODUCTION/PRINTING Two-color on recycled paper

FORMAT 8½" x 11"; eight pages

DESIGN Danette C. High

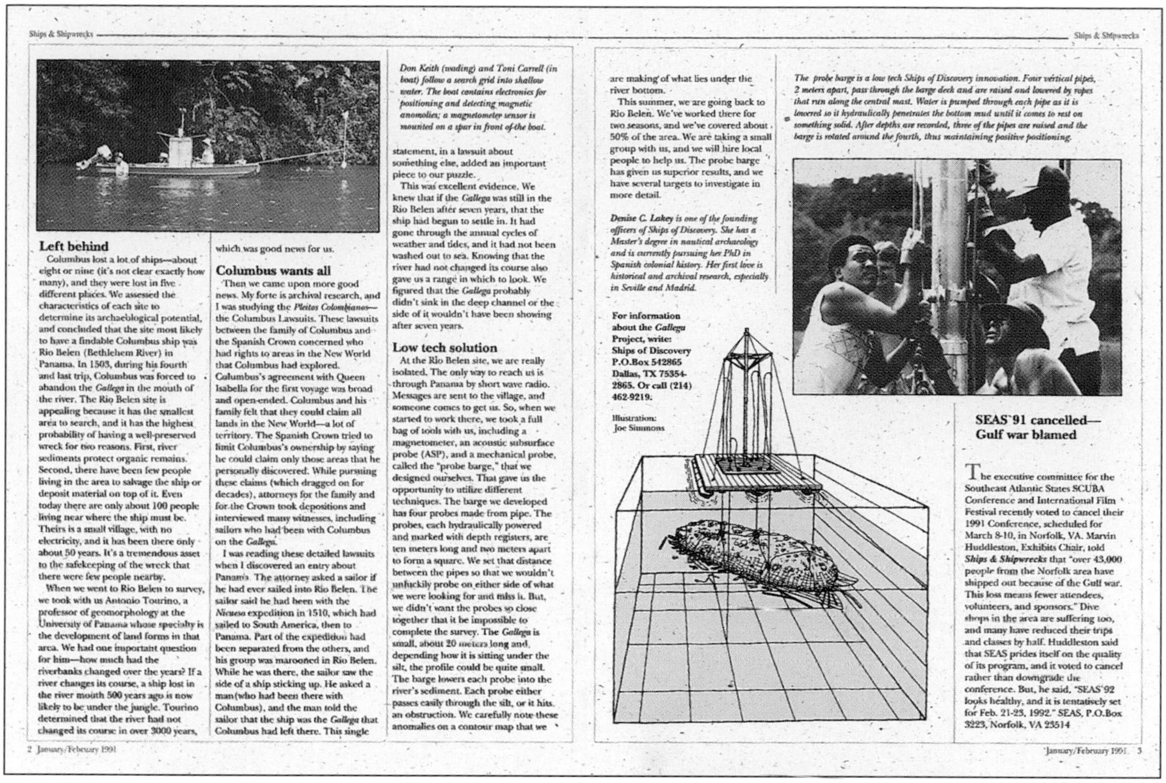

Ships & Shipwrecks

Left behind

Columbus lost a lot of ships—about eight or nine (it's not clear exactly how many), and they were lost in five different places. We assessed the characteristics of each site to determine its archaeological potential, and concluded that the site most likely to have a findable Columbus ship was Rio Belen (Bethlehem River) in Panama. In 1503, during his fourth and last trip, Columbus was forced to abandon the *Gallega* in the mouth of the river. The Rio Belen site is appealing because it has the smallest area to search, and it has the highest probability of having a well-preserved wreck for two reasons. First, river sediments protect organic remains. Second, there have been few people living in the area to salvage the ship or deposit material on top of it. Even today there are only about 100 people living near where the ship must be. Theirs is a small village, with no electricity, and it has been there only about 50 years. It's a tremendous asset to the safekeeping of the wreck that there were few people nearby.

When we went to Rio Belen to survey, we took with us Antonio Tourino, a professor of geomorphology at the University of Panama whose specialty is the development of land forms in that area. We had one important question for him—how much had the riverbanks changed over the years? If a river changes its course, a ship lost in the river mouth 500 years ago is now likely to be under the jungle. Tourino determined that the river had not changed its course in over 3000 years, which was good news for us.

Columbus wants all

Then we came upon more good news. My forte is archival research, and I was studying the *Pleitos Colombianos*—the Columbus Lawsuits. These lawsuits between the family of Columbus and the Spanish Crown concerned who had rights to areas in the New World that Columbus had explored. Columbus's agreement with Queen Isabella for the first voyage was broad and open-ended. Columbus and his family felt that they could claim all lands in the New World—a lot of territory. The Spanish Crown tried to limit Columbus's ownership by saying he could claim only those areas that he personally discovered. While pursuing these claims (which dragged on for decades), attorneys for the family and for the Crown took depositions and interviewed many witnesses, including sailors who had been with Columbus on the *Gallega*.

I was reading these detailed lawsuits when I discovered an entry about Panama. The attorney asked a sailor if he had ever sailed into Rio Belen. The sailor said he had been with the *Nicuesa* expedition in 1510, which had sailed to South America, then to Panama. Part of the expedition had been separated from the others, and his group was marooned in Rio Belen. While he was there, the sailor saw the side of a ship sticking up. He asked a man (who had been there with Columbus), and the man told the sailor that the ship was the *Gallega* that Columbus had left there. This single statement, in a lawsuit about something else, added an important piece to our puzzle.

Don Keith (wading) and Toni Carrell (in boat) follow a search grid into shallow water. The boat contains electronics for positioning and detecting magnetic anomolies; a magnetometer sensor is mounted on a spar in front of the boat.

This was excellent evidence. We knew that if the *Gallega* was still in the Rio Belen after seven years, that the ship had begun to settle in. It had gone through the annual cycles of weather and tides, and it had not been washed out to sea. Knowing that the river had not changed its course also gave us a range in which to look. We figured that the *Gallega* probably didn't sink in the deep channel or the side of it wouldn't have been showing after seven years.

Low tech solution

At the Rio Belen site, we are really isolated. The only way to reach us is through Panama by short wave radio. Messages are sent to the village, and someone comes to get us. So, when we started to work there, we took a full bag of tools with us, including a magnetometer, an acoustic subsurface probe (ASP), and a mechanical probe, called the "probe barge," that we designed ourselves. That gave us the opportunity to utilize different techniques. The barge we developed has four probes made from pipe. The probes, each hydraulically powered and marked with depth registers, are ten meters long and two meters apart to form a square. We set that distance between the pipes so that we wouldn't unluckily probe on either side of what we were looking for and miss it. But, we didn't want the probes so close together that it be impossible to complete the survey. The *Gallega* is small, about 20 meters long and, depending how it is sitting under the silt, the profile could be quite small. The barge lowers each probe into the river's sediment. Each probe either passes easily through the silt, or it hits an obstruction. We carefully note these anomalies on a contour map that we are making of what lies under the river bottom.

This summer, we are going back to Rio Belen. We've worked there for two seasons, and we've covered about 50% of the area. We are taking a small group with us, and we will hire local people to help us. The probe barge has given us superior results, and we have several targets to investigate in more detail.

Denise C. Lakey is one of the founding officers of Ships of Discovery. She has a Master's degree in nautical archaeology and is currently pursuing her PhD in Spanish colonial history. Her first love is historical and archival research, especially in Seville and Madrid.

For information about the *Gallega* Project, write: Ships of Discovery P.O.Box 542865 Dallas, TX 75354-2865. Or call (214) 462-9219.

Illustration: Joe Simmons

The probe barge is a low tech Ships of Discovery innovation. Four vertical pipes, 2 meters apart, pass through the barge deck and are raised and lowered by ropes that run along the central mast. Water is pumped through each pipe as it is lowered so it hydraulically penetrates the bottom mud until it comes to rest on something solid. After depths are recorded, three of the pipes are raised and the barge is rotated around the fourth, thus maintaining positive positioning.

SEAS'91 cancelled—Gulf war blamed

The executive committee for the Southeast Atlantic States SCUBA Conference and International Film Festival recently voted to cancel their 1991 Conference, scheduled for March 8-10, in Norfolk, VA. Marvin Huddleston, Exhibits Chair, told ***Ships & Shipwrecks*** that "over 43,000 people from the Norfolk area have shipped out because of the Gulf war. This loss means fewer attendees, volunteers, and sponsors." Dive shops in the area are suffering too, and many have reduced their trips and classes by half. Huddleston said that SEAS prides itself on the quality of its program, and it voted to cancel rather than downgrade the conference. But, he said, "SEAS'92 looks healthy, and it is tentatively set for Feb. 21-23, 1992." SEAS, P.O.Box 3223, Norfolk, VA 23514

2 January/February 1991

January/February 1991 3

Syva drug abuse feature

THE FIRST CLIA '88 INSPECTIONS

On January 20th of this year, the laboratory Mary Jemison supervises was inspected for compliance with regulations of the Clinical Laboratory Improvement Amendments of 1988 (CLIA '88). This inspection, unlike others, was unannounced. "When the inspector introduced herself and told me that she was there to do my CLIA inspection, of course my heart rate just increased dramatically. You must realize that I'm at a small hospital laboratory. I was the only person there that day."

It was the third inspection Jemison had undergone in a supervisory position at the Perry County Hospital laboratory, which services a 30-bed hospital plus 51 skilled nursing home beds in a small town in Alabama. "Each inspection had made me a little nervous. But this was CLIA, and it just wasn't the same. I had most of the information I needed—I thought I did—because I'd gone to a lot of the workshops on CLIA in Montgomery. I had a lot of information together; but it wasn't all in place, and I wasn't ready to be inspected by CLIA."

This sounds like every laboratorian's CLIA '88 nightmare. But apparently Jemison was better prepared than she realized: Perry County Hospital passed its inspection without a single deficiency.

Having a Good Inspection

The key to a good inspection (or survey, as it is called in the CLIA '88 regulations) is largely preparation. Because nearly all of the laboratories inspected so far were previously regulated under CLIA '67, these laboratories are having mostly positive experiences. Larry Miller at the Madison Avenue Laboratory in Indianapolis, Indiana, saw nothing in his recent inspection to upset him. "Why be upset? We've been doing this for a long time." He admits that his inspection under the new CLIA '88 regulations was longer, "but they didn't ask for anything I wasn't expecting. You have to remember that we've been regulated for a long, long time. And we've been inspected by the same agencies doing these inspections for a long time. So, why would there be any surprises?"

At the Louisville and Jefferson County Health Department in Louisville, Kentucky, Elwood Stroder has been getting ready for his inspection for the past year and a half. The lab has had three or four inservices, and Stroder feels "fairly prepared." He hasn't had his formal CLIA '88 inspection yet, but his state inspector gave the lab what he calls "the CLIA preview" when she came for their regular state inspection.

This inspection was a little tougher than previous inspections. "She was much more adamant about certain things like quality control and record keeping," Stroder found. But having so much time to prepare made things easier. "We went through some of the panic stages in the beginning, and we were over some of those humps when she actually got here. For the most part, health departments haven't been heavily regulated. But our director saw CLIA coming a long time ago. He got us certified through the state, which was the only thing that we could get certified through at the time. And that's helped us out a lot since we've been certified for 7 or 8 years, and we've been having inspections for that many years. Plus, 4 or 5 years ago, even before CLIA, he got us on to the CAP [College of American Pathologists] surveys, our proficiency programs—all the things that we needed to be on—so that's been a big help, too. He was really a big help because he was worried about it early on in the process, and he prepared us for it. I think it's the places like doctors' labs that haven't been regulated before that are going to feel the most panic."

First-ever Inspections

But even the laboratories that haven't been inspected before need not fear their first inspections. CLIA inspector Mary Azbill, who is program director for the Indiana State Board of Health, assures them, "The first year, we will not be taking sanctions on deficiencies unless we see it's a real hazard or problem to a patient. So, on the first survey, it may be that we document a lot of deficiencies, but the labs will have 12 months to correct them—unless there's a serious problem, and then they would have 45 days or so. We're not coming in to shut them down. The survey will be done according to the regulations. They will be told what's wrong, they'll be given time to submit a plan of what they're going to do to fix it, and they'll be given, again, depending upon the seriousness, a time frame up to 12 months to correct the deficiency."

The laboratories that were not previously regulated under CLIA '67 can also take some comfort from knowing that, in most cases, they will receive somewhat more time to prepare for their inspections than the currently regulated laboratories. Azbill was given directions last September, "and I'm assuming all the other regions had the same directions, to do any problem labs first. After inspecting all of those labs, we were to do the previously regulated labs that are not also accredited." Inspection of accredited laboratories is being postponed because accreditation programs such as CAP may be permitted (ie, given what is called "deemed status") to

6 Volume II Number 2 1993

Volume II Number 2 1993 7

St. Louis Children's Hospital
One Children's Place
P.O. Box 14871
St. Louis, Missouri 63178-4871

NON-PROFIT
ORGANIZATION
U.S. POSTAGE
PAID
St. Louis, Mo.
Permit #617

ST. LOUIS
CHILDREN'S
HOSPITAL

BJC HEALTH SYSTEM™

454-KIDS *or Toll Free, 1-800-678-KIDS*

St. Louis Children's Hospital *Answer Line*

Available 7 a.m. to 11 p.m., Monday-Friday;
Noon-8 p.m., Weekends; 9 a.m.-5 p.m., Holidays
St. Louis Children's Hospital, a member
of BJC Health System, is recognized as one
of the nation's leading pediatric hospitals.
Our 235-bed facility, designed especially to
care for kids, offers a full range of pediatric
health services to families throughout our
200-mile service area and beyond.

Nested newsletters

The self-mailer unfolds to a two-column, letter-size *Kids Today* which
unfolds to a four-column tabloid *Kids
Today* which unfolds to a 22" x 17"
fact-filled poster that includes a calendar of events. Green and blue spot
inks give color to the fun, childlike
illustrations.

NAME *Kids Today*

PUBLISHER St. Louis Children's Hospital, St. Louis,
Missouri

PURPOSE/AUDIENCE Service and marketing to
customers

PRODUCTION/PRINTING Three-color on white
60# offset

FORMAT 8½" x 11"; opens to four 11" x 17" pages

DESIGN St. Louis Children's Hospital

Kids Today

Winter 1997

A quarterly publication from St. Louis Children's Hospital

Happy, Healthy New Year! How To Make Those New Year's Resolutions Last

Right after the holidays, you probably made a list of resolutions for the new year. If you're like most parents, you
included your children in a family-style improvement plan
that included eating more nutritious foods, cutting down on
snacks, getting more exercise, watching less television, reading more books and...if you're like most people, you've
already begun to toss aside some of those resolutions.

"It's so tempting to set really high goals for ourselves —
and for our children — especially when it comes to changing eating habits," says Christy Gilcrease, a registered dietitian at St. Louis Children's Hospital. "The truth is, it's just not
realistic to banish potato chips or candy bars from your
home forever. Instead, teach
children that any food is fine in
moderation — and then
make sure there are
plenty of nutritional
options in the
kitchen."

Snacks and Kids Belong Together

While adults may decide to cut out snacks, children
from 1 to 10 years old need between-meal snacks to grow.
"Kids should consume between 1,300 and 2,000 calories
per day — about the same number of calories that most
adults need," says Gilcrease. "Since children's stomachs are
smaller, they need to eat more frequently to keep up energy
levels and meet daily nutritional needs." Snacks should be
planned as mini-meals, says Gilcrease. Remember that each
day, a child needs to consume:

▲ six to 11 servings of bread, cereal, rice or pasta
▲ three to five servings of vegetables
▲ two to four servings of fruit
▲ two to three servings of milk, yogurt or cheese
▲ two to three servings of meat, poultry, fish, beans,
   eggs or nuts

See calendar page for some healthy snack substitutions.

Family Exercise: Help Yourself, Help Your Kids

Regular exercise is usually right at the top of
the family resolution list. It should stay there,
too, according to national fitness statistics,
because many Americans are passing on
their sedentary lifestyles to their children.
A recent U.S. Surgeon General report
shows that only about half the nation's
children are physically active for more than
20 minutes each day.

Just as children model parents' eating habits,
they also tend to follow in their family's footsteps regarding exercise — whether those
footsteps lead to a brisk walk or to the
couch. "The best way to help your kids is
to help yourselves," says Paul Jenkins,
physical therapist at St. Louis Children's
Hospital. "Pick an activity you and your child enjoy,
and just get started," he says.

If you're starting the year with a shiny new piece
of home exercise equipment, remember that it's
designed for adults. "The 'ab flex' equipment is too big
for kids — they'll just end up flexing their hips," says
Jenkins. "With the exception of properly adjusted treadmills, children don't benefit from adult-size exercise
equipment."

And even if the weather outside is frightful, bundle
up (in layered, loose-fitting outerwear) and go on
walks, head for a skating rink or show your kids how
to zip past those stores during a brisk mall-walk. Doing
this 20 minutes a day, three to five days a week, will
help establish a life-long pattern of activity for your
children — and you'll be well on your way to a healthier lifestyle.

Help keep those resolutions by enrolling your
child in the "Head to Toe" class, Feb. 18. For information, call **454-KIDS (press 3)**.

Kids Today

Winter 1997

A quarterly publication from St. Louis Children's Hospital

Air Bag Safety Update: Buckle Them Up — In the Back Seat

Air bags are effective because they deploy rapidly — faster than the blink of an eye — by coming out of the dashboard at rates of up to 200 miles per hour. Air bags save hundreds of lives each year; but, tragically, several children nationwide have been killed or injured by the force of an air bag opening during an accident.

The National Highway Traffic Safety Administration reports that in many of these cases, the children were either riding in the front seat in a rear-facing child safety seat, or they were "out of position" — unbuckled or not wearing the shoulder portion of the seat belt.

"The National Safety Council is conducting a campaign aimed at educating the public on air bag safety," says Nancy Litzinger, child advocacy spokesperson for St. Louis Children's Hospital. "The campaign stresses one simple road rule: kids belong in the back seat," she says.

Drivers can virtually eliminate air bag dangers to children by insisting that they ride — properly belted or in child safety seats — in the back seat. Additional studies show that regardless of the presence of air bags, children are up to 30 percent safer when riding in the rear rather than the front seat of cars.

Any adult — or caregiver— who drives children should review the following air bag safety tips, developed by the National Safety Council:

- **Kids ride in back.** Infants should NEVER ride in the front seat of a vehicle with a passenger-side air bag. Children, typically up to age 12, also should ride buckled up in the back seat.
- **Child safety seats.** Young children and infants ALWAYS should ride in age- and size-appropriate child safety seats. The safety seat should be installed and anchored properly, and the child should be correctly buckled into the safety seat. A child who has outgrown a convertible safety seat needs to ride in a booster seat in order for the vehicle's safety belts to fit properly.
- **Wear both lap AND shoulder belts.*** The shoulder strap should cross the collarbone, and the lap belt should fit low and tight on the hips. The shoulder strap should never be slipped behind the back or under the arm.
- **Move the front seat back.** Driver and front passenger seats should be moved as far back as possible, particularly for children ages 12 and older and for shorter adults.

*Cut the slack: Seat belt slack can be dangerous. Tests conducted by the National Highway Traffic Safety Administration show that two inches of slack in a car's shoulder harness increases the incidence of serious head injury by 81 percent. So make sure everybody's "tucked in" snugly while driving.

Sweet Dreams or Bedtime Blues?

"Good night noises...good night room...good night stars...good night moon." Those soothing lines from *Good Night Moon*, Margaret Wise Brown's classic bedtime story, have helped lull many children to sleep. But many others seem to resist a good night's sleep with every fiber of their being.

"Sleep problems nearly always rank among parents' top concerns," says Mary Beth Casso, pediatric nurse educator at St. Louis Children's Hospital. "As we mature, we learn ways to 'comfort' ourselves back to sleep — by changing positions or adjusting the pillow, for example," she says. "Parents can help babies and young children learn ways to lull themselves back to sleep."

What's "Normal?"

As almost every parent can confirm, there is no established sleep cycle for the first three to four months of life — babies sleep an average of 16 hours a day and awake when they're hungry. Sleep patterns vary, Casso says, but as the baby gets older, nightly (or daily!) sleep averages:

- 14 hours beginning around six months
- 13 hours by age 2
- 11 hours by age 5
- 8 or 9 hours by age 12

Six months is not too early to begin establishing some nighttime routines, Casso says. In classes, she presents techniques from well-known pediatricians and sleep experts, but stresses that families should look at their own individual goals — and their individual children — when trying to achieve bedtime tranquility.

Rituals help make bedtime easier, Casso says. She offers the following suggestions:

- Avoid boisterous play; substitute a half-hour of quiet activities before bedtime.
- Use a bedtime snack — followed by brushing the teeth — as a signal to begin the bedtime countdown.
- A warm, quiet bath — not too much splashing! — can be soothing.
- Allow your child to select a favorite pair of pajamas and pick a special book — saved just for bedtime.

Sleep Apnea

Although occasional sleeping problems are a common part of infancy and early childhood, some sleeping disturbances — like sleep apnea — signal a medical problem. Symptoms include excessive snoring and cessation or reduction of air flowing through the airways, despite efforts to breathe. Causes include obesity, or enlarged tonsils or adenoids that block the upper air passage. "It's not unusual for infants to have pauses in their breathing, but a breathing cessation of 20 seconds is significant at any age, and should be evaluated by a physician," says George B. Mallory Jr., MD. Dr. Mallory and James B. Kemp, MD, pediatric pulmonary specialists, are co-directors of sleep diagnostic services at St. Louis Children's Hospital. Susan Arnold, MD, pediatric neurologist, is also a consultant to the team.

"Obstructive sleep apnea is not uncommon in children and adolescents," Dr. Mallory says. In severe cases, the condition can cause heart failure, but new treatment options and monitoring devices make the condition manageable. "Any time your child is having a breathing difficulty — awake or asleep — contact your pediatrician," says Dr. Mallory.

To find out more about helping your child — and yourself — get a good night's sleep, attend the Parenting Enrichment Group, "Lights Out," at the Magic House on March 20.

All shapes and sizes

No fixed size makes a newsletter a newsletter. Your news can appear on a postcard, U.S. letter, legal, tabloid or international A4 size. It doesn't even have to be in print at all. See pages 21, 26, 61, 94-95, 110-111, 126, 127, for newsletters via e-mail and on the Web.

Weight Loss & Exercise

We're sure that many of you have made New Year's resolutions, including the annual rite of promising to lose weight.

So, to help you accomplish your goals, let's take a short quiz courtesy of Weight Watchers International to test your knowledge of weight loss and exercise.

1. The best type of physical activity for losing weight is: (a) housework; (b) weightlifting); or (c) aerobic exercise.

2. Which of the following is not true about aerobic exercise? (a) it uses large muscle groups, such as leg muscles and large portions of the upper body; (b) it requires a great deal of oxygen; (c) for weight loss, it is best performed at a rapid pace for no more than 20 minutes.

3. Rank the following activities from the highest burner of calories to the lowest: (a) swimming; (b) cooking; (c) light office work; or (d) aerobic dancing.

4. True or false? Exercising before a meal uses more calories than exercising after a meal.

Now the answers!

1 — (c) Aerobic exercise, with its stimulation of the cardiovascular system and use of large muscle groups, is the most conducive to weight loss.

2 — (c) Aerobic exercise is best performed at a low-to-moderate pace for at least 20 minutes.

3 — Swimming: 264 calories
Aerobic dancing: 214 calories
Light office work: 129 calories
Cooking: 94 calories.
All measures based on 30 minutes by a 154-pound person.

4 — Neither. Researchers do not know whether exercising before or after a meal will help you burn more calories. But any exercise burns calories, no matter when it is done.

Dieta y Ejercicio

Estamos seguros que muchos de ustedes han tomado resoluciones de Año Nuevo, incluyendo promesas de perder peso.

Para ayudarles, trate de contestar las siguientes preguntas, cortesía de Weight Watchers Internacional:

1. El mejor tipo de actividad física para perder peso es: (a) tareas domésticas; (b) levantar pesas; o (c) gimnasia aeróbica.

2. De las siguientes preguntas sobre gimnasia aeróbica, diga cual es falsa: (a) usa un grupo grande de músculos, como los de las piernas y el torso; (b) requiere mucho oxígeno; (c) para perder peso, es mejor ejercitar en forma rápida por unos 20 minutos.

3. Liste de mayor a menor cual de estas actividades quema más calorías: (a) natación; (b) cocinar; (c) trabajo de oficina liviano; o (d) gimnasia aeróbica.

4. ¿Verdadero o falso? El hacer ejercicio antes de las comidas quema más calorías que el ejercicio que se hace después de las mismas.

¡Y ahora las respuestas!

1 — (c) Gimnacia aeróbica; con la estimulación cardiovascular y el uso de grandes grupos de músculos, es la mejor forma de perder peso.

2 — (c) Gimnasia aeróbica; ejercitada en forma rápida por unos 20 minutos.

3 — Natación: quema 264 calorías
Gimnasia aeróbica: 214 calorías
Trabajo de oficina liviano: 129 calorías
Cocinar: 94 calorías
Basado en 30 minutos y en una persona que pesa 154 libras.

4 — Ninguno. Investigadores no saben con certeza si el hacer ejercicio antes de comer ayuda a quemar más calorías. Lo que sí se sabe, es que el hacer ejercicio ayuda a quemar calorías.

The new CAC Medical Center in North Miami Beach is located at 1701 N.E. 164th Street.
El nuevo Centro Médico CAC de North Miami Beach esta situado en el 1701 N.E. 164 Calle.

Have You Had Your Annual Mammogram?

According to the American Cancer Society, the following are the recommended guidelines for screening of breast cancer:

✓ All women over 50 years of age should have a mammogram once a year.

✓ Women 40 years of age and older with prior breast cancer or those with a first-degree relative with a history of breast cancer.

✓ Women 35 years of age with a prior history of breast cancer.

We urge you to contact your CAC Medical Center to schedule a mammogram as part of your preventative health care program.

—Lourdes Agundez, RN
Director of Quality Assurance

¿Se Hizo Usted Su Mamografía Anual?

La Sociedad Americana del Cáncer le ofrece las siguientes pautas a seguir para detectar el cáncer del seno:

✓ Todas las mujeres mayores de 50 años deben hacerse un mamograma todos los años; así como:

✓ Todas las mujeres de 40 años o mayores con historia de cáncer del seno en cualquiera de sus familiares de primer grado.

✓ Mujeres de 35 años o mayores con historia de cáncer del seno.

Póngase en contacto con su centro médico CAC más cercano para hacer una cita para una mamografía como parte del cuidado preventivo de salud.

—Lourdes Agundez, RN
Directora de Seguridad de Calidad

WELCOME NEW DOCTORS

We welcome the following doctors who have joined CAC-Ramsay:

BIENVENIDOS NUEVOS DOCTORES

Los siguientes doctores se han unido a la familia de CAC-Ramsay:

Ray Acevedo, M.D.
Rafael Alfonso, M.D.
Janellie Azaret, M.D.
María Betancourt, M.D.
James Blair, M.D.
Jorge Caridad, M.D…
José Carreras, M.D…
Mayra Cordero, M…
Mario Cuervo, M.D…
Jesús Escar, M.D.
Yolanda Galarraga…
Manuel García, M…
María González, M.D.
Rodolfo Gutiérrez, M.D.
Luis Hernández, M.D.
Juana Julien, M.D.

Generic vs. Brand-Name Drugs

(The following questions and answers were designed for our members who receive pharmacy benefits.)

Question: Are companies which produce generic drugs under the same regulations as those which make brand-name prescription drugs?
Answer: Yes. The company manufacturing the brand-name drug has proven to the Food and Drug Administration, which monitors all drugs sold in this country, that the drug is safe. The company distributing the generic drug only has to show the FDA that it has correctly followed the formulation using the same amount of the identical active ingredient.

Question: Are brand-name drugs of better quality than their generic counterparts?
Answer: No. While 80% of the generic drugs sold today are made by the same companies which make brand-name drugs, all companies manufacturing drugs are subject to FDA inspections to ensure that they meet federal guidelines for equipment, workplace environment, drug quality, purity and strength.

Question: Can a patient demand the brand-name drug?
Answer: Yes. A patient always has the right to request a brand-name drug. However, that patient will be responsible for paying the difference in the cost of the two drugs, in addition to any applicable copayment.

Question: Will CAC-Ramsay be adding pharmacy facilities to their centers?
Answer: Yes, in our continuing effort to better serve our members, we are planning to open pharmacies in 4–5 of our centers during the next few months.

Medicinas Genéricas vs. Medicinas de Marca

(Hemos recibido cartas de asociados que tienen beneficios de farmacia con preguntas acerca de medicinas genéricas.)

Pregunta: ¿Tienen las compañías que fabrican medicinas genéricas las mismas regulaciones que las compañías que fabrican medicinas de marca?
Respuesta: Si, porque las compañías de medicinas de marca han probado que las mismas son eficaces y seguras. Una compañía de medicinas genéricas debe ser aprobada por el Food and Drug Administration, (FDA), organización que se encarga de controlar todas las medicinas que se venden en el país. Las medicinas genéricas deben usar la misma fórmula y los mismos ingredientes que las de marca.

Pregunta: ¿Son las medicinas de marca mejores que las genéricas?
Respuesta: Absolutamente no. El FDA inspecciona regularmente los diferentes laboratorios, tanto los de medicinas genéricas como los de marca, para asegurarse que todo esté en perfecto estado de limpieza y calidad.

Pregunta: ¿Puede un paciente especificar que desea solamente la medicina de marca?
Respuesta: Por supuesto. Sin embargo, el paciente deberá pagar la diferencia de precio entre la medicina genérica y la de marca, más el copago cuando sea aplicable.

Pregunta: ¿Tiene CAC-Ramsay planes de abrir farmacias en diferentes centros?
Respuesta: Si, en nuestro continuo esfuerzo por brindar un mejor servicio a nuestros asociados, planeamos abrir farmacias en 4 o 5 centros en los próximos meses.

Just a Reminder...

Always contact your CAC-Ramsay Primary Care Physician or nearest CAC Medical Center for all of your medical service needs.

All Specialist services and hospital admissions must be authorized in advance by CAC-Ramsay.

Para Recordarles...

Póngase siempre en contacto con su médico de CAC-Ramsay o con el Centro Médico más cercano cuando necesite servicios.

Todos los servicios especiales y las admisiones en el hospital deben ser autorizados con CAC-Ramsay.

NEW AFFILIATED PROVIDERS

We welcome these new affiliated providers:

NUEVOS PROVEEDORES AFILIADOS

Bienvenida a los siguientes proveedores afiliados:

Medical Center of Broward
Alan J. Saltzman, D.O.
7762 N.W. 44 St., Sunrise
Rajiv R. Chokshi, M.D.
4701 N. Federal Hwy., #21,
Bldg. A, Fort Lauderdale
Broward Medical Center
Dr. Robert Hunt, D.O.
2601 Davie Blvd., Davie
Marie Adam, M.D.
1011 N.W. 54 St., Miami
Ira Jacobson, M.D.
1190 N.W. 95 St., #401, Miami
John T. McAdory, M.D.
11350 Dunbar Drive,
Richmond Heights
Maritza Diaz, M.D.
900 S.W. 27 Avenue, Miami
North Miami Beach Center
1701 N.E. 164 Street,
North Miami Beach
CAC Kendall Lakes Medical Center
13600 No. Kendall Dr., Miami
Broward Medical Center of Hollywood Hills
Francisco Albites, M.D.
6100 Hollywood Blvd.,
Suite 106, Hollywood
Pan American Hospital Network – Primary Care Physicians
Ramón Báez, M.D.
630 N.W. 33rd Ave., Miami
Andrés Cao, M.D.
8782 S.W. 8th St., #21, Miami
Armando Cruz, M.D.
825 S.W. 87th Ave., Miami
René De Lamar, M.D.
5799 N.W. 7th St., Miami
976 East 25th Street, Hialeah
Armando Fleites, M.D.
729 S.W. 8th Street, Miami
Carlos O. Ocho, M.D.
1871 Coral Way, #202, Miami
Gustavo Ortega, M.D.
747 Ponce de Leon Blvd., #411,
Coral Gables
Antonio Sarda, M.D.
7000 SW 97th Ave., #106, Miami
390 West 49th Street, Hialeah
Emilio Trujillo, M.D.
330 S.W. 27th Avenue, Miami
Charles Villoch, M.D.
2075 SW 27th Ave, #100, Miami
Pan Am Health Center
701 S.W. 57th Avenue, Miami

训练一提供良好素质服务的关键

大东方人寿为了更好地为各界人士提供一广泛系列的寿险计划，除了不断增进使客户感到便利的措施外，更全心全力地改进其有礼与高效服务。而为了实现这些目标，我们十分重视专业性的训练。

为了使您，投保者获得更好的服务，我们的代理员都必须参予项改进他们专业知识与技能的训练发展计划，同时也必须参加"新加坡保险学院专业考试"。我们设备最时代化的训练中心便位于哥里门街的The Adelphi。它齐备了最先进的多元教学媒体配备。在这儿，我们的代理员参予各类适合各别需求的训练课程，如大东方人寿产品与服务，专业性促销技巧和代理处管理等。他们也有机会参加其他的课程，如契约前考试研讨课，代理员发展课程，产品知识模式，管理前方针确定及商业保险等等。

公司董事兼执行总裁Mr A.J. Pathmarajah评论道"为了使我们的保险促销人员走向专业化道路，我们鼓励他们参加不同的训练课程。他们拥有了足够的知识后，才有能力分析客户们的财务需要，并在迎合他们的预算和可能面对较主要的风险下，选购适合自己的保险计划。"

How To Calculate Tax Relief From Insurance Premiums

In Singapore, life insurance premiums paid are eligible for tax relief (i.e. deduction from the taxpayer's assessable income), subject to the following conditions.

1) The policy must be on the life of the taxpayer or the life of his wife. The premiums paid by you for the policy on your own life fulfills this condition. The premiums you pay for the policy insuring your wife's life also qualify for tax relief.
In the reverse situation where a wife buys a policy on her husband's life, premiums paid by her will not qualify for tax relief.

2) The policy must be issued by a life insurance company which has an office or branch in Singapore. This condition is not applicable to policies issued before 10 August, 1973.

3) The amount of premiums deductible shall not exceed 7 per cent of the capital sum assured payable on deaths excluding bonuses, if any.

The total deduction for the premiums paid together with contributions to the CPF or any other approved pension funds should not exceed S$5,000.

Example 1

A self-employed man who does not contribute to CPF, has a life insurance policy with a capital sum assured of $100,000 and an annual premium of $2,500. He also owns a $10,000 life insurance policy insuring his wife with an annual premium of $800.

Maximum tax relief on premiums paid on his own life policy.	$2,500
Maximum tax relief allowed on premiums paid on his wife's policy. (restricted to 7% of $10,000)	$ 700
Total tax relief	$3,200

If the taxpayer buys additional life insurance for himself or his wife, he can claim tax relief of up to another $1,800 (i.e. $5,000 minus $3,200).

Example 2

An employee who contributes $3,500 to CPF, has a life insurance policy with a capital sum assured of $100,000 and an annual premium of $2,500.

CPF contribution	$3,500
Maximum tax relief on premiums paid ($5,000 minus $3,500)	$1,500
Total tax relief	$5,000

Although the premium paid is $2,500, the maximum tax relief on premiums paid is $1,500. This is because total deduction for premiums paid together with contributions to the CPF or any other approved pension funds should not exceed $5,000.

如何根据保费来计算所得税扣除额？

若符合以下的条件，在新加坡所缴交的人寿保费能够用以扣除所得税（也即是从纳税人的估值收入项目中扣除）：

(a) 保单必须是投保纳税人本身或其妻子的生命。
您为自己的保单所缴交的保费符合这个条件。您投保妻子寿命的保单所缴交的保费也能用以扣除所得税。
相反的，若妻子为丈夫投保，她所缴交的保费将不允许扣除所得税。

(b) 保单必须由在新加坡设有办事处或分公司的人寿保险公司所发出，此条件不适用于那些在1973年10月以前所发出的保单。

(c) 保费的扣税数额不能超过被保人去世时所能获得赔偿的保额之百分之七，不包括红利在内(若有)。

保费的扣税总和，连合公积金缴交额或其他政府所批准的养老金不能超出S$5,000。

以下的例子详细说明了如何用所缴付的保费来扣除所得税。

例案1：

某位不缴交公积金的自雇人士拥有一份保额$100,000的人寿保险。他每年所付的保费是$2,500。他也为妻子投保了一份保额$10,000，常年保费$800的人寿保险。

他的保费最高扣税额是$2,500，他的妻子的保费最高扣税额(以$10,000的7%为限)则是$700。
所以，所得税扣除额总和是$3,200。
若纳税人为自己或其妻子投保额外的人寿保险，他的所得税扣除额可以增多$1,800(即$5,000减去$3,200)。

例案2：

某位雇员缴交$3,500的公积金，并拥有一份保额$100,000，常年保费$2,500的人寿保险。

公积金缴交额—$3,500，用保费扣除所得税的最高数额是$1,500。
虽然所缴付的保费是$2,500，但允许扣除所得税的最高数额却只是$1,500。(即$5,000减去$3,500)。

Going global

Side-by-side bilingual columns expand the reader base and aid those readers who want to improve their language skills. While difficult to translate and lay out, this format proves more cost-effective than back-to-back bilingual formats because the photos and other visuals are used only once. Text and sidebar directories need two headlines but only one body of information. The facing page of the Chinese/English newsletter includes the top article in English, with another photograph further illustrating the message.

From Web to mailbox

Earth's Best Baby Food uses a newsletter posted on its website to encourage parents to sign up for the newsletter in printed form.

The home page offers a newsletter button. When the button is selected, the opening screen for *Family Times* offers registration for a free print subscription.

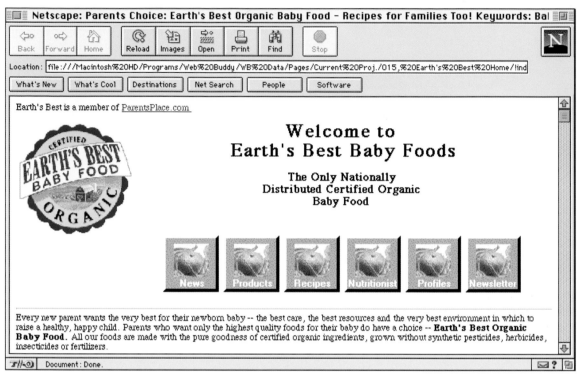

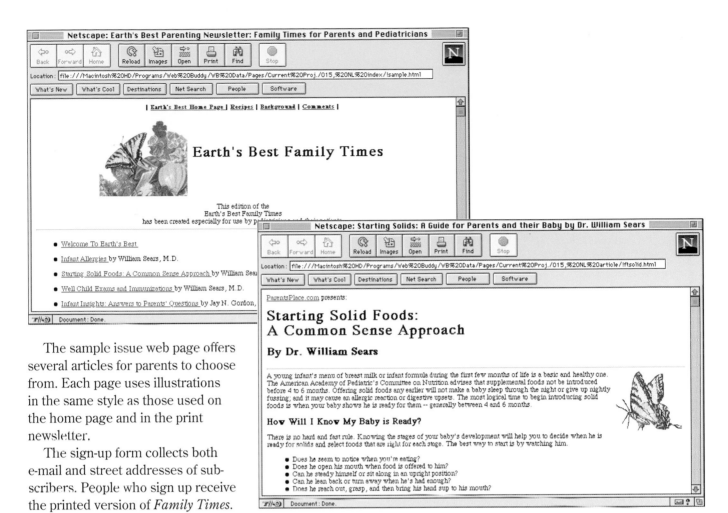

The sample issue web page offers several articles for parents to choose from. Each page uses illustrations in the same style as those used on the home page and in the print newsletter.

The sign-up form collects both e-mail and street addresses of subscribers. People who sign up receive the printed version of *Family Times*.

NAME *Family Times*

PUBLISHER Earth's Best Baby Food, Boulder, Colorado

PURPOSE/AUDIENCE Service and marketing to customers

PRODUCTION/PRINTING Four-color process on cream 60# offset

FORMAT 8½" x 11"; six pages (with foldout)

DESIGN Lisa Bell, Earth's Best Baby Food

chapter three

TYPE

Studies of eye movement and reading comprehension point to the following hallmarks of effective typography:

CONSISTENCY. Good type design uses one or two type families for text, headlines, captions and all other elements. Designers build interest and create emphasis by changing size and weight—not by switching from one type family to another.

FAMILIARITY. People read by the shapes of whole words, not by the forms of individual letters. Familiar letterforms create words whose meanings readers perceive instantly.

Familiar typefaces used for body copy promote efficient reading. Although most designers and editors have hundreds of typefaces at their fingertips, there are only eight or ten faces that are suitable for most newsletters. This small pool includes standards such as Times Roman, Optima, Garamond, Palatino and Helvetica.

COLOR. Print copy in black. Use color in paper, tints and other graphic elements, but not for type. Although many designers feel that printing headlines in color makes readers pay more attention, research shows the opposite: Color slows readers down. Print headlines in black.

CONTRAST. Keep background colors light to ensure good contrast between type and paper or screen.

In addition to these general rules for type, consider the following for headlines and subheads:

TYPE. Use a single typeface—serif or sans serif. If you prefer a serif face, use the same face as your text type. Make headlines larger and bolder.

DOWNSTYLE. To aid in quickly identifying words by their entire shape rather than the shapes of their individual letters, words that normally begin with lowercase letters should do so consistently. This is especially important for headlines. Set downstyle, they look like bold sentences.

Guidelines for body copy include the following:

SERIFS. Dozens of research efforts show that readers comprehend text in serif type much more easily than text in sans serif type. Good design sticks with serif typefaces such as Garamond and Palatino for text, and saves sans serifs typefaces such as Helvetica and Avant Garde for headlines.

ALIGNMENT. Readers understand text in justified type more easily than text set in ragged type.

PLACEMENT. Put captions under or next to photos — never on top. Pull quotes may be used to break up columns of type, but should not compete with headlines or subheads.

Messages readers remember appear in type that is large enough and that has ample space between lines. If yours won't fit, reduce the word count, not the type size and leading.

Fractally Speaking

U S WEST TODAY
NEWS
ON LINE

Volume 2, No. 2   March 1991

HEMISFILE
Perspectives on Political and Economic Trends in the Americas

Labor's

Many of Latin America's labor unions today are vigorously resisting the free market economic policies and privatizations of public enterprises

✓ check

safety

Griffin's
Signature
A NEWSLETTER FOR THE PUBLISHING INDUSTRY

MCHUGH ON PUBLISHING

VOLUME 6, NO. 3

SUMMER 1991

INSIDE THIS ISSUE

John B. McHugh

This newsletter is printed on recycled paper.

Book Publishing and N...
Publishing Organizatio...
PART II: *Issues, Opportunities and Management*

by John B. McHugh

Part I of this article was in our July/August 1990 issue. Part III will appear in our Fall 1991 issue. A reprint of Part I and/or a copy of the balance of the article (Part III) are available on request.

Unclear and Unspecific Responsibility

Many book publishing executives in a non-publishing organization are unsure about their specific responsibilities and accountabilities. The executive over the book publishing entity and book publishing manager may not have reached agreement on the *objectives* of the book publishing program. In many organizations that sponsor book publishing programs, I find the publishing manager's job description is either outdated or nonexistent. It is important to establish the responsibilities and expectations of the book publishing executive. Much of this organizational confusion and ambiguity will disappear if a

book publishing mission statement is prepared by top management. The mission statement should define exactly the expectations of the parent organization and the results expected from the book publishing entity. What are the expectations for: product support? service to members? generating profits? breaking-even? Unspecified goals will

> ### With in-house providers, where is the incentive to please the customer?

lead to poor financial performance.

Centralized Promotion: A Concern

Many organizations centralize their marketing and promotion function. The centralized promotion group provides promotional support and services for the *entire* organization.

From an organizat... standpoint, central... makes sense as the... many economies an... efficiencies to be ach... However, there may... drawbacks for the bo... publisher.

Consider the matt... service. Who gets take... care of first? If the book... in production are on... schedule and the promo... tion is not timed with th... book production schedule... then book sales will suffe... The book publishing executive is responsible fo... sales, while someone else, not accountable for either sales or Profit & Loss, can affect the publisher's performance. The promotional group can (and will) bump the book publisher's work for someone else. That "someone else" may be considered more important politically or financially to the organization.

Let's talk about quality and accuracy of the promotional materials. A major problem of being an internal customer is the "forced" use of someone

(Cont'd on page 2)

Into the 21st Century
MAT chairs and representatives meet to learn what their role will be as we head toward the year 2000...

Great energy, creativity and challenges marked the second annual "Meet Me in St. Louis" program April 19-20. The focus of the program —the importance of community outreach—was heard and affirmed. Also, relationships among the members were established and deepened, facilitating the networking process. The following "Points to Ponder" —quotations from the speakers— provide a flavor of the meeting.

MAYO CLINIC HEALTH LETTER

RELIABLE INFORMATION FOR A HEALTHIER LIFE

VOLUME 14   NUMBER 7   JULY 1996

Inside this issue

Coming in August

SPEECH AFTER STROKE
Even small gains in your ability to communicate can improve your quality of life.

DIETARY FIBER
It can do more than just contribute to regularity.

EMERGENCY MEDICAL HELP
Assistance can be a button push away.

Heel pain

It's usually a symptom of plantar fasciitis

That first step out of bed in the morning really catches your attention — it feels just like someone poked you in the heel with a knife. But after walking for a few minutes, the pain slowly disappears.

Heel pain is very irritating, but rarely serious. Although it can result from a pinched nerve or a chronic condition, such as arthritis or bursitis, the most common cause is plantar fasciitis (PLAN-tur fas-e-I-tis).

Plantar fasciitis is an inflammation of the plantar fascia, the fibrous tissue that runs along the bottom of your foot and connects to your heel bone (calcaneus) and toes (see illustration).

The plantar fascia also acts as a bowstring for the arch of your foot to keep the arch from collapsing.

Treatment for plantar fasciitis involves simple steps to relieve the pain and inflammation. But don't expect a quick cure. It can take six months or longer before your heel is back to normal.

Stretching under stress

A flattening of your arch or overuse can cause your plantar fascia to stretch and pull on your heel bone. That can result in microscopic tears in the fascia, inflammation, and a piercing pain or burning sensation.

The pain usually develops gradually, but can come on suddenly and severely. It tends to be worse in the morning, when the fascia is stiff.

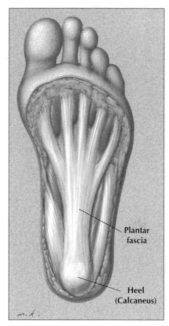

Plantar fascia

Heel (Calcaneus)

Heel pain most often results from stress on the plantar fascia, the tough, fibrous tissue that runs along the bottom of your foot and connects to your heel bone and toes.

Although both feet can be affected, it usually occurs in only one foot.

The pain generally goes away once your foot limbers up. But it can recur if you stand or sit for a long time. Climbing stairs or standing on your tiptoes can also produce pain.

In severe cases, your foot may hurt whenever you put pressure on it, making walking difficult.

You may also develop a bone spur that forms from tension on your heel bone. In most cases, the spur doesn't cause pain. ▶

One type fits all

The Optima family of typefaces used in *Mayo Clinic Health Letter* works equally well for the nameplate, headlines, subheads, body text, contents, callouts and captions. Optima is strong and bold for flush left downstyle headlines and holds up well in small sizes for captions and the masthead. Note the reserved use of color, even though full color is available. Screens in yellow and blue organize the information.

NAME *Mayo Clinic Health Letter*

PUBLISHER Mayo Clinic, Rochester, Minnesota

PURPOSE/AUDIENCE Service to subscribers

PRODUCTION/PRINTING Four-color process on natural 50# offset; three-hole punched

FORMAT 8½" x 11"; eight pages

DESIGN George E. DeVinny and David E. Swanson

Self-help steps that may relieve the pain

To treat plantar fasciitis yourself, you can:

■ *Find alternative activities* — Cut back on jogging or walking. Substitute exercises, such as swimming or bicycling, that put less weight on your heel.

■ *Ice it* — Apply ice to the painful area for up to 20 minutes after activity.

■ *Stretch daily* — Stretching increases flexibility in your plantar fascia, Achilles' tendon and calf muscles (see illustration, page 3).

Stretching in the morning before you get out of bed helps reverse the tightening of the plantar fascia that occurs overnight.

■ *Do strengthening exercises* — Strengthening muscles in your foot can help support your arch.

■ *Wear appropriate shoes* — Buy shoes with a low to moderate heel (1 to 2 inches) and good arch support and shock absorbency. High-quality running or walking shoes are a good choice.

■ *Use pain relievers* — Over-the-counter medications may ease the pain. Taper their use as your condition improves.

■ *Lose weight* — If you're overweight, shedding excess pounds will reduce pressure on your feet.

■ *Try heel pads or cups* — They help cushion and support your heel. You can find them in most medical supply, shoe and drug stores.

Common causes

Plantar fasciitis can affect people of all ages. Factors that increase your risk include:

■ *Age* — As you get older, your plantar fascia loses some of its elasticity and doesn't stretch as well. In addition, the fat pad covering your heel bone thins out and isn't able to absorb as much shock when you put weight on your foot. That places more stress on your heel bone and the tissues attached to it.

■ *Weight-bearing activities* — Walking, jogging, lifting heavy objects and standing for long periods place added pressure on your feet. When performed regularly, they may stress your plantar fascia.

Plantar fasciitis can also occur if you've been physically inactive and then plunge into a weight-bearing activity, such as playing golf or walking more than you're used to while vacationing.

■ *Shoes* — Shoes with thin soles, poor arch support, that are too loose around your heels, lack shock absorbency, or are worn out can be harmful to your feet.

In addition, regularly wearing high heels (greater than 2 inches) can shorten your Achilles' tendon, which attaches to your heel bone, and tighten your calf muscles. This increases the strain on your heels when you switch to a flatter shoe.

■ *Weight* — Excess weight increases pressure on your feet.

■ *Poor biomechanics* — A flat foot, high-arched foot, or abnormalities in your gait may prevent your weight from being evenly distributed when you walk or run. This stresses your plantar fascia.

Treatment steps

The goal of treatment is to heal the tears and decrease inflammation, as well as prevent the condition from recurring. Although you may find the slow course of healing frustrating, patience is important.

There are several steps you can take to relieve plantar fasciitis (see "Self-help steps that may relieve the pain"). But if these aren't effective, or you believe your condition is due to a foot abnormality, see your doctor. Treatment options include:

■ *Custom orthotic devices* — If you have a foot deformity, a custom shoe insert from an orthopedist or podiatrist can compensate for the deformity and distribute pressure to your foot more evenly.

■ *Night splints* — While you sleep, your plantar fascia relaxes

MAYO CLINIC HEALTH LETTER

Managing Editor
Christopher C. Frye

Medical Editor
Charles C. Kennedy, M.D.

Associate Editors
Jill P. Burcum
Donna H. Cortese
Karen R. Wallevand

Associate Medical Editor
Philip T. Hagen, M.D.

Customer Service Manager
Ann M. Allen

EDITORIAL BOARD

Mayo Clinic Rochester
Steven C. Adamson, M.D., *Family Medicine*; Susan L. Ahlquist, R.N., *Patient and Health Education*; Daniel J. Berry, M.D., *Orthopedic Surgery*; Mary M. Gallenberg, M.D., *Medical Gynecology*; Philip T. Hagen, M.D., *Preventive Medicine*; Loren W. Hunt, M.D., *Allergy*; Charles C. Kennedy, M.D., *Internal Medicine*; Randolph S. Marks, M.D., *Medical Oncology*; Michael D. McGoon, M.D., *Cardiology*; M. Molly McMahon, M.D., *Endocrinology and Metabolism*; Kevin G. Moder, M.D., *Rheumatology*; Gregory A. Poland, M.D., *Internal Medicine*; John J. Poterucha, M.D., *Gastroenterology*; Marc D. Silverstein, M.D., *Internal Medicine*; Christopher C. Frye, *Health Information*. *Ex-officio:* Jill P. Burcum, Donna H. Cortese, Vicki L. Moore, Karen R. Wallevand.

Mayo Clinic Jacksonville
Kay M. Mitchell, M.D., *Internal Medicine*; W. Andrew Oldenburg, M.D., *Vascular Surgery*.

Mayo Clinic Scottsdale
Brent A. Bauer, M.D., *Internal Medicine*; Matthew A. Butters, M.D., *Physical Medicine and Rehabilitation*.

Mayo Clinic Health Letter (ISSN 0741-6245) is published monthly by Mayo Foundation for Medical Education and Research, a subsidiary of Mayo Foundation, 200 First Street SW, Rochester, MN 55905. Subscription price is $24 a year, which includes three eight-page Medical Essays and a Five-Year Cumulative Index published in December. Periodicals postage paid at Rochester, MN, and at additional mailing offices. POSTMASTER: Send address changes to *Mayo Clinic Health Letter*, Subscription Services, P.O. Box 53889, Boulder, CO 80322-3889.

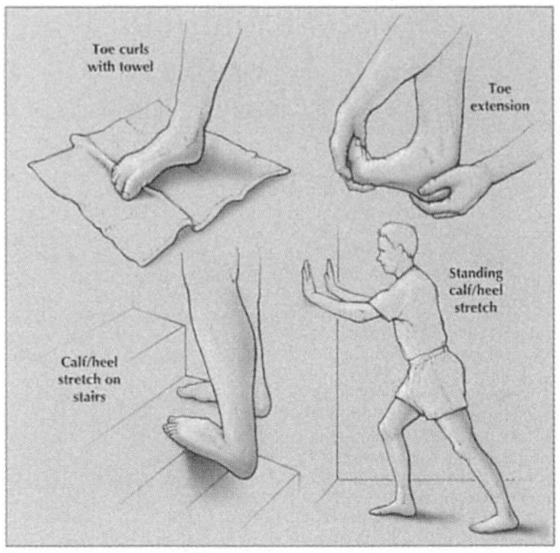
Toe curls with towel
Toe extension
Standing calf/heel stretch
Calf/heel stretch on stairs

These exercises stretch or strengthen your plantar fascia, Achilles' tendon and calf muscles. Hold each for 20 to 30 seconds, and do one or two repetitions two to three times a day.

and starts to heal in that position. When you bear weight on the foot, you can stretch and tear your fascia all over again. Splints worn at night keep tension on the tissue so it heals in a stretched position.

■ *Ultrasound* — Deep heat may increase blood flow and promote healing.

■ *Corticosteroids* — An injection in your heel can often help relieve the inflammation when other steps aren't successful. But multiple injections aren't recommended because they can weaken and rupture your plantar fascia, as well as shrink the fat pad covering your heel bone.

■ *Surgery* — Doctors can detach your plantar fascia from your heel bone, but this is only recommended when all other treatments have failed. Side effects can include continued pain and weakening of your arch.

Additional options may be available in the future. Mayo Clinic and other medical centers are investigating a number of alternative therapies, including low-intensity laser treatments.

Stepping away from the pain

Heel pain can be frustrating, but it doesn't have to keep you from your daily routine or favorite exercise program. Most people are able to relieve the pain by following simple treatment recommendations and gradually working back into normal activities.

Maintaining a stretching program and continued attention to proper footwear may help prevent the condition from returning. ❐

Health tips

Relieving swollen feet and ankles

When you wake up, your feet and ankles are fine. But by the end of the day they're swollen and wearing shoes is painful.

The swelling, called dependent edema, results from a buildup of fluids in your skin tissue. During the day, gravity pulls the fluids to your feet and ankles, causing them to swell.

To reduce swelling:

■ *Cut back on sodium* — Sodium causes fluid retention.

■ *Maintain proper weight* — Excess weight slows circulation of body fluids and puts extra pressure on your veins, causing fluid buildup.

■ *Get some exercise* — Regular exercise improves circulation in your legs and feet.

■ *Put your feet up* — Place them at least 12 inches above the level of your heart. Do this for 10 to 15 minutes, three or four times a day.

■ *Use support stockings* — They compress your legs, promoting circulation and limiting gravitational movement of excess fluid. Elastic stockings are available at most medical supply or drug stores.

■ *Take a break when traveling* — Long periods of sitting can promote swelling in your feet and ankles. Get up and walk around at least every one to two hours.

If swelling is persistent, or accompanied by shortness of breath and weight gain, see your doctor. ❐

Update '96

News and our views

Study shows tobacco may be more deadly than alcohol

A Mayo Clinic study has sobering news for alcoholics who smoke. You're more likely to die of tobacco-related causes than from illnesses related to your alcohol addiction.

The study appeared in the April 10 issue of the *Journal of the American Medical Association*. It examined medical records of 845 Olmsted County, Minn., patients treated for addiction at Mayo Clinic between 1972 and 1983. Ninety-six percent were hospitalized for alcohol addiction. Almost all smoked.

By December 1994, 26 percent had died. But lung cancer and other diseases caused by tobacco accounted for 51 percent of deaths. In contrast, alcohol-related conditions, such as liver disease, caused 34 percent of the deaths.

The study has implications for alcoholism treatment, according to its author, Richard D. Hurt, an internal medicine specialist and director of Mayo's Nicotine Dependence Center. Although the majority of alcoholics smoke, alcoholism treatment traditionally focuses on sobriety from alcohol and non-nicotine drugs. Mayo doctors believe nicotine addiction can be treated effectively at the same time.

"Tobacco produces more mortality in alcoholics than any other cause," Hurt said. "By showing this, hopefully we will convince more in the addictions treatment community of the serious nature of nicotine dependence and the need to treat it." ❐

Cholesterol medications may help heart attack survivors

If you've had a heart attack, taking a cholesterol-lowering drug may reduce your risk for another "cardiovascular event" — even if your total cholesterol is under 240.

That's the conclusion of a five-year study of more than 4,000 heart attack survivors in the United States and Canada. The study group given the cholesterol-lowering drug pravastatin (Pravachol) had 24 percent fewer second heart attacks and heart disease deaths than the group that didn't take the drug. The decline in deaths was most pronounced among women.

The pravastatin group also underwent 26 percent fewer bypass operations and 22 percent fewer balloon angioplasties.

All participants in the study, which was presented at the March annual meeting of the American College of Cardiology, had total cholesterol levels under 240. In Mayo Clinic experience, the majority of heart attack patients fall into that group.

National Cholesterol Education Program guidelines recommend that you reduce your LDL, or "bad" cholesterol, to below 100 if you have heart disease. To reach this, your total cholesterol will usually be 180 or less. Desirable levels for healthy adults without known heart disease are below 200 for total cholesterol and below 130 for LDL. ❐

Nutrition drinks

Keys to a healthy diet?

It's hard to miss the advertisements for nutrition drinks aimed at our aging population. Open a magazine or turn on your TV and you'll likely see a smiling couple toasting their golden years with cans of their favorite liquid supplement.

After seeing these ads, you may wonder about your diet and lifestyle. Should you be drinking Ensure, Sustacal, or one of the other brands available?

While nutrition drinks aren't rocket fuel for your body, as ads claim, they do contain vitamins and minerals you need to stay healthy. But so do many other foods. If your diet includes a variety of foods and three meals a day, chances are you're already getting all the ingredients for a healthy, active lifestyle.

But, if you're at dietary risk (see "Determining your nutritional health"), liquid supplements may help you get the calories and nutrients you need.

New marketing strategies

Liquid nutritional supplements have been available for nearly 30 years. Until recently, their use was generally confined to nursing homes and hospitals to help those with nutritional problems maintain their weight and get essential vitamins and minerals.

But now, the drinks' manufacturers are marketing them for healthy, active adults.

In the past year, sales of liquid nutritional supplements in the United States rose to $669 million. Sales of the Ensure brand alone topped $300 million.

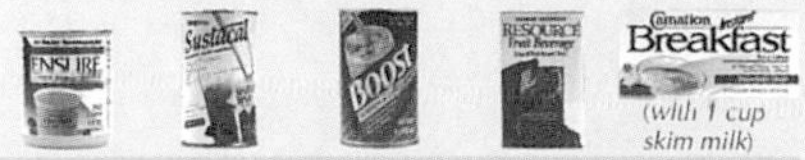

How nutrition drinks stack up	ENSURE	Sustacal	BOOST	RESOURCE	Breakfast (with 1 cup skim milk)
Serving size	8 ounces	8 ounces	8 ounces	8 ounces	8 ounces
Calories	250	240	240	180	220
Fat	6.1 grams	5.5 grams	4 grams	0 grams	0 grams
% of calories from fat	22%	21%	14.5%	0%	0%
Carbohydrates	40 grams	33 grams	40 grams	36 grams	39 grams
Protein	8.8 grams	14.5 grams	10 grams	8.8 grams	13 grams
Servings for 100% RDA of vitamins and minerals	4	4	4	8	4
Cost per serving	$1.62	$1 to $1.50	$1 to $1.50	$1.35	$.64

Not a food replacement

Liquid supplements contain water, sugars, oils, vitamins, minerals and milk and soy proteins. But they aren't better than food, or a replacement for it.

In fact, other than brightly packaged cans and catchy slogans, there's little difference between them and a vitamin pill dissolved in a milk shake.

The best way to ensure your nutritional health is to eat enough of the right foods — breads, fruits, vegetables and dairy and meat products. Depending on your age and lifestyle, you need between 1,600 and 2,800 calories a day.

If you have a less active lifestyle, particularly if you're a woman, your caloric intake should stay at the lower levels of this range.

A dietary option

Your nutritional status is an important vital sign, just as your blood pressure and pulse are.

If age, illness or other factors are affecting your diet and appetite, liquid supplements are one option for meeting your nutritional needs. But if you have a balanced diet and aren't at nutritional risk, you probably don't need them. ❐

Determining your nutritional health

Circle the points for the statements that apply to you, then add up your score.

I have an illness or condition that has made me change the kind or amount of food I eat.	2
I eat fewer than two meals a day.	3
I eat few fruits, vegetables or milk products.	2
I have three or more drinks of beer, liquor or wine almost every day.	2
I have tooth or mouth problems that make it hard for me to eat.	2
I don't always have enough money to buy the food I need.	4
I eat alone most of the time.	1
I take three or more prescription or over-the-counter drugs a day.	1
Without wanting to, I've lost or gained 10 pounds in the last six months.	2
I'm not always physically able to shop, cook or feed myself.	2
Your total	☐

0 to 2 — Good. Recheck your score in six months.

3 to 5 — You may be at moderate nutritional risk. Check with your physician, senior citizens center or health department for information on improving your eating habits and lifestyle. Recheck your score in three months.

6 or more — You may be at high nutritional risk. Discuss this checklist with your doctor, dietitian or another health professional.

Source: The American Academy of Family Physicians, the American Dietetic Association and the National Council on Aging. Note: This checklist suggests risk but does not represent diagnosis of any condition.

The Business Woman's
Advantage

JANUARY/FEBRUARY 1997

An interactive newsletter for women with entrepreneurial spirit

Technology... know when to shut down

by Mershon Shrigley

Being connected is great if you know when to shut down. According to Joe Mullich, the winner of the National Headliners Award for humor writing, "The New Age technology mantra of 'work anytime, anywhere' has really come to mean 'work all the time, everywhere.' Take this new call-forwarding service. From 8 am to 9, you can have callers connect to your car phone; from 9 to 5 to your office phone; from 5 to 6 back to your car; and after 6 to your home phone. The service is named the 'Time Manager'. I call it the 'Terminator'. . .no matter where you go, that thing would be in your rear-view mirror, relentlessly chasing you, giving you no peace."

Waiting for a red light to change? Grab your laptop and crunch that spreadsheet. I'm not kidding. . .I recently saw an advertisement for a device that fits over your steering wheel to accommodate a laptop. The ad said it was only to be used while the car was parked. . .yeah, right.

Obviously, some of us need technology to keep technology in check. Joe explains, "There are now 'bozo filters'. . .computer programs that read e-mail and decide what messages should be forwarded to you. On one level, I miss the days when it took a human receptionist to decide my calls were insignificant enough to be ignored. On another, more profound level. . .I'll have my bozo filter installed by tomorrow!"

Brian Woerner, director of the mobile and portable radio research group at Virginia Tech, predicts this type of computerized gatekeeping will increase. Phones, for instance, will have embedded intelligence to route business calls after 5 pm to voice mail while calls from our children to the same number will go through.

"Who knows," says Joe, "technology might reach a state that calls from our kids telling us they got an 'A' in chemistry will reach us no matter where we are, while their calls asking for money will be shunted to a prerecorded voice saying, 'This number is out of service.'"

We love to be connected. But to whom or to what are we connecting? Are we managing technology or is technology managing us? Joe comments, "As beepers,

Continued on page 4

Software...the #1 tool for business

To stay ahead in today's fast-paced environment, entrepreneurs must have the right tools. The standard for nearly all businesses today includes: a computer system (computer, monitor, printer, modem), fax machine, answering machine or voice mail, multiple line phone system.

The software you use in your computer system is fundamental. The following is a list of software programs used by many of our readers and recommended by successful entrepreneurs.

Of course the big hype last year was **Microsoft Windows 95**. Those who made the switch have found that there are many advantages to this operating system over the older models. Increased speed and ease of use are primary. Icons and folders are right on the desktop and a Taskbar puts applications just a click away. The 32-bit architecture provides the speed and ability to manage memory. Approximate cost: $210, Microsoft Corp., 800/426-9400, www.microsoft.com/windows.

For Mac users there's the **Macintosh System 7.5**. Approximate cost: $100, Apple Computer Inc., 800/776-2333.

Office suites are software packages that integrate several applications into one. Although a wonderful opportunity to "have it all," you must consider

that a full install of the most popular suite, **Microsoft Office Professional**, can take up 124MB of hard-drive space. The suite includes: Word 95, a word processor; Excel 95, a spreadsheet; PowerPoint 95, a presentation program; Access 95, a database; Schedule+ 95, a scheduling program; Word Internet Assistant, a simple HTML editor; Internet Explorer, a Web browser and more. Office Professional provides all the applications a business needs. With Office you have total integration of all the programs, a big plus for entrepreneurs.

Unlike office suites, integrated programs are designed primarily for home office use. The components are not full-fledged program but competent enough to perform common functions. The most popular is **Claris Works 4.0** for the Macintosh. This programs has a word processor, spreadsheet database, and graphics and presentation capabilities. It also offers cross-platform compatibility between the Macintosh and Windows 95 versions. All functions require just 14MB of hard-drive space and can run on 4MB RAM. Approximate cost: $130, Claris Corp.

800/544-8554, www.claris.com. Note: ClarisWorks 4.0 for Windows 95 is $50.

If all you need is word processing, consider **Microsoft Word 95**. Although the front runner is still WordPerfect, Word is catching up fast. It's notable that WordPerfect can no longer be purchased as a stand-alone product but is available in two Corel Suites: WordPerfect Suite 7 for Windows 95 and Corel Office Professional 7. Microsoft Word 95 approximate cost is $340; Corel WordPerfect Suite 7 is $400.

For that all important accounting/bookkeeping package, consider **QuickBooks Pro 4.0**, this year's best seller. QuickBooks Pro needs about

16. . .BWA

*Patricia Smith-Pierce, Ph.D.
President, Power Speaking Consultants*

Communicating with the technology of video

Using videotape for training or marketing is a good use of technology as a communication tool. It is, however, natural to feel nervous when being videotaped. After all, videotapes can be played over and over again with both glaring and subtle errors recorded for all to see.

How many times have you watched a taped message or presentation that contained annoying distractions such as negative facial expressions, squinting, excessive hand gestures or very little audience eye contact? Didn't you wonder why the person didn't realize the effect of her body language on the camera?

Here are a few helpful hints to remember when you're being videotaped:

Posture—Stand or sit straight ahead with as little slouch as possible. Slouching makes you appear uninterested and too casual.

Eye contact—Look directly at the camera. . .your audience. Looking away makes you look less than truthful.

Hand gestures—Make the gestures purposeful when standing. Try to avoid them at all when

seated. Gestures can be very distracting.

Stance—Place your feet evenly on the floor, not quite a shoulder width apart. Keep your knees slightly bent so you don't rock or weave.

Clothing—Avoid distracting patterns, jewelry or accessories. Dark suits frame you best and minimize size. . .cameras do enhance size. Avoid stark white shirts or blouses and red dresses. Medium blue is always a good choice in front of the camera.

It's important to discuss your presentation with the camera-person. Include such things as approximate length, use of visual aids and props such as podium, desk, or chair. If there is a live audience, look at them rather than the camera. Let the camera-person capture your interaction with them.

Most important, remember that you are the expert. It's likely that no one will notice if you make a mistake unless you point it out. However, if you're unhappy with any portion of your presentation ask for a retake and/or editing. Request a practice session or rehearsal if necessary. ■

BWA. . .13

Downstyle ensures readability

According to research reported in Colin Wheildon's book *Type & Layout*, readers find downstyle headlines easiest to read. "Downstyle" means following grammatical rules for capitalization in headlines, just as in text. This newsletter uses downstyle italic headlines combined with lowercase kickers for a professional, yet approachable, look.

NAME *Advantage*

PUBLISHER Shrigley & Associates, Schaumburg, Illinois

PURPOSE/AUDIENCE Service to subscribers

PRODUCTION/PRINTING Two-color on 80# gloss-coated

FORMAT 8½" x 11"; twenty pages

DESIGN Marshon Shrigley, Shrigley & Associates

Retirement Today

Financial strategies for retired Canadians   Vol. 1, No. 1

The best strategies to help you keep more retirement income

According to Statistics Canada, more than half of Canadian seniors received 80% of their income from government benefit programs in 1991. Today, with Canada's social safety net being affected by the government's desire to reduce costs, the message to retirees is clear: You can no longer afford to rely on the government for that much of your retirement income.

Fortunately, Canadians enjoy incentives to fund their own retirement dreams. Among these, the Registered Retirement Savings Plan (RRSP) is the most powerful. But once you've retired, there are still a variety of tax-saving opportunities available.

A regular income stream

With a little ongoing planning and attention, your registered and non-registered holdings can provide a regular income stream to see you comfortably through retirement, while at the same time preserving more of your capital and reducing the annual tax bite. Here are some ideas on how to get the most from your retirement income.

Just because you've retired doesn't

mean you can't do not have to the end of the (Because of rec who turn 69 or to mature their the end of this

Keep your RRS
In many cases, RRSP intact as

Marketing to tired eyes

Retirement Today serves an older audience, but the design is suitable for a variety of publications because excessive computer use leaves almost all audiences with weary eyes. Readability is enhanced with down-style headlines and subheads, drop caps and ample leading. The type never looks crowded on the page.

NAME *Retirement Today*

PUBLISHER Investors Group, Winnipeg, Manitoba, Canada

PURPOSE/AUDIENCE Service and marketing to customers

PRODUCTION/PRINTING Four-color process on white 60# offset

FORMAT 8½" x 11"; four pages

DESIGN Ariad Custom Publishing

Get the most for your house:
Before selling, check for any tax advantages

One of the few tax breaks left to Canadians is the principal residence exemption. The way you use that exemption, however, can make a big difference.

Most homeowners will be familiar with the concept, which has been entrenched in Canadian tax laws for decades. Essentially, any gain you make when you sell your principal residence is free of tax. If you own more than one property, however, you may be able to get even more mileage from this valuable tax break.

Know the rules
In order to qualify for the exemption, the property in question must be a principal residence as defined by the Income Tax Act.

A variety of homes can qualify. That includes part-time residences, cottages, recreational properties, hobby farms — even a houseboat or trailer home. The only stipulation is that you or a family member must have occupied the home at some point during the year, and you must be a Canadian resident for each year you make

the designation.

In addition, you and your spouse are allowed to claim only one home between you in any given year.

How to decide
Suppose you own both a home in the city and a lakeside cottage. You probably think of the city house as your principal residence. But for tax purposes, it may make more sense to make the cottage your principal residence. Suppose, for example, you bought your cottage property in 1975, and paid just $30,000. Today, that property might be worth as much as $200,000 or more. Claim the cottage as your principal residence, and that entire gain will be yours, tax-free, when you sell.

If you purchased your city property just before the bottom dropped out of the real estate market in the mid-1980s, chances are it hasn't appreciated as much.

Strategic planning
Determining which property has generated a greater exemption is pretty straightforward. But there

are a number of factors that can complicate the issue, and a number of special tax planning opportunities that are easy to miss:

1 If you and your spouse owned two homes prior to 1982, when the one-principal-residence-per-family rule was introduced, you may be able to claim the exemption on the increase in value on both homes up to that date.

2 If you have adult children, you may be able to shift ownership of one of the properties to them, so they can claim it as their principal residence subject to the requirement that they occupy the property at some time during the year. Remember that the transfer of ownership is a disposition for income tax purposes and may trigger a capital gain for you.

3 Until 1994, real estate qualified for a $100,000 capital gains exemption. Under special tax rules, you were allowed to claim the exemption on accrued capital gains to that date when you filed your return by April 30, 1995. If you didn't do so, you may still be able to claim this exemption. Late-filing penalties will apply, and in most cases claims can be filed no later than two years after the original filing deadline. For most taxpayers, the cutoff date will be April 30, 1997.

Retirement Today is published by Investors Group Financial Services Inc. Head Office: One Canada Centre, 447 Portage Avenue, Winnipeg, Manitoba R3C 3B6. Les Services Investors Limitée, 1501, av. McGill College, bureau 1488, Montreal (Quebec) H3A 3M8. © Investors Group Inc. 1997.

Clients should ask their consultant for advice based on their specific circumstances.

Illustrations: Margox Thompson

 Investors Group

December 1995 Issue 136

IN HOUSE Graphics™

*Where to turn for design ideas & techniques...
on a desktop or not*

INSIDE INFORMATION

The 10 most common web-design crimes... *& how to avoid them*

To paraphrase an old saw, you can lead visitors to your web page — with the promise of useful content — but you can't make them stay. *But...* with good design (and fulfilled content promises), you *can* make them feel at home.

How? To start, avoid the most common visual crimes committed on web pages, says designer Fred Showker in his workshop, "PowerHouse Web Design," presented at MultiCom '95 in Washington, DC:

1. Avoid inappropriate color selections
Garish colors may be popular among Web page designers, but that doesn't mean they're effective. Unless you're promoting, say, a rock band, use colors to shout and you'll chase away many who just can't bear the glare. In fact, use restful, subtle colors and you'll create a haven for garish-page escapees.

That doesn't mean you've got to cross bright colors off your list. They're useful for some audiences and messages, as long as you keep them in their place.

Cool colors (blues, greens, grays) recede and warm colors (reds, oranges, yellows) advance, as you probably know. That visual law applies to web pages as much as to printed materials. With that law in mind, you'll never think of running a background in bright yellow, magenta or hot pink (like the design above right), or the main features in subtle blue.

Then you might think, why doesn't Stan's page (on our next page) work?

The graphic's grea... with a dandy 3-d, ... yellow type below ... the designer kept t... the choice of hot p... much, in fact, it's ...

Let's forget for... readable typefi... lets it run as t... the overtexture... red and white... over a blue ba...

Fair Employment Practices Guidelines
redesign specs
colors: teal (#328) and black
paper: Cougar Opaque
Typefaces:
• *heads:* Century Bold
• *text:* Century Book (10/12)
frequency: twice monthly
number of pages: 8
audience: Human resource departments, upper level management
redesigner: Sue Connah
editor: Mary-Lou Devine

NEWSLETTER REDESIGN

How to redesign... ask your readers *part 3*

What a concept! Listen to readers and let their needs help you redesign your newsletter. In the past two issues, you watched how Bureau of Business Practices (BBP), Waterford, CT, wisely consulted its readers before *and* after redesigning its 33 newsletters. Let's look at more of the results of that process.

Why the massive redesign?
BBP's newsletters' designs showed their age, as you see in this month's "before" examples. It was also time to reevaluate newsletters' rates of financial success and editorial effectiveness; BBP planned the redesigns to coincide with the merging of some of the newsletters and the refocusing of others.

If the tas...

in a year sounds daunting — and it should — it was eased by the company's structure: Each newsletter is produced by its own team: an editor and a designer, although some designers work on more than one newsletter. And each editor sent out its own version of the surveys that preceded and followed the redesign.

Teams met to share typical reader requests — like hole-punching, more white space and less clutter. But assigning individual teams ensured that each redesign would be a unique interpretation of the newsletter audience's specific needs and editorial focus.

A newsletter in need
None of the BBP originals we saw

"Redesign me,... loudly. Below ... belongs with ... tents. If black ... the acronym, r...

PUBLIC RELATIONS

Looking for a few good press releases

This is "Crud," the best part of a press kit that promotes a greasy-hand cleaner (there's a textbook example of a needed hyphen!). A plastic bag of the stuff came to challenge editors to a product test. The supplied product sample's meant to clean hands rubbed with crud.

Anywhere, USA — Editors have announced they'll no longer accept press releases that don't address the needs of their readers and that don't come to the point quickly. "My time is limited, and I don't have time to search for the facts hidden in the hype," said one. They made the announcement in the wake of a worldwide corporate ban on actual news in press releases.

Although we made up the press release lead above, it's not all that farfetched. That's because, as we said in the October issue, it's hard to serve two audiences — editors and your senior management — and cross purposes when you write press releases.

For one thing, we pointed out, you've got to put your company in the best light. But editors need solid information... few will print hype-only releases. In October, we gave tips for serving both audiences. So let's use those tips to grade some actual press releases on their newsworthiness, brevity and degree of hype.

Check your press list
The first press release we show here was sent to us in the hope we'd include it in *In House Graphics*. If not for this story, we wouldn't, because it doesn't fit your needs or the newsletter's focus.

"Many of your readers work with heavy grease, adhesives, tar, inks and other stubborn soils daily at their job site," insists the letter that accompanied a press kit for a product called Scrubs. Must be thinking of some other publication's readers.

How can you know if you're hitting the mark with your release? Survey your press list. Send a prepaid reply postcard that's brief and easy to respond to. Let editors know you respect their time. Tell why you're asking... to find out their needs so you can send them only what they can use. Ask about the type of news

they write about, the publication they write for and the people who read it.

Pressing releases get to the point fast
Although the release didn't get to its intended audience — a publication for printers — we salute its style. Writing's mostly economical and clear. "New invention makes soap, pumice and water unnecessary to clean greasy, soiled hands," says the press release's headline.

Even the presence of a headline is useful. Headlines are less common in a press release than you might think. A headline helps editors decide whether to go further. They appreciate that service and may remember it the next time they see your return address on the news-release envelope. It's a myth that leaving out headlines force any but the most copy-desperate editors into the release.

In this case, the head clearly says what the product's about... the word, "invention" rather than "product" suggests there are no competitors so it eliminates a typical editor question: "Is this product exclusive? If not, how is it better than competitors'?"

Finetuning...
Now put the benefit on the first line. Making soap, pumice and water unnecessary isn't the point of the product; it's cleaning hands. So let's say that first: "New invention cleans greasy, soiled hands without soap, pumice or water."

"Soiled" seems redundant — any word that doesn't add meaning doesn't belong — until we realize the writer wanted to include audiences who attribute dirty hands to substances other than grease. In the lead, the writer does a good job of laying out seven possible audiences and six kinds of soil they get into:

"Mechanics, painters, printers, machinists, plumbers, construction workers and assembly line personnel — just to name a few — work with heavy grease, lubricants, adhesives, tar, asphalt, inks and other stubborn soils day in and day out, often

---

Left vs. centered heads

Since the reader's eye always starts at the left, these headlines hook the eye and get it started. With very large type stretching across the page, the second-line indention of the headline avoids stacking (big type in one column) or creating a headline that looks too long.

NAME *In House Graphics*

PUBLISHER United Communications Group, Rockville, Maryland

PURPOSE/AUDIENCE Service to subscribers

PRODUCTION/PRINTING Two-color on natural 70# offset

FORMAT 8½" x 11"; eight pages

DESIGN Ronnie Lipton

NAME *US West Today*

PUBLISHER US West, Englewood, Colorado

PURPOSE/AUDIENCE Service to employees

PRODUCTION/PRINTING Three-color on white
50# offset

FORMAT 11" × 17"; four pages

DESIGN US West Communications

FEBRUARY 12, 1996 VOL. 9 NO. 2

US WEST
Today

This special edition of *U S WEST Today* reports on the Telecommunications Act of 1996, which will have far-reaching effects on U S WEST, its businesses, customers and shareowners.

REFLECTING THE PEOPLE, EVENTS & ISSUES SHAPING OUR BUSINESS

Telecommunications Act just the start of changes

With pen in hand, President Clinton signed into law the Telecommunications Act of 1996.

"This legislation is a major step toward catching up with consumer demand and technological advancement," says Dick McCormick, chairman and chief executive officer of U S WEST. "Consumers will be the major beneficiaries of the updated national policy."

What happens next?

"It's taken years to get this bill written and signed into law, but the real work for U S WEST is just beginning," says Laird Walker, U S WEST vice president Federal Relations. "While the legislation provides a policy framework, we anticipate an extensive amount of activity will occur with federal regulators and state policy makers in the months ahead as they develop the necessary rules to implement the new law."

The Federal Communications Commission is charged with deciding how to most effectively carry out Congress' instructions. Among its tasks, the FCC must:

• Within six months, establish all the necessary regulation to implement the bill's interconnection requirements.

• Within six months, complete the specifics of a 14-point competitive checklist designed to

> 'This legislation is a major step toward catching up with consumer demand and technological advancement. Consumers will be the major beneficiaries of the updated national policy.'
>
> **– Dick McCormick**
> U S WEST chairman and chief executive officer

Freedom — President Clinton watches Thursday's signing of telecommunications. The ceremony commitment to connecting the upcoming electronic age.

provide the framework for companies to open up their

• Within one month, establish a state joint board to define and recommend funding

• Within 90 days, prescribe lution process for industry

New law a long

The White House changed six times, companies merged and divided, competition exploded, and technology rapidly evolved since the first cry for telecommunications reform was heard. But getting a fair bill was a difficult and arduous task.

An electronic signature on Thursday, however, finally — and symbolically — brought national communications policy in line with the immense changes of the past few decades and a cyberspace future. As

President Clinton digitally Telecommunications Act he said, "The Information been held back by outdate laws will catch up with ou

"As far back as 1974, the went to Congress with the Communications Reform A new rules written for our i Laird Walker, U S WEST vi Federal Relations in Washi Divestiture in 1984 and

Long-distance team to deliver on one-stop shopping promise

As President Clinton signed the sweeping telecommunications reform bill into law, U S WEST Communications began moving quickly to compete for customers' long-distance business.

Rick Coleman, U S WEST Communications president-Long Distance, and his team are finalizing the business plan to enter the $70 billion-a-year national inter-LATA long-distance market.

"We intend to be in the inter-LATA long-distance business as soon as we can meet the checklist requirements of the new legislation," Coleman says. "Customers are eager to receive benefits of this new law as soon as possible.

"The inter-LATA long-distance potential is a tremendous business opportunity for the company," says Coleman. "Customers have made it clear that they want one-stop shopping for both their local and long-distance service. We are preparing to give them exactly what they've been asking for."

Coleman estimates that U S WEST will be able to reach a reasonable resolution on the bill's checklist requirements in the majority of its states within 12 to 18 months. He expects U S WEST to capture 15 percent to 20 percent of the inter-LATA long-distance market in its 14-state territory within five years of entry.

Although Coleman's highest priority is to provide long-distance service to existing customers, his team also is exploring a full range of service options and developing targeted solutions to deliver on the one-stop

> 'The inter-LATA long-distance potential is a tremendous business opportunity for the company. Customers have made it clear that they want one-stop shopping for both their local and long-distance service. We are preparing to give them exactly what they've been asking for.'
>
> **– Rick Coleman**
> U S WEST Communications president-Long-Distance

shopping promise that customers have long been asking for.

Industry analysts have noted that the cost of entry for the regional Bells from a capital standpoint is very low. They point out that the RBOCs have high brand recognition and are already well-positioned with the customer base in their operating regions.

According to industry figures, the national inter-LATA long-distance market is between $65 billion and $70 billion a year. About 10 percent of that market is in the region served by U S WEST.

Business as usual changes with new law

The Federal Telecommunications Act of 1996 will change the way U S WEST does business by transferring jurisdiction over activities and conduct dealt with by the **Modified Final Judgment** to the Federal Communications Commission. U S WEST will continue to use the MFJ compliance manager network within the business units to facilitate legal reviews until new business review practices are developed and put into place.

Some **Open Network Architecture (ONA)** rules may be modified by the legislation, but employees should continue to follow the current ONA compliance policies regarding fair competition found in Regional Practice and Procedure 1005, the 1995 ONA Training Manual and established departmental methods and procedures.

U S WEST will be able to provide many **inter-LATA services**, including out-of-region inter-LATA and "incidental" services such as audio and video programming, cellular, two-way interactive video and network signaling. Almost all of these services can be provided without a separate subsidiary. However, U S WEST must obtain FCC authorization before providing in-region inter-LATA services through a separate subsidiary.

Electronic publishing is defined within the legislation as content-based information services such as news, entertainment, advertising, educational, instructional and technical materials. U S WEST has one year from enactment to move all electronic publishing into a separate subsidiary.

The legislation gives U S WEST significant freedom in **manufacturing.** The company may work closely with manufacturers of customer equipment and telecommunications equipment during the design and development of hardware and software. U S WEST also may engage in research activities relating to manufacturing and can enter into royalty agreements. The full scope of the manufacturing freedom is still being evaluated. U S WEST Communications can manufacture telecommunications equipment and customer equipment through a separate subsidiary when the FCC allows U S WEST Communications to enter into the inter-LATA services business. U S WEST may not manufacture in conjunction with another Bell operating company.

The **Customer Proprietary Network Information (CPNI) and Privacy Rules** legislation may impose broader requirements on how local service records can be used in marketing competitive services. Employees involved in CPNI and/or Privacy Rules should continue to follow current practices and procedures until new ones are developed.

> **ANSWERS TO COMPLIANCE ISSUES**
>
> For questions, contact a local business unit compliance manager or one of these FCC compliance managers: Sandra Sanchez, 303-965-8054; Harry Mertz, 303-896-9549; Mike Jude, 303-896-7345; Ivy Stevens, 206-345-3547; Sara Van Home, 303-965-8086.

...S REFORM

1994:
Congress proposed letting all communications companies into all segments of the industry. The House had passed a telecom reform bill by a wide margin and similar legislation was heading to the Senate, but was withdrawn after strong opposition.

...990 — 1995 — 1996

1995:
Congress elected in November 1994 introduced bills which win favor of U S WEST and other baby Bells.

Feb. 8, 1996:
President Clinton signed the Telecommunications Act of 1996 into law.

...gs in some states had opened the local loop to ...invested $2.5 billion in Time Warner Entertain- ...began shaping the telecommunications landscape.

TELECOMMUNICATIONS *from page 1*

specific rules for the entire industry. Our job is to stay actively engaged in the debate to ensure the FCC's rulemakings do not add cumbersome processes, do not advantage one player over another and that they keep the interests of consumers in mind."

According to Jim Stever, executive vice president-Public Policy, the state regulators will have their work cut out for them, too. Although the states have a requirement to certify that companies like U S WEST have met the checklist, there is no hard and fast timetable for compliance. "When we think we've satisfied the requirements, we'll petition the states and the FCC. In addition, the states will need to revisit and update their statutes, many of which

are now out of sync with the new federal legislation. We expect new legislation will be introduced in most of the 14 states in the U S WEST territory because of that."

Stever says the challenge for U S WEST over the next couple of years will be to make certain "that we're positioned to effectively compete in the new environment. A few components of the critical work we'll be overseeing from a state standpoint include cost recovery, interconnection and resale.

"This will be the most difficult task that employees shaping public policy have to face. Our first step will be to make sure that the rules are fair to everyone. Given that, we'll be able to take advantage of all our new marketing opportunities," Stever says.

Centered vs. left heads

In this large format, *US West Today* has the luxury of plenty of white space to frame the centered heads, which are written to utilize most of the line width. Design does not leave any single- or double-word lines dangling at the bottom of the centered heading.

THE TICKET™

Helpful News For Atlanta-Based Business Travelers →

AUGUST 1996

AIRLINE NEWS

As we go to print, ValuJet is busy submitting paperwork to the FAA by an August 1 deadline set back in June. Once the papers are filed and the FAA approves them, ValuJet hopes to start flying again in **early August**. At first, it will be allowed to fly only 15 aircraft, so you can expect a slow crawl back to its previous 31 destinations. *(POSSIBLE WRENCH IN THE WORKS:* If the recent TWA crash was a result of the use of old aircraft or due to FAA negligence, ValuJet's re-start might be even slower.)

The TWA tragedy, which as we go to print remains unresolved, has no upside for the airline industry— if is was a terrorist attack, people will shy away from international travel. If it was a mechanical malfunction, the "planes falling out of the sky" scenario will dominate. *(You can bet this issue will arise over and over as presidential*

Blimpie sandwiches on lunch flights—the sandwiches will now be made with only Healthy Choice meats and include fat-free cole slaw or pasta salad, low-fat Snackwell cookies, and a Sweet 'n Low mint. *(Sounds like an enforced weight-loss regime to us.)*

TICKET readers at Delta Sky Magazine passed along an interesting number to us: 2.3 million people read Sky every month, making it the MOST read in-flight among all U.S. carriers.

Interesting: The weight of the documentation associated with the development and manufacture of a single aircraft is more than the weight of a Boeing 747.

Q: Do you know what KLM, as in "Royal Dutch Airlines" stands for?
A: *Koninklijke Luchtvaart Maatschappij*

United is negotiating to by the old Denver Stapleton airport property to build the world's largest flight training center . . . GTE Airfones grossed $5.7

BIZ TRAVEL BOMBS:
Based on an informal poll of *TICKET* readers, we discovered a few superfluous items. *Do we REALLY need these things??*
• In-room fax machines, computers
• Indoor pool at the hotel health club
• Showers at the airport
• In-flight shopping
• Chocolate on the pillow
• Business/first class amenities kits
(Shave on the plane? Not me!)

AIRPORT NEWS

Helpful: Now hanging from the ceiling between the main security checkpoint and the atrium is a bank of **color monitors** listing the departure and arrival gate and time of all flights. Now passengers do not have to wait until they get to the bottom of the escalator in the transportation mall to determine from which concourse and gate their flights depart.

AFSEEE UPDATE

The New Forest Doublespeak

By Andy Stahl

A well-orchestrated campaign is tuning up to exploit the first anti-environmental U.S. Congress in 30 years. Like interlocking corporate directorates, each piece of this campaign is superficially disconnected from the others. However, the melody sounds the same: fix the environmental laws that obstruct forest management.

The feel-good part of the campaign is led by the 7th American Forest Congress, which bills itself as a grassroots democracy whose purpose is the development of a "shared vision" and new forest policies that are "ecologically sound, economically viable, and socially responsible." The forest congress will culminate Feb. 20 to 24, 1996, in a Washington, D.C., conference to which "everyone" is invited.

The forest congress' founding board of directors includes three current or former Weyerhaeuser employees, two from International Paper, the head of the Society of American Foresters, seven university foresters, two wise-use front groups (with

Earth-friendly names), a state forestry department spokesperson, and two staff members from American Forests, which has championed the forest health "crisis." Also included are a Forest Service regional forester (known for having been the only agency wildlife biologist willing to testify in court that the Forest Service's first illegal spotted owl plan would save the owl) and the agency's head of ecosystem management.

Finding out what the 7th American Forest Congress wants to accomplish is like trying to

meddlesome courts enforcing environmental laws. Although this may not be the agenda of some participants, the mere existence of the forest congress is a bold statement by its promoters that current policies are broken and need fixing.

That's also the U.S. Department of Agriculture's theme in a soon-to-be-released report that chronicles alleged inconsistencies among environmental laws. The report drawn on a recent study by two University of Montana forestry professors, funded by the Forest Service,

Executive Director Andy Stahl.

but on eliminating citizen oversight of agency behavior.

This campaign may succeed in the next legislative or budget-cutting wave. It is supported by many foresters and land managers who are uncom...

Finding out what the 7th American Forest Congress wants to accomplish is like trying to catch a cloud

---

FRONTLINES

Read the Fine Print

The Clinton administration is protecting buyer's remorse over its signing of the timber salvage bill (dubbed "logging without laws"). Apparently, the White House and U.S. Department of Agriculture failed to read the bill's fine print, which directs the Forest Service to sell old timber sales that violate the president's Northwest Forest Plan.

Subsection (k) of the new law (titled "Award and Release of Previously Offered and Unawarded Timber Sale Contracts") directs the Forest Service to sell "all" su...

cades-old timber sales be resurrected from the dead, even if those sales now fall within a wilderness area, such as the Three Sisters, Mt. Hood, or Mt. Jefferson wildernesses. The bill even requires logging within national parks, such as Mt. Rainer and Olympic National Parks, which were national forests in the first half of the century.

The timber industry, for its part, is playing coy on this section of the bill. Their spokesperson, Ross Mickey, suggests that Congress meant the law to apply only to sales offered since (although no such language exists in the bill). The Forest Service, for its part, says that it applies only to sales offering 1990, although the bill does not say so. Environmental groups support the Forest Service's interpretation; they believe that timber sales offered in 1990 but not complying again on no specific statutory language).

In a remarkable display of the timber industry...

filed a motion for contempt of court, asking U.S. District Court Judge Michael Hogan to fine and/or imprison Undersecretary of Agriculture James Lyons for not moving fast enough with these old timber sales. Although Lyons' predecessors in the Reagan and Bush administrations violated virtually every environmental law on the books (according to federal Judges William Dwyer, Helen Frye, and Thomas Zilly, not to the mention the 9th U.S. Circuit Court of Appeals) in their zeal to log ancient forests, not one of those officials was ever threatened with jail time. Crimes against the environment must not be as serious as crimes against industry.

The latest word from the White House should not come as a surprise for those who have followed this drama. President Clinton, who first vetoed the "logging without laws" bill and then flip-flopped to sign the bill two weeks later, has now reversed course again and has asked Congress to repeal the law — which just goes to show: You should always read the fine print.

Pulp Friction

The Inner Voice staff was excited by the prospect of not only doing an Issue on kenaf but also doing it on recycled paper. It is an opportunity to make amends for the countless trees we consume each year (albeit recycled ones), as well as a way to rub elbows with enlightened folks who buck the current system of liquidating nations' forests for paper pulp.

The process was far from effortless. But the fact that you're reading this issue proves it can be done. It's also prudent to keep in mind that this issue cost us roughly three times more than an issue printed on recycled paper — and the initial quote from our regular printer was almost five times as high.

Our regular printer was hesitant to print on kenaf paper. This is probably typical of any printer who has enough grief using traditional papers. They couldn't guarantee the quality of the print job and were unwilling to purchase the paper directly from the supplier. Left with the question of what to do with surplus rolls of kenaf, the possibility of an inferior print job, and an exorbitant price tag

...ployees Lead the Way

BACK PAGE

AFSEEE Goes Online

AFSEEE is working on establishing a presence on the information superhighway. We currently offer a site on the World Wide Web that features information about AFSEEE, ways to contact Forest Service employees electronically, back issues of Inner Voice, links to other useful WWW sites, and much more. We have many future plans for our site, but we encourage you to see what we're offering today and to keep checking for new options. In the coming months, we hope to offer more new, useful services and information.

AFSEEE also offers two listservs to members or anyone who wants inside information on what's happening — one for Forest Service employees in 8-6 and one for citizen activists. As other regions become listserv-enabled, new listservs will no doubt form.

Lastly, you can contact any AFSEEE staff member directly by using their personal email address. We want to hear from you. Please make a note. Thanks.

AFSEEE WWW SITE
Point your WWW browser to
http://www.afseee.org

STAFF EMAIL ADDRESSES
Dennis Bishop, Information Director, dennis@afseee.org
Erin Bonner, Information Director, erin@afseee.org
Cheri Brooks, Inner Voice editor, cheri@afseee.org
Shannon Cantrell, Administration and Finance Director, shannon@afseee.org
Bob Dale, Field Director, bobdale@afseee.org
Jim Desmond, Grant Administrator, jim_d@afseee.org
Joe Fox, Science and Policy Coordinator, joefox@afseee.org
Suzanne Johnson, Administrative Assistant, suzanne@afseee.org
Don Sanders, Southeast Program Director, donsand@afseee.org
Andy Stahl, Executive Director, a_stahl@afseee.org

AFSEEE LISTSERVS
To subscribe to the Region 6 Environmental News send an email message to the list moderator dennis@afseee.org

To subscribe to the Activist...

Inner Vo...

Inner Voice (ISSN 1062-9491) is published bimonthly by the Association of Forest Service Employees for Environmental Ethics, PO Box 11615, Eugene, OR 97440, (541) 484-2692 — Voice: (541) 484-3004 — Fax.

E-mail address via the Internet: afseee@afseee.org or via the USFS DG: internet:afseee.org@internet@att.x400 WWW access: http://www.afseee.org

BOARD OF DIRECTORS

Dave Iverson (President), Regional Economist, Intermountain Region; Cynthia Reichelt (Secretary/Treasurer), Public Affairs Specialist, Colville National Forest; Sally Claggett, botanist, Georgia Forest; Richard Fairbanks, Timber Sale Planner, Willamette NF; Jackie Canterbury, Wildlife Biologist, Tongass National Forest; District Ranger (retired), Wildlife Staff, Forest Service Region 1; Jim Horne, Staff Archaeologist, Los Padres National Forest (Vice President); District Ranger, PAO (retired), Forest Service...

AFSEEE STAFF

Dennis Bishop, Information Director; Erin Bonner, Development; Cheri Brooks, Editor, *Inner Voice*; Shannon Cantrell, Administration; Director; Bob Dale, Field Director; Jim Desmond, Grant Administrator; Joe Fox, Science and Policy Coordinator; Suzanne Johnson, Assistant; Don Sanders, Southeast Program Coordinator; Andy Stahl, Director.

INNER VOICE PRODUCTION

Cheri Brooks, Editor; Dennis Bishop, Production Editor; Additional help; Lori Howard, Designer; Alonzo Printing Company, Inc...

AFSEEE is a nonprofit corporation 501(c)(3). The association is dedicated to promoting ecologically sustainable management practices and an environment-sensitive resource ethic by public resource management agencies, especially the Forest Service, through educational and outreach activities.

Membership comprises current, retired, and former Forest Service employees...(a contributor category allows non-Forest Service individuals, organizations and resource managers in other agencies an opportunity to support our cause)...a subscription to Inner Voice.

The views expressed by the contributors are those of the authors and do not necessarily reflect AFSEEE's position or that of the U.S. Forest Service.

DICK DAVIS DIGEST

Investment Ideas From The Best Minds On Wall Street

12 YEARS

Vol. 12 No. 271 September 6, 1993

In This Issue

PERSONAL NOTE

THIS TIME IS DIFFERENT ... OR IS IT?

Who are you? Thousands of readers participated in our recent survey, giving us a profile of the "typical" Digest subscriber. I thought you might be interested in the results. The average respondent to the survey is 57 years old, with ages ranging from 16 to 87. The average annual income of our readers is $90,000, and the average value of their portfolios is $600,000. Our largest group of readers comprises investment professionals, followed by retirees. The typical reader has 71% of their assets in equities and holds stocks for an average of 2.6 years. I would also like to thank our readers for the encouragement in the section that was left for comments: Phrases such as "if it ain't broke, don't fix it" and "don't change a thing" appeared repeatedly. In line

with this sentiment, the average Digest reader has so far maintained their subscription for four years; in addition, almost half our readers first learned about the Digest from a friend or a broker. In all, the survey shows that Digest readers are among the nation's most successful citizens and investors. Congratulations!

I was also able to meet many Digest readers who attended the recent ISI Money Show in San Francisco. The conference was the largest investor show ever held, with over 8,000 attendees. The turnout -- nearly double that of any previous investor conference -- reflects the broadening appeal of stocks to the public. In many ways, my encounters with investors and advisors at the ISI

(Cont. on page 2)

SPOTLIGHT STOCK

TELMEX: EHRENKRANTZ LOOKS SOUTH OF THE BORDER

Louis Ehrenkrantz, who has long been one of our favorite analysts, has formed his own investment firm, Ehrenkrantz King Nussbaum. Coming on board as senior market analyst is William LeFevre, who has also been frequently, and favorably, featured in this publication. Thankfully, LeFevre's Monday Morning Market Memo, as well as The Ehrenkrantz Report (635 Madison Ave., New York, NY 10022, 12 issues, $120, 8/25/93), will continue to be published. In his latest issue, Ehrenkrantz notes, 'Our focus will be anticipatory in character, one that is able to make courageous and even unpopular calls. Successful investing, we believe, requires the ability to detect impending changes in the economic and social spheres.

No longer can analysts be content with assembling reported number and consensus options. A portfolio for the 1990s had better reflect a keen understanding of the political and social changes before they become reflected in prices of securities. Whether we're analyzing the fall of communism, a war, or the water supply, our ultimate goal is to build portfolios that anticipate this change." His latest featured buy recommendation -- **Telefonos de Mexico** (TMX 50 NYSE) -- reflects this focus; it is a controversial stock that is heavily influenced by the heated political and social debate concerning the North American Free Trade Agreement (NAFTA). Here's his review:

(Cont. on page 8)

Editor/Publisher ....Steven Halpern
Assoc. Editor ....Dona Walker
Office Manager ....Roberta Noonan
Asst. Manager ....Lynne Walbzestein
Customer Service ......Jodie Corbett
Marketing Director .....Jaye Lasion

Standing heads stand out

Standing heads, such as those in *Inner Voice*, *The Ticket News* and *Dick Davis Digest*, help readers find their favorite information in each issue. Including a graphic element along with the typography is a handsome way to pull these kinds of heads away from the body copy and other headlines.

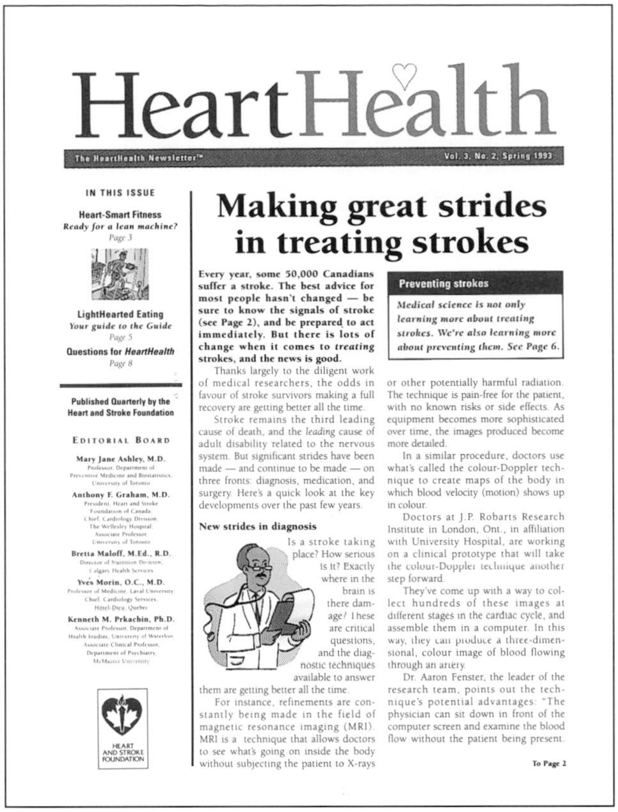

HeartHealth

The HeartHealth Newsletter™ Vol. 3, No. 2, Spring 1993

IN THIS ISSUE

Heart-Smart Fitness
Ready for a lean machine?
Page 3

LightHearted Eating
Your guide to the Guide
Page 5

Questions for *HeartHealth*
Page 8

Published Quarterly by the Heart and Stroke Foundation

EDITORIAL BOARD

Mary Jane Ashley, M.D.
Professor, Department of Preventive Medicine and Biostatistics, University of Toronto

Anthony F. Graham, M.D.
President, Heart and Stroke Foundation of Canada; Chief, Cardiology Division, The Wellesley Hospital; Associate Professor, University of Toronto

Bretta Maloff, M.Ed., R.D.
Director of Nutrition Division, Calgary Health Services

Yves Morin, O.C., M.D.
Professor of Medicine, Laval University; Chief, Cardiology Services, Hôtel-Dieu, Quebec

Kenneth M. Prkachin, Ph.D.
Associate Professor, Department of Health Studies, University of Waterloo; Associate Clinical Professor, Department of Psychiatry, McMaster University

HEART AND STROKE FOUNDATION

Making great strides in treating strokes

Every year, some 50,000 Canadians suffer a stroke. The best advice for most people hasn't changed — be sure to know the signals of stroke (see Page 2), and be prepared to act immediately. But there is lots of change when it comes to *treating* strokes, and the news is good.

Preventing strokes

Medical science is not only learning more about treating strokes. We're also learning more about preventing them. See Page 6.

Thanks largely to the diligent work of medical researchers, the odds in favour of stroke survivors making a full recovery are getting better all the time.

Stroke remains the third leading cause of death, and the *leading* cause of adult disability related to the nervous system. But significant strides have been made — and continue to be made — on three fronts: diagnosis, medication, and surgery. Here's a quick look at the key developments over the past few years.

New strides in diagnosis

Is a stroke taking place? How serious is it? Exactly where in the brain is there damage? These are critical questions, and the diagnostic techniques available to answer them are getting better all the time.

For instance, refinements are constantly being made in the field of magnetic resonance imaging (MRI). MRI is a technique that allows doctors to see what's going on inside the body without subjecting the patient to X-rays or other potentially harmful radiation. The technique is pain-free for the patient, with no known risks or side effects. As equipment becomes more sophisticated over time, the images produced become more detailed.

In a similar procedure, doctors use what's called the colour-Doppler technique to create maps of the body in which blood velocity (motion) shows up in colour.

Doctors at J.P. Robarts Research Institute in London, Ont., in affiliation with University Hospital, are working on a clinical prototype that will take the colour-Doppler technique another step forward.

They've come up with a way to collect hundreds of these images at different stages in the cardiac cycle, and assemble them in a computer. In this way, they can produce a three-dimensional, colour image of blood flowing through an artery.

Dr. Aaron Fenster, the leader of the research team, points out the technique's potential advantages: "The physician can sit down in front of the computer screen and examine the blood flow without the patient being present.

To Page 2

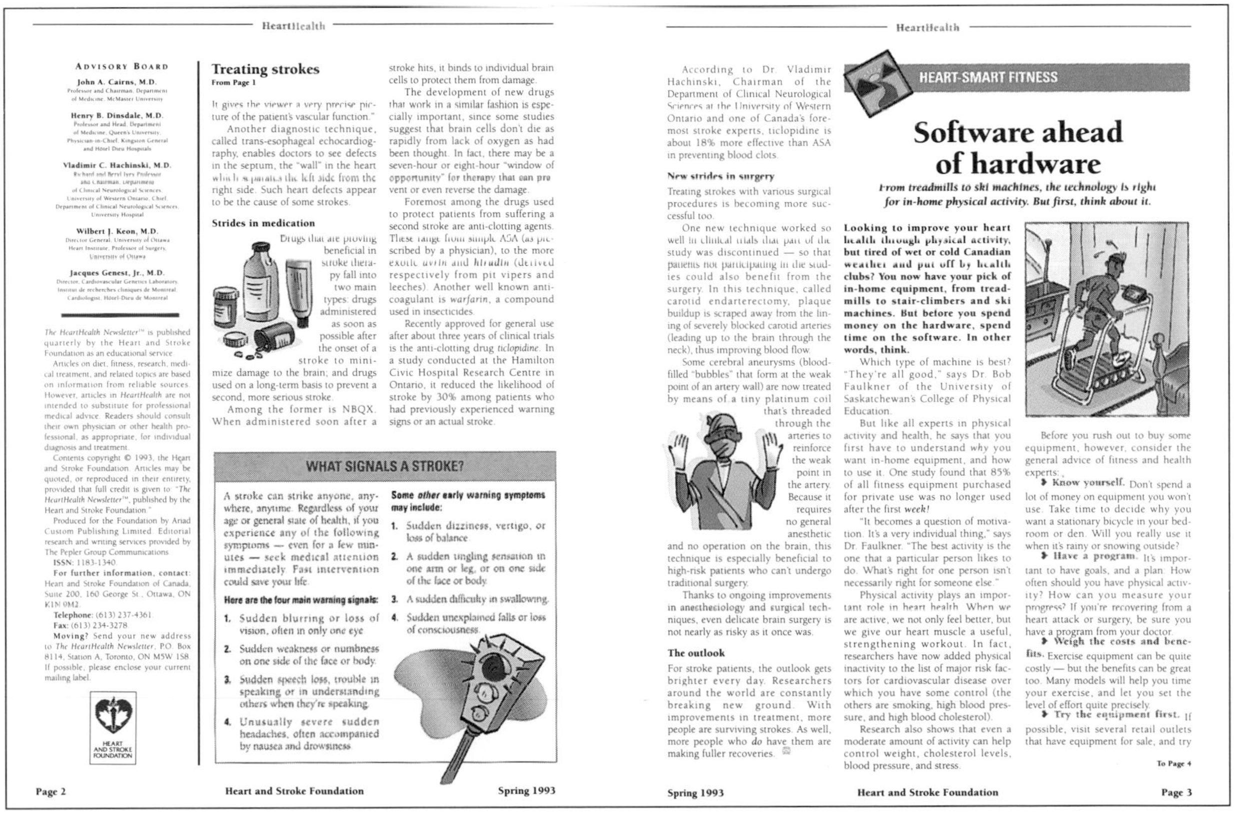

HeartHealth

ADVISORY BOARD

John A. Cairns, M.D.
Professor and Chairman, Department of Medicine, McMaster University

Henry B. Dinsdale, M.D.
Professor and Head, Department of Medicine, Queen's University; Physician-in-Chief, Kingston General and Hôtel Dieu Hospitals

Vladimir C. Hachinski, M.D.
Richard and Beryl Ivey Professor and Chairman, Department of Clinical Neurological Sciences, University of Western Ontario; Chief, Department of Clinical Neurological Sciences, University Hospital

Wilbert J. Keon, M.D.
Director General, University of Ottawa Heart Institute; Professor of Surgery, University of Ottawa

Jacques Genest, Jr., M.D.
Director, Cardiovascular Genetics Laboratory, Institut de recherches cliniques de Montréal; Cardiologist, Hôtel-Dieu de Montréal

The HeartHealth Newsletter™ is published quarterly by the Heart and Stroke Foundation as an educational service.

Articles on diet, fitness, research, medical treatment, and related topics are based on information from reliable sources. However, articles in *HeartHealth* are not intended to substitute for professional medical advice. Readers should consult their own physician or other health professional, as appropriate, for individual diagnosis and treatment.

Contents copyright © 1993, the Heart and Stroke Foundation. Articles may be quoted, or reproduced in their entirety, provided that full credit is given to: "*The HeartHealth Newsletter*™, published by the Heart and Stroke Foundation."

Produced for the Foundation by Ariad Custom Publishing Limited. Editorial research and writing services provided by The Pepler Group Communications.

ISSN: 1183-1340.

For further information, contact: Heart and Stroke Foundation of Canada, Suite 200, 160 George St., Ottawa, ON K1N 9M2.

Telephone: (613) 237-4361.

Fax: (613) 234-3278.

Moving? Send your new address to *The HeartHealth Newsletter*, P.O. Box 8114, Station A, Toronto, ON M5W 1S8. If possible, please enclose your current mailing label.

HEART AND STROKE FOUNDATION

Treating strokes

From Page 1

It gives the viewer a very precise picture of the patient's vascular function."

Another diagnostic technique, called trans-esophageal echocardiography, enables doctors to see defects in the septum, the "wall" in the heart which separates the left side from the right side. Such heart defects appear to be the cause of some strokes.

Strides in medication

Drugs that are proving beneficial in stroke therapy fall into two main types: drugs administered as soon as possible after the onset of a stroke to minimize damage to the brain; and drugs used on a long-term basis to prevent a second, more serious stroke.

Among the former is NBQX. When administered soon after a stroke hits, it binds to individual brain cells to protect them from damage.

The development of new drugs that work in a similar fashion is especially important, since some studies suggest that brain cells don't die as rapidly from lack of oxygen as had been thought. In fact, there may be a seven-hour or eight-hour "window of opportunity" for therapy that can prevent or even reverse the damage.

Foremost among the drugs used to protect patients from suffering a second stroke are anti-clotting agents. These range from simple ASA (as prescribed by a physician), to the more exotic *avrin* and *hirudin* (derived respectively from pit vipers and leeches). Another well known anticoagulant is *warfarin*, a compound used in insecticides.

Recently approved for general use after about three years of clinical trials is the anti-clotting drug *ticlopidine*. In a study conducted at the Hamilton Civic Hospital Research Centre in Ontario, it reduced the likelihood of stroke by 30% among patients who had previously experienced warning signs or an actual stroke.

WHAT SIGNALS A STROKE?

A stroke can strike anyone, anywhere, anytime. Regardless of your age or general state of health, if you experience any of the following symptoms — even for a few minutes — seek medical attention immediately. Fast intervention could save your life.

Here are the four main warning signals:

1. Sudden blurring or loss of vision, often in only one eye.
2. Sudden weakness or numbness on one side of the face or body.
3. Sudden speech loss, trouble in speaking or in understanding others when they're speaking.
4. Unusually severe sudden headaches, often accompanied by nausea and drowsiness.

Some *other* early warning symptoms may include:

1. Sudden dizziness, vertigo, or loss of balance.
2. A sudden tingling sensation in one arm or leg, or on one side of the face or body.
3. A sudden difficulty in swallowing.
4. Sudden unexplained falls or loss of consciousness.

Page 2 Heart and Stroke Foundation Spring 1993

HeartHealth

According to Dr. Vladimir Hachinski, Chairman of the Department of Clinical Neurological Sciences at the University of Western Ontario and one of Canada's foremost stroke experts, ticlopidine is about 18% more effective than ASA in preventing blood clots.

New strides in surgery

Treating strokes with various surgical procedures is becoming more successful too.

One new technique worked so well in clinical trials that part of the study was discontinued — so that patients not participating in the studies could also benefit from the surgery. In this technique, called carotid endarterectomy, plaque buildup is scraped away from the lining of severely blocked carotid arteries (leading up to the brain through the neck), thus improving blood flow.

Some cerebral aneurysms (blood-filled "bubbles" that form at the weak point of an artery wall) are now treated by means of a tiny platinum coil that's threaded through the arteries to reinforce the weak point in the artery. Because it requires no general anesthetic and no operation on the brain, this technique is especially beneficial to high-risk patients who can't undergo traditional surgery.

Thanks to ongoing improvements in anesthesiology and surgical techniques, even delicate brain surgery is not nearly as risky as it once was.

The outlook

For stroke patients, the outlook gets brighter every day. Researchers around the world are constantly breaking new ground. With improvements in treatment, more people are surviving strokes. As well, more people who *do* have them are making fuller recoveries.

HEART-SMART FITNESS

Software ahead of hardware

From treadmills to ski machines, the technology is right for in-home physical activity. But first, think about it.

Looking to improve your heart health through physical activity, but tired of wet or cold Canadian weather and put off by health clubs? You now have your pick of in-home equipment, from treadmills to stair-climbers and ski machines. But before you spend money on the hardware, spend time on the software. In other words, think.

Which type of machine is best? "They're all good," says Dr. Bob Faulkner of the University of Saskatchewan's College of Physical Education.

But like all experts in physical activity and health, he says that you first have to understand *why* you want in-home equipment, and how to use it. One study found that 85% of all fitness equipment purchased for private use was no longer used after the first *week!*

"It becomes a question of motivation. It's a very individual thing," says Dr. Faulkner. "The best activity is the one that a particular person likes to do. What's right for one person isn't necessarily right for someone else."

Physical activity plays an important role in heart health. When we are active, we not only feel better, but we give our heart muscle a useful, strengthening workout. In fact, researchers have now added physical inactivity to the list of major risk factors for cardiovascular disease over which you have some control (the others are smoking, high blood pressure, and high blood cholesterol).

Research also shows that even a moderate amount of activity can help control weight, cholesterol levels, blood pressure, and stress.

Before you rush out to buy some equipment, however, consider the general advice of fitness and health experts:

- **Know yourself.** Don't spend a lot of money on equipment you won't use. Take time to decide why you want a stationary bicycle in your bedroom or den. Will you really use it when it's rainy or snowing outside?
- **Have a program.** It's important to have goals, and a plan: How often should you have physical activity? How can you measure your progress? If you're recovering from a heart attack or surgery, be sure you have a program from your doctor.
- **Weigh the costs and benefits.** Exercise equipment can be quite costly — but the benefits can be great too. Many models will help you time your exercise, and let you set the level of effort quite precisely.
- **Try the equipment first.** If possible, visit several retail outlets that have equipment for sale, and try

To Page 4

Spring 1993 Heart and Stroke Foundation Page 3

Springboarding into articles

Bold introductory paragraphs under the headlines, such as "Making great strides..." and "Software ahead...," lead readers into the longer articles. The decks, in conjunction with subheads, illustrations, bulleted lists, sidebars and pull quotes, create pages that are easy to skim.

NAME *HeartHealth*

PUBLISHER Heart & Stroke Foundation, Ottawa, Ontario, Canada

PURPOSE/AUDIENCE Service and education for the community

PRODUCTION/PRINTING Four-color process on white 60# offset

FORMAT 8½" x 11"; eight pages

DESIGN Ariad Custom Publishing

NEWS BRIEFS

Telecommuting is in future of the American workforce . . . Federal Express announces an online service to allow customers to schedule and track deliveries themselves . . . U.S. Postal Service offers free, one-time cleanup of your mailing list to meet USPS Zip+4 standards . . . DAZzle envelope software adds POSTNET coding to envelopes and labels . . .

Workforce 2000: Will Your Staff Be Working from Home?

FOR ALL OF YOU WHO HAVE THOUGHT TO SUGGEST TELE-COMMUTING IN YOUR WORKPLACE (BUT WERE AFRAID TO ASK), you may not need to. Business trends analyst Link Resources Corp. estimates that 8.8 million American workers were officially telecommuting this year—not counting the many more who unofficially telecommuted a day or so a week to get work done without office interferences. Even more, according to a study by the Gartner Group, a Stamford, Connecticut consulting firm, more than 80 percent of all organizations will have at least half of their employees telecommuting by 1999. In fact, due to the Clean Air Act (which requires employers to look for alternate means of getting their employees to work during peak commuting hours), many larger employers in the Delaware Valley are already at least considering telecommuting. Other alternatives to nine-to-five workdays include flextime and compressed work weeks (e.g., four 10-hour days).

Other findings of the Gartner group study include:

- Average increase in productivity of telecommuting employees: 10% to 16%

- Average amount of time each telecommuter spends in the office: one day each week

- Average investment of employer per telecommuter per year: $1,000 to $1,500

- Equipment employer typically provides: 486 PC, fax-modem, telephone and telephone line, dot-matrix printer, office furniture, to an average investment of about $3,000 (equipment *Read Me* readers probably already have at home)

If you're interested in finding out more about working telecommuting programs and trends in the Delaware Valley, contact Steve Russel at the Delaware Valley Telecommuting Advisory Council. You can reach Steve at (610) 667-4088. 🔲

About *Read Me*

Editor/Publisher: Cheryl Lockett Zubak
President, Work Write™
128 South Eastview Avenue
Feasterville, PA 19053
Phone: (215) 357-3453
Fax: (215) 357-0695
74654.1532@compuserve.com

ISSN: 1077-8845

Read Me is the quarterly newsletter of Work Write™, a corporate and technical communications consulting organization located in Bucks County, Pennsylvania. Work Write™ specializes in online and print user's guides, training materials, technical reports, and newsletters.

Read Me is offered free of charge to Work Write™ customers and contacts. Other interested persons may receive a yearly subscription (4 issues) by sending a check or money order for $29 made payable to Cheryl Lockett Zubak, Work Write™, 128 South Eastview Avenue, Feasterville, PA 19053.

Colophon. *Nameplate, headlines:* Presidents type art (Image Glub Graphics); *Reverse Headings:* Centaur; *Body headings:* Stone Sans; *Body text:* Stone Serif.

Toolbox. Aldus PageMaker 5.0 on a 486/33 with 8MB of RAM and a 1.2GB hard drive. Proofs are output to a QMS 860 at 600 dpi; final copy is output to a Xerox DocuTech printing system (also at 600 dpi).

Print Shop: Graphic Reproductions, 1957 Pioneer Road, Building F, Huntingdon Valley, PA 19006. (215) 957-6120. Speak with Kim Ayling. 🔲

What Makes a Successful Telecommuter?

Been pondering whether you have what it takes to tele-commute? Jack M. Nilles, President of JALA International, says the characteristics of a successful telecommuter include:

- *Self-motivated:* will get the job done despite the distractions of being at home

- *Self-disciplined:* don't need frequent urging to complete a job successfully; can determine own pace and work style

- *Job skills and experience:* already has the skills and experience for the job

- *Flexibility and innovation:* can adjust to new ways of working

- *Socialization:* can work in an isolated environment with little outlet for office socialization

- *Family:* supports the fact that the telecommuter is working in the home office 🔲

Summarized from **Making Telecommuting Happen: A Guide for Teleman-agers and Telecom-muters***, by Jack M. Nilles (Van Nostrand Reinhold, 1994). Another recently published guide is* **Home Sweet Home** *by Jeff Meade (Peterson's, 1994).*

For further information on this study, contact the Gartner Group at (800) 645-6395.

Readable type runs in the family

The typography of *Read Me* makes the reader do just that. Stone Serif body type and Stone Sans headlines, subheads, sidebars, decks and folios create an attractive page. Note how the dark icons, soft drop shadows, headlines, rules and boxes create a page that pops using only one ink color on recycled gray paper. *Working Solo Newsletter*, shown on pages 26 and 27 uses the same type combination.

NEWS BRIEFS

FedEx Goes Online

NEVER LET IT BE SAID THAT THE OVERNIGHT MAIL SERVICES WILL BE THE LAST to get on the infamous Information Superhighway. Federal Express, at least, has decided it won't be left behind. The company has recently announced an online service that will allow customers to schedule and track Federal Express deliveries from their personal computers.

The free service, called FedEx Ship, provides a Windows or Macintosh interface to connect to a FedEx server in Memphis, Tennessee, through your modem. Using the service, you can print FedEx shipping labels (you need a laser printer), schedule pickups, verify shipment and delivery times, and access other FedEx other services.

FedEx customers can order FedEx Ship now. Federal Express has also signed agreements to provide FedEx Ship on American Online and Commercenet.

For further information, call Federal Express at (800) 463-3339.

From a conversation with a Federal Express customer service representative, January 1995.

Postal Service Cleans Up Mailing Lists—Free!

IF YOU NEVER THOUGHT TO ASK THE U.S. POSTAL SERVICE for help with fast mail delivery (gosh, why not?), you may want to reconsider. The Postal Service is offering a free, one-time service called Zip+4 Zip Coding to help you update your mailing lists so it's easier for Postal Service employees to sort your mail. As a result (in theory, anyway), your mail will be delivered more quickly.

To take advantage of the service, pick up an application at a Postal Business Center or call (800) 238-3150. Then send the application and the mailing list (in ASCII format only) on a Mac or PC diskette to the specified address. Within three or four weeks, you'll receive the Postal Service-approved list with addresses updated to the USPS standards, Zip+4 codes added, incomplete addresses identified, and so forth.

And Then Add Bar Codes . . . .

DURING THE LAST SIX MONTHS, I'VE BEGUN TO USE a software application called DAZzle Designer, which, among other things, adds bar codes to single addresses or lists of addresses. Certified by the U.S. Postal Service, DAZzle can update zip codes to Zip+4 and even standardize the address, if it's in the correct database structure.

The product works like this: you design an envelope or mailing label with DAZzle and add the address (or open a list of addresses in a supported file format, such as ASCII or dBase). Then you dial out through DAZzle to one of the Postal Service centers listed in the program (9600 baud is the top transmission speed, by the way). Your address list is compared against the Postal Service database and updated if necessary. At the end of the transmission, you can choose to print out a form the Postal Service needs for bulk mailings to verify that you've coded your envelopes or labels from a CASS mailing list and with a certified POSTNET coding product.

DAZzle can add delivery point or standard bar codes, FIM codes, and carrier-route information on domestic or international mail. You can also calculate postage (yes, the new postal rates are present), add graphics, and design envelopes or labels (which you can then save as a new layout).

I use DAZzle quite frequently, for both bulk and non-bulk mailings. I've noticed that adding the bar code greatly decreases the time it takes for my mail to be delivered—both first class and third class mailings.

Of course, I don't use DAZzle when I pay my bills!

DAZzle Designer is available for $149 from Envelope Manager Software, 247 High St., Palo Alto, CA 94301-1041. Call (800) 576-3278. Other versions of DAZzle are also available.

Read Me Editor to Speak at Annual Conference

Interested in learning more about Windows online help tools? Or how to design and manage newsletters? Then you may want to attend the workshops being presented by Cheryl Lockett Zubak at the Annual Conference of the Society for Technical Communication, to be held in Washington, D.C. this April.

Cheryl will present "A Real-World Look at Windows Help Authoring Tools," a review of the major authoring tools for Windows help authors. She will also copresent (with Cheryl Disch of BE&K) "Newsletter Design for Nondesigners" and "Getting to Best of Show: Managing Chapter Newsletters."

PHILLY AREA DATES

March 13–18. *13th Annual National Conference on Ada Technology.* Valley Forge, PA. (310) 397-6338

April 6–7. *Going Online: How to Design Effective Online Manuals, Help Systems, and tutorials.* Malvern, PA. (610) 658-2735

April 20–21. *Fundamentals of T1/T3 Networks, Technologies, and Services.* Penn Tower, Philadelphia, PA. (201) 478-5400

AROUND THE NATION

March 16. *A Business Guide to the Internet.* Local satellite seminar. (800) 643-4668

March 19–23. *Object World.* Boston, MA. (508) 879-6700.

March 27–31. *Network+ Interop.* Las Vegas, NV. (800) 488-2883

March 27–31. *Microsoft Tech Ed '95* Ernest N. Morial Convention Center, New Orleans, LA. (800) 433-9996 or (612) 550-6390

April 9–13. *NAB MultiMedia World.* Las Vegas, NV. (800) 342-2460

April 20. *Internet Business Tools.* Local satellite seminar. (800) 643-4668

April 20–21. *Usability Testing: How to Plan, Design & Conduct Effective Tests.* Washington, D.C. (800) 34-TRAIN

April 23–26. *Annual Conference of the Society for Technical Communication.* Washington, D.C. (703) 522-4114

April 26–28. *Spring Comdex '95.* Atlanta, GA. (617) 449-6600

May 4. *Building Your Internet Business Case.* Local satellite seminar. (800) 643-4668

NAME *Read Me*

PUBLISHER Work Write, Feasterville, Pennsylvania

PURPOSE/AUDIENCE Service and marketing to customers

PRODUCTION/PRINTING Black on gray 60# recycled offset

FORMAT 8½" × 11"; twelve pages

DESIGN Cheryl Lockett Zubak, Work Write

Justified type looks official

The justified type helps *Warren Boroson's Mutual Fund Digest* look official and authoritative. News briefs on the second page are separated with a rule and triangle. Note how top and outside margins are design elements that clearly frame the text and allow space for three-hole punching.

NAME *Warren Boroson's Mutual Fund Digest*

PUBLISHER Warren Boroson, Glen Rock, New Jersey

PURPOSE/AUDIENCE Service to subscribers

PRODUCTION/PRINTING Black ink on white 50# offset

FORMAT 8½" x 11"; eight pages

DESIGN Jerry Szubin

★ NEWS ★

Strong Common Stock is reopening—until April 15, and only for IRA money. This is a five-star Morningstar fund with a five-year annualized return of 199.13% a year. Last year it climbed 20.47%. Richard Weiss and Marina Carlson are a gifted team, and this mid-cap blend fund is hard to resist. In its seven years it has never landed below the top 50% of similar funds. (800) 368-1030.

"Eleven Superior Funds to Buy Now" include Brandywine (800-656-3017), Managers Special Equity (800-638-5660), EuroPacific Growth (800-421-4120), Ivy International A (800-456-5111), Merrill Lynch Developing Capital Markets B (800-637-3863), T. Rowe Price Equity-Income (800-638-5660), Vanguard Bond Index-Total Bond (800-851-4999), Merrill Lynch Corporate High Income B (800-637-3863), Loomis Sayles Bond (800-633-3330), Vanguard Municipal Intermediate Term (800-851-4999), and Dodge & Cox Balanced (800-621-3979). (Money, Feb.)

Comment: Money foolishly promises that "you will profit for years to come by investing in these stars...." And it calls Merrill Lynch Corporate High Income "king of the junkyard." Like heck. Northeast Investors Trust (see page one) has done better over one year, three years, and five years—and doesn't have a deferred sales charge.

The "seven best mutual funds 1997" are supposedly Legg Mason Value Trust (800-577-8589), Third Avenue Value (800-443-1021), Janus Worldwide (800-525-8983), Longleaf Partners Small-Cap (800-445-9469), T.

Rowe Price Growth Stock (800-638-5660), Mairs & Power Growth (612-222-8478), and Scudder Growth & Income (800-225-2470).

SmartMoney's 1996 choices rose 16% versus 27.85% for the S&P 500 (roughly from December to December). Worst performer: Wasatch Mid-Cap, up a mere 3.57%. (SmartMoney, Feb.)

Comment: Good, sound choices.

Are short-term bond funds always better than money market funds—even if you can stand a little volatility? Not if interest rates are rising quickly. Only money market funds can keep up. (Value Line Mutual Funds, 1/7)

Is Fidelity too big? Maybe. "It is no coincidence, Fidelity analysts say, that the relatively small $370 million Fidelity Export fund has been a top performer, with a 37% return through Nov. 22. Manager Arieh Coll concentrates about a third of his assets in his top ten holdings, mainly small and mid-sized technology and gaming stocks. Magellan would have had great difficulty jamming 33% of its assets, $17.7 billion, into those ten stocks." (Business Week, Dec. 9)

Comment: With stock funds, other things being equal, smaller is better than bigger. Magellan has an almost impossible task.

Morningstar's publisher, John Rekenthaler, recommends smaller funds that invest in undervalued stocks: Skyline Special Equities, Fidelity Low-Priced Stock, T. Rowe Price Over-the-Counter Securities,

and Schroder U.S. Smaller Companies Fund. He's leery of smaller growth funds: some from the Aim, Alger, American Century (Twentieth Century), PBHG, and Van Wagoner families. (New York Times, 1/9)

Which members of the Schwab Select List "are most likely to show signs of bloat in the coming months?" The Select List "too often...has proven to be a jinx." Among funds on the list that disappointed: Berger 100, Founders Discovery, Warburg Pincus Growth & Income, Crabbe Huson Special. Candidate to be "particularly wary of": Oakmark and PBHG Growth. But Third Avenue Value should continue to do well, despite its being on the list. (Critical Investor, Feb.)

Comment: I wouldn't bet against Oakmark, big as it is.

Is it okay that fund families kill their poor-performing funds, moving their shareholders and assets over into their better-performing funds? "Mergers hurt the ability of investors to make informed decisions because they don't have the complete picture," says Morningstar's John Rekenthaler. Among the fund families practicing such disappearing acts: Smith Barney, PIMCO, Dreyfus. Says Rekenthaler: "Fund companies tell investors to stay in for the long haul, and when they shut down funds after a few years, they aren't following their own advice."

Comment: Personally, I want poor-performing funds to close down and good funds to take them over. But what if the same manager ran both funds? What if the same analysts

Ragged right looks friendly

The ragged-right type in *Artes Liberales Today* gives the copy an informal, friendly feeling and lends to an overall open design. Note the good use of the second ink color for the standing head, pull quote and bullets, while keeping headlines in black.

▼▼▼ ASK THE PROFESSOR ▼▼▼

Wanted: A few really good neutrinos!

As part of our ongoing series, we passed along a question on astronomy to neutrino expert, Bob Morse. Morse is Senior Scientist in the Physics Department and Co-Principal Investigator on the Amanda Project. He recently completed his ninth trip to the South Pole.

Question:

I read recently in the *New York Times* that the UW Physics department is participating in research in Antarctica where they drill holes in the ice looking for neutrinos. Can you explain to me what a neutrino is, and why physicists are looking for them at the South Pole?
Roberta Bassman Krinsky, BA 1958; MA 1960.

Answer:

Amanda, which stands for "Antarctic Muon and Neutrino Detector Array," is an NSF-funded project involving scientists from UW–Madison and universities in California, Sweden, and Germany. The goal of the project is to detect high energy neutrinos to learn about astronomical events that cannot be seen by ordinary telescopes.

A neutrino really started as a bookkeeping particle. It's what we call the missing energy released from the decay of a neutron to a proton and electron.

High-energy neutrinos (with energies about a billion times that of visible light) could be the ultimate messenger particle, giving us information on cataclysmic processes occurring in the Milky Way and other galaxies. Because they travel in a straight line at the speed of light and rarely interact with other matter, they could carry reliable messages through clouds of intergalactic dust from the "hot spots" in the universe.

On rare occasions, neutrinos do interact with matter. The collision that occurs creates **muons, or daughter particles,** and causes the emission of Cerenkov light. This emitted light is like the bow wave from a boat going

Bob Morse demonstrates drill ... neutrino detectors that may l... type of astronomy.

Pole in 1993, and each year since then we've enlarged the grid.

The neutrinos we're interested in are the ones travelling up through the earth. We get a lot of junk coming down on us from space. By analyzing only the upward travelling neutri-

Neutrinos could carry reliable messages through clouds of intergalactic dust from the "hot spots" in the universe.

nos we are using the whole earth as a filter. Only high-energy neutrinos can travel through the earth without changing.

The selectors have logged millions of par...

through water. It can be m... to determine the origin of t...

We designed light sens... regularly shaped grid. To b... tors must be placed in a m... plentiful and transparent, i... scientific establishment to s... ment. The ice at the South...

At depths of 1 km, we d... which the bubbles had all b... out—ice of almost glass-lik... ing downward to depths of... and installed the first detect...

We are the world *continued from page 1*

Speaking at the November 12 dedication, Chancellor David Ward praised the Institute as exemplifying objectives outlined in his 1995 *Vision for the Future:* a "cross-college, collaborative and interdisciplinary activity that challenges outmoded forms of organization and makes the most of human, financial and physical resources."

The Institute is a new unit, a federation of programs both old and new. It brings the eight area studies programs—African Studies, East Asian Studies, European Studies, Latin American and Iberian Studies, Middle East Studies, Center for South Asia, Center for Southeast Asian Studies, and Center for Russia, East Europe and Central Asia, together with Global Cultures, Global Studies, and the International Relations major. Two affiliated programs, International Academic Programs (IAP, which now manages study abroad) and the World Affairs and Global Economy (WAGE) Initiative, are also part of the Institute.

"Having all of these different programs under one roof will encourage the sharing of ideas and resources," said Phillip Certain, Dean of Letters and Science.

Already under way at the International Institute are:

► A proposal to the Ford Foundation for major program support.

► A series of events on glo... change and regional bus... offered to the public thr... the Management Institut... Economics Professor D...

► Development, with the ... of new courses in intern...

► An International Festiva... gram of Asian films, spe... art exhibit, a student co... cross-regional workshop...

► Continuing programs o... tors, with planned interc... nars and social activities...

► Activities designed to bu... friends constituency, cap... coming event in Washin... prominent alumni about... grams and faculty.

As we enter a new cent... increasing cross-cultural ex... national initiatives, trade ag... peace negotiations, the Inte... has an important role to fill... programs will be tomorrow... teachers, international poli... leaders, and secretaries of s... prime ministers and preside... shaping the future political... of our planet. Now, more t... the world.

NAME *Artes Liberales Today*

PUBLISHER College of Letters and Science, Madison, Wisconsin

PURPOSE/AUDIENCE Service to alumni

PRODUCTION/PRINTING Two-color on offset

FORMAT 11" × 17"; eight pages

DESIGN Nancy B. Rinehart, University Publications

Artes Liberales
TODAY

College of Letters and Science
Volume 2, Number 2

SPRING 1997

THE NEWSLETTER OF THE COLLEGE OF LETTERS AND SCIENCE AT THE UNIVERSITY OF WISCONSIN–MADISON

Morning mist at the Taj Mahal. L&S students gain global perspective in international programs.

We are the World!

International Institute promotes collaboration

L&S grads are a far-flung population. Just in the past months we've heard from a chief librarian in Nigeria, a professor of South Asian History at the University of Oslo, a Peace Corps volunteer in Nepal, the director of an AIDS education program in South Africa, a partner in a recording business in London, the director of the Mindanao Development Center in the Philippines, and the director of a bilingual theater company in Paris. What they have in common is that they all got their start in one of the vast array of international programs on the UW campus.

Because of the growing number and importance of these programs, L&S and the Office of International Studies and Programs (OISP) this fall established the International Institute as a major step toward coordinating international offerings.

The 57 campus international offices listed in a recent directory range in size from small, individual faculty projects to degree programs such as the Center for Development, which trains international graduate students for government service in their home countries. Curricular offerings include a span of options from specific courses such as *Introduction to Southeast Asia: Vietnam to the Philippines,* to fully-developed undergraduate certificate and degree programs. There are 21 internationally-oriented majors in L&S, such as African Languages and Literature, Chinese, International Relations, and Scandinavian Studies; and a wide array of graduate research degrees and training programs.

The International Institute was conceived as a framework to foster interdisciplinary teaching, research and outreach in area and international studies.

Language programs undergird the area studies programs and many of the other international activities. The UW has the capability to teach more than 60 different languages— the largest offering of foreign language of any North American university. They include, of course, major languages such as French, Italian, and Spanish, but also less common offerings such as Thai and Kazakh. Faculty who teach in international programs hold dual appointments in such departments as Political Science, Sociology, Anthropology, Geography, History, and languages and literature departments like East Asian Languages and Literature.

As you might imagine, coordinating the burgeoning programs, seminars, visitors, and research proposals has been a challenge. And yet, coordination is essential if we are to make the most of our resources without unnecessary duplication.

The International Institute was conceived as a framework to foster interdisciplinary teaching, research and outreach in area and international studies. For the first time, leaders of the major area studies programs are housed in one location—the newly refurbished Ingraham Hall (see story p. 4). *continued on page 3*

CONTENTS

Embrace readers

This makeover of *Eastern European Outreach* by David Gustafson includes changing small, justified type to larger ragged-right type. Other improvements include shifting headlines from centered to flush left, a flexible two-column format instead of three columns and a scholar margin with graphics and captions.

EASTERN EUROPEAN OUTREACH

Volume 11, No. 3   April 1992

PERM FOR CHRIST

Over 900 miles east of Moscow, in the forests of

By Jan Wilbrink

A young girl waited at the door. A former medical student, her English was excellent. "There is no God!" she yelled. "If there is, why does He allow my life to be so miserable in this terrible place? Why doesn't He change this world?" I didn't know her circumstance, but it was obvious she was hurting.

"God hasn't made your life miserable," I answered. "Neither has He brought you into this situation. He wants to save you." She looked at me, turned around, and silently followed the guard back into the barracks. I felt so frustrated inside, I didn't know what to say. Finally I called after her, "Jesus loves you!" She turned around and looked me in the eyes, tears streaming down her cheeks. That was the last time I saw her.

for New Testaments and follow arvest is great but the laborers

The Perm City Crusade

Our citywide crusade began on a Tuesday night in a downtown theater seating 600 people. Two Ukrainian Christians moved to Perm last year to start a church and had baptized 81 people already before our meetings. Together with members of the Mission DVIM, (acronym for Good News & Mercy) they printed posters, ran ads in newspapers and television, and organized follow up for new believers.

Cities like Perm are usually overlooked in the work of western mission agencies because they are so remote. However, we have concentrated on those cities where the Gospel hasn't been preached. Each evening the theater was full and the morning Bible study for new Christians was always packed.

Continued on page 2

EASTERN EUROPEAN

Outreach

VOLUME 12, NUMBER 6   SEPTEMBER 1993

Hope for Romania

EEO missionary delivers good news
By Dorel Ursachi

"He who is gracious to a poor man lends to the Lord, and He will repay him for his good deed."
Proverbs 19:17

This month I was given the opportunity to serve God in a special way. During a Sunday evening service at church, a Christian Gypsy lady began to feel sick. My wife signalled me to come help. We drove her home and I carried her up three flights of stairs. Her condition became worse and we called an ambulance.

The next day I visited Rita in the hospital. She was a little better, and besides some food I left a gospel booklet. That night she got out of bed, walked to a nursing station, and called asking if I could bring more booklets the next day. "And by the way," she said, "do you have any Bibles?"

Mother's Day Surprise
On Mother's Day I visited Rita again. I filled my suitcase with New Testaments, prayed that God would touch the hearts of the ladies in Rita's room, and left for the hospital. When I reached Rita, I greeted the ladies in her room, opened the suitcase and said: "Dear ladies, I know you celebrate Mother's Day today. I am sorry I do not have any flowers. Instead I am bringing you a special

present. I have brought a New Testament for each of you." While they watched in astonishment, I walked around the room and gave each one their own New Testament.

Entire Hospital Receives Gospel
What happened in that room on Mother's Day spread like a spark in dry grass over the whole hospital. Rita began phoning me asking for more and more Bibles and book-

"And by the way," she said, "do you have any Bibles?"

lets. Three times I returned bringing the precious gift of God's Word. I finally met with the director and asked if I could provide Bibles for all of the patients in the entire hospital. He was very kind and even provided a nurse to guide me through the various wards. Together with Rita and the nurse we distributed 250 New Testaments and many more booklets to every patient and hospital staff worker! In the meantime, Rita has become well known and respected by the doctors and nurses throughout the hospital. In normal circumstances in our country, gypsies are shown very little respect. They have a terrible reputation and are hated by a majority of Romanians. This has encouraged me to give as much love and attention to all people, irrespective of race or color, for God can use anyone as an instrument of His blessings.

Children receive a bible as part of EEO activities throughout Romania.

Dorel Ursachi is a regional coordinator for the Child Sponsorship Program. Dorel lives in the Moldavian region of Romania, in the city of Iasi near the Russian border. This is his first article to appear in *Outreach.*

NAME *Eastern European Outreach*

PUBLISHER Eastern European Outreach International, Sun City, California

PURPOSE/AUDIENCE Service and marketing to donors

PRODUCTION/PRINTING Two-color on white 60# offset

FORMAT 8½" x 11"; four pages

DESIGN David Gustafson, Alta Loma, California

Orchestrating type

Effective design of each typographical element—headlines, decks, drop caps, text, captions and standing heads—combines with a refined format to compose a symphony on the page.

NAME *Strategies*

PUBLISHER Manulife Financial, Buffalo, New York

PURPOSE/AUDIENCE Service and marketing to customers

PRODUCTION/PRINTING Four-color process on 60# matte

FORMAT 8½" × 11"; four pages

DESIGN Ariad Custom Publishing

Strategies

Ideas and information from Manulife Financial

Winter 1996
Volume 3, Issue 3

RETIREMENT PLANNING STRATEGIES

Getting the most from your retirement planning team

Even if your anticipated retirement is 10 or 15 years away, planning now can make a substantial difference to your quality of life when you retire.

If you expect to retire sooner, establishing or updating your retirement plan is even more urgent. A solid plan is also

all your advisors. With this team approach, you and your attorney, accountant, life insurance agent, financial advisor, and be able to create and t can address all your

of the key issues to eam:
sociated Press recently that found that 67% cans worry that their provide an acceptable income.
ow much income you your savings and they liquid enough to urce of cash? To fund you'll probably need investments structh adequate, long-term

sidered the impact of a modest inflation rate

OVER 65
Retired 51% / Still working 49%
1950

OVER 65
Retired 84% / Still working 16%
1990

Retirement: back to the future?

Mid-century, a majority of Americans over 65 worked because they had to. Times changed, but the Census Department now estimates that one million "boomers" will live beyond age 100. While that's good news, it may mean re-evaluating your retirement plan.

of 2.5%, your cost of living will double in 29 years!

Life expectancy. Many people underestimate how long they will live. If you

To Page 2

TAX-PLANNING STRATEGIES

Protect your family and add to your retirement income

Variable Universal Life (VUL) policies combine the protection of life insurance with a variety of investment options and the

opportunity to defer tax on any of the policy's earnings.

Are they right for you? Here's what you need to know.

VUL policy premiums are flexible, allowing you to vary the amount you pay. The policy will remain in force as long as the cash value is sufficient to meet the costs of the insurance protection and the policy expenses.

You can choose from a level or varying death benefit to provide estate planning flexibility and meet changing needs. The death benefit and cash value

reflect the performance of
stment accounts.
your beneficiaries can
me-tax-free death benefit
l amount of the policy's
ess any loans or with-

ner, you can choose from quity- and bond-based unts that offer long-term th potential.

a VUL policy may also y tax-saving benefits.
's investment earnings grow on a tax-deferred 70½.
g from one investment r incurs no capital gains

tax liability for the policy owner.

• Withdrawals are usually income tax free until the value of the withdrawals exceeds the total value of premiums paid. Additionally, policy loans usually do not generate income tax liability if the policy remains in force and is not transferred to another owner.

If the policy is a modified endowment contract, loans or withdrawals may be subject to income tax when they are made. A penalty tax may also apply if the loan or withdrawal is taken before age 59½.

• At death, proceeds are generally received income tax free and may pass directly to the contract's named beneficiary without going through probate.

Is VUL right for you?

Of course, like any insurance policy, VUL is purchased primarily to provide a death benefit. To determine if VUL's other benefits make it the right option for you, consider the following:

• A VUL policy is most effective with a time horizon of 10 years or more.

• Although VUL's flexibility offers more growth potential, it can also mean more downside risk.

• Loans and withdrawals from the policy may reduce its death benefit and cash surrender value. ●

Strategies • Winter 1996   3

Your advisors can show you how to use a VUL policy to protect your family, lifestyle, and long-term goals.

tection ends when employment ends. Consider setting up individual plans now, even if you don't expect to retire for several years. Generally, the younger you are when you purchase life insurance, the lower the premiums. Remember that regular reviews can ensure that your protection matches your needs.

You should also take this opportunity to find out about long-term-care insurance and to establish a health care proxy or living will. These documents outline the treatments you would deem acceptable in the event of life-threatening injury or illness. Be sure that copies of the documents are included with your medical records and that your family and care-givers are aware of your wishes.

What to do next

This issue of *Strategies* provides key points to discuss with your advisory team. Together, you can continue to build a solid foundation for your future and for the future well-being of your

WELLNESS & LEISURE

Consider mentoring *after* retiring

During the working years, most people look forward eagerly to retirement. But many recent retirees are surprised to find that they

miss the responsibilities of the workplace, and the daily interaction with co-workers or clients.

Increasingly, many of today's retirees are channeling their time and energy into the community. Across the country, mentoring programs, adjunct professorships, and volunteer organizations are

reaping the benefits of their wisdom and their desire to "give something back."

Feel good, help others

Mentoring programs cover a variety of objectives, but the most common ones tend to focus on education, career counseling, and personal development.

One of the first, and still best known of these organizations is Big Brothers/ Big Sisters. Its "buddy system" has become the standard for many other mentoring organizations, such as those that provide extra guidance to physically or developmentally challenged adults, young offenders, and academically gifted or challenged students.

Hospitals are adapting this approach by teaming survivors of cancer with patients who have been recently diagnosed.

Back to school

Career mentoring is another area which seems particularly well-suited to retirees. These programs can be as informal as speaking to kids in grade school, or more personal one-on-one guidance sessions with teens and recent graduates.

Entrepreneurs can participate in business mentoring programs that provide

support and direction to those just getting started, and ultimately benefit the whole community.

At the college and university level, adjunct professorships give experienced professionals the opportunity to share their knowledge with students. In some cases, these positions are filled by retired teachers or professors. Other times, they are staffed by former engineers, social workers, executives or designers—anyone with years of hands-on experience in the area of study.

Getting involved

Whatever your area of interest or expertise, chances are there's an organization that would welcome your participation.

For information on mentoring programs, the U.S. Department of Education has published a pamphlet called the *Consumer Guidebook to Mentoring*, by Gregory Dennis. To obtain a copy, send your name and address to: Consumer Guides, OERI, U.S. Dept. of Education, Room 610, 555 New Jersey Ave., NW, Washington, D.C., 20208. Or visit their site on the World Wide Web at: http://www.ed.gov/pubs/OR/ConsumerGuides/mentor.html.

To find out about programs and groups in your area, contact local schools, libraries, hospitals, religious institutions, community centers, or municipal offices. If you are interested in college-level professorships, call your alma mater or state university. ●

Manulife Financial

4   *Strategies* • Winter 1996

NAME *Piedmonitor*

PUBLISHER Piedmont Hospital, Atlanta, Georgia

PURPOSE/AUDIENCE Service to employees

PRODUCTION/PRINTING Two-color on offset

FORMAT 11" × 17"; six pages

DESIGN John Kems, Jr., Piedmont Hospital

Piedmonitor

A Publication for the Employees of Piedmont Hospital

Volume Five • • • May/June 1993 • • • Number Three

An Invitation to the White House

Editor's Note: May 5 is a day Connie Whittington, RN, ONC, won't soon forget. As incoming president of the National Association of Orthopaedic Nurses, Connie was invited to the White House as one of 100 nursing leaders for a briefing on President Clinton's proposed healthcare plan. The invitation was extended in an effort to inform nursing leaders on the issues. Here is her report:

I never expected to receive an invitation to the White House! A perfectly normal day at work was turned upside down when the NAON office called to extend the invitation. Excited is the only word to describe my feelings!

It was difficult to continue working that day as the news of my pending trip moved through the Hospital and congratulations and words of encouragement poured in.

In Washington, our group of nurses arrived at the Old Executive Office Building and were cleared to enter. Eddie Bernice Johnson, a nurse and freshman Represen-

tative from Texas, welcomed us and introduced Ira Magaziner, President Clinton's Senior Policy Advisor, who presented an overview of the 13-point plan. When asked why nurses were hearing the package first, Mr. Magaziner replied that the President wanted his plan presented to us in a non-biased fashion without the opinions of the press and other factions.

We adjourned to the Rose Garden where President Clinton and Donna Shalala, Secretary of Health and Human Services, welcomed us and introduced Virginia Trotter-Betts, President of the American Nurses Association, who extended thanks to the President from nurses around the country for his emphasis on healthcare reform. President Clinton emphasized the importance of the plan to U.S. citizens and to the economy and voiced concerns over the lack of access to healthcare and the inequity of insurance coverage.

When I returned to my hotel, flowers had arrived from my nursing colleagues at Piedmont with a note of congratulations. This expression of

support was so important and appreciated, because we can make a difference nationally only after we have made a difference locally — in our workplace, in our city, and in our state government. You may not need to visit the White House for your ideas to be considered. Nurses, the largest group of healthcare professionals in America at 1.8 million, can have tremendous impact on the healthcare reform process. Study the proposals for healthcare reform when they appear in the media and determine your stand. Then make your legislators aware of your thoughts, questions and ideas. You can impact national issues individually and through your professional organizations, your voice in Washington.

Connie Whittington, RN, ONC

Connie Whittington, RN, ONC

Record Number Receive Service Awards During National Hospital Week

All 336 Piedmont employees who observed an employment anniversary this year were honored with service awards, a delicious brunch, a carnation, and much recognition for their dedication. The large number of recipients required two brunch events due to space limitations in the Cafeteria. The celebration took place during National Hospital Week, May 9 through 15, as the theme "Partners for a Healthy America" took on special meaning. In addition, all employees and volunteers were treated to free dessert on May 11 in the Piedmont Grille or Cafeteria. Enjoy these photo highlights of National Hospital Week!

For a complete list of service award honorees and retirees, please see inside.

25 years: Guster Lupoe, Rehabilitation Services, with Wright Alcorn, Vice President, Patient Services II

20 years, l-r: Hattie Neal, Housekeeping; Tom Cook, Radiology; Jimmie Pruitt, Laboratory; Maria Bobo, OR; Tengier PowPong, OR; Shirley Thomas, Piedmont Grille; Gaby Aguirre, Pharmacy; Maggie Parker, McDonnell Surgical Center; Ola Schley, Housekeeping; Phil Vizba, OR

Not Pictured

20 years: Mary Anderson, Selida Boyd, Thelma Dailey, Connie Duran, Francine Dyer, Arnold Holder, Pam Medland, Joan Pilger, Brucie Roberts, Micheline Rothman, and Virginia Smallwood.

25 years: Olga Luttrell and Alline Wood.

25 years: Beatrice Dubose, Nutrition and Food Service, with Director, Dan Salas

20 years: l-r: Jeanne Hutto, Vascular Lab; Dianne Spigner, 2 Center

30 years: Pat Nation, RN, (center) NICU with Shirley Thomas, RN, Vice President, Nursing Service and Ann Blackwelder, RN, Unit Director, Nursery / Labor and Delivery

Joshua Ludecke, age 8, son of David Ludecke, accounting clerk, Business Office: "My Dad's David Ludecke. He counts all the money four the hospital. My dad types on the computer and the calculator. He also helps sends people on trips."

...rah Leamon, RN, ...on: "I am lucky ...Piedmont Hospital ...lly works as a ...O.R., helps ...supplies, counts ...ble for medications ...So as you see mom ...y reason she's ...rk in the

Ja'Qonna Manley, age 12, daughter of Jackie Manley, lead EKG tech, EKG Department: "My mother dedicated herself to the community, by helping people in a hospital which is known as piedmont. My mother...she gave it all her best. She even made success. By being very sharp and smart and helping people with their heart. She makes the patients laugh not cry and gives them a warming welcome before saying goodbye. She meets new people every day and makes friends each and every way. So if you think your heart is breaking, Go to Piedmont's EKG technicians and they'll stop the acting."

...r Martin, age 6, son of Jenny ...cial worker, Social Work ...t: "My mommy is a social ...r helps people get wheelchairs ...s. She helps people if they need ...learning hospitals — like if ...y has to learn to swallow again. ...s people get a nurse if ...ed one. She gets a dirt ...d takes it to her office ...inks it."

Rebecca Sigman, age 4, daughter of Marilyn Sigman, neurodiagnostic technologist, Neurophysiology Department: "My mommy works at Piedmont Hospital. She does tests on little babies to check their hearing. She works on patients in case their sick and there's something wrong. She does EG tests and tests spines in surgery. I want to be a mommy when I grow up!"

Jesse Davis, age 6, son of Matilda Davis, phlebotomist, Clinical Laboratory: "My mom works in the lab and draw peoples blood. She works very hard to make us lots of money. My mom is Matilda Davis. My name is Jesse Davis. I'm six years old."

Crissie Montanare, age 10, daughter of Nina Montanaro, Director, Public Affairs: "I think my mom just writes letters about abbreviations such as ICU, ER, CCU, NICU, OB, PHO, DRG, PPO, HMO, & RTU. I think that's just baby talk. But I like it because I can help with the Peachtree Road Race. But I know she works hard all day!"

Captions stick by subjects

Place captions as close as possible to the image they describe, especially when using several captions per page. When tilting photos, avoid placing the caption askew: Run captions straight on the page, as is done here in *Piedmonitor*.

Piedmonitor

A Publication of the Piedmont Hospital Public Affairs Department
1968 Peachtree Road, N.W., Atlanta, Georgia 30309 • Phone (404) 605-3372

Address correction requested

Non-Profit Org.
U.S. Postage
PAID
Atlanta, GA
Permit No. 2529

PIEDMONT HOSPITAL

The College installed 200 workstations and servers in fall 1990. Over the next two years, 550 more workstations will arrive. Dr. William Willis, director of Computer Operations, helps with the first arrivals.

From her home desk area designed by her husband to meet her working needs, Kathy Werdahl, Transportation Planning Technician 2, is one of seven employees taking part in the Washington State Energy Office's Puget Sound Telecommuting Demonstration Project. While telecommuting, Kathy is able to work out of her home three days a week and avoid the morning and evening commute.

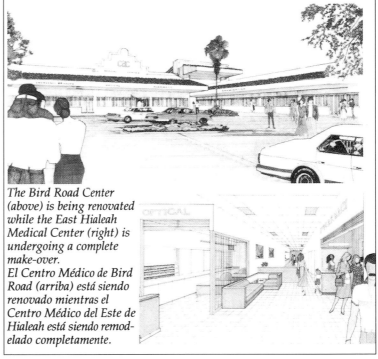

The Bird Road Center (above) is being renovated while the East Hialeah Medical Center (right) is undergoing a complete make-over.
El Centro Médico de Bird Road (arriba) está siendo renovado mientras el Centro Médico del Este de Hialeah está siendo remodelado completamente.

Cynthia Mackey, left, of ISD and Linda Lindley of CUNA & Affiliates were recently named the Credit Union Center's first "Community Service Volunteers of the Year." Judges recognized Mackey for her work at Briarpatch, a United Way family counseling agency. Lindley is a leader of the Waunakee Parent Support Network, an organization providing a forum for adults to work together to share parenting skills. The award was established this year to recognize employees who have made a significant volunteer contribution to their community.

Make every caption count

Readers read captions first, often before reading stories or even headlines. Go beyond merely identifying people or places, and use captions to draw readers into the story. Count on captions to convey vital information. Even readers who don't read the article will get your message.

"Allen James has the ingenuity to come up with ways to make something work to keep the plant running reliably."

- Gregg Coffin

Getting organized is a process, not an end result. The key lies in setting up a simple program for maintenance.

Be on the lookout for outstanding employee efforts!

"

A first class stamp on a reply envelope says you really want a response.

"

Right now, it costs more to make paper from kenaf than from cheap, heavily subsidized wood pulp. This is essentially a problem of start-up and of scale.

It felt like we were in an Indiana Jones movie sometimes. We didn't know what to expect next and had to totally rely on God.

"It was overhearing unsolicited comments from attendees talking to each other that, 'This was the best symposium yet...' "

"The release must reach the right editor. It must do so in a manner and format that makes it easy to use. This is the goal of PR Newswire's daily feature service and of our special feature packages."

Fred Ferguson
Feature News Service editor

"My gratitude goes to Devorah Gallagher. Her initiative, persistence and constant encouragement supported me through some very frustrating and tough times."

"Ms. Vaughn exemplified superior consumer relations and communication skills that allowed her to take efficient action to address and resolve my credit problems. Her ability to calm me down, in the midst of my frustration, assure me the problem would be addressed reaffirmed confidence that TRW is sensitive to customer complaint and will take actions to immediately correct the problem. This was my first time dealing with TRW and it was a positive experience."

"KPFCU could not have been as successful without your (Maria Parker) ongoing support. You've done a terrific job!"

Any unauthorized vehicle left in the lot at the end of the business day should be towed to avoid offering a place to hide a bomb.

Making pull quotes pull

The "pull" in pull quotes has two meanings: (1) You pull the quote out of the story and (2) The quote pulls readers into the story. Effective pull quotes capture the essence of the story in the words of one of its main speakers. Massive, ornate or colored quotation marks signal that the item is a quote, not a headline or an excerpt. Design elements such as rules, reverses, boxes, screen tints or large type separate the quote from the text of the story.

Fan Mail

"Wow! If more companies had employees like Ms. Miscik, the country would be a much happier place. Many thanks from Feduke Inc. for her friendly, efficient, methodic knowledgeable help."

"Priscilla (Harrison), your promptness, willingness to help, professional attitude and follow-up makes working with you a great pleasure."

Safety on the beach

four times every day. When the tide

The ocean's power
safety. To avoid a tr
self or someone you
four simple guidelin

Stay off the logs. Do
stump to watch
around your fe
wave can roll
heartbeat.

Watch the waves. T
tent, but it rout
much larger th
wave can run
feet almost ins

In addition to dange
waves often c
breakers can t
as if it were a

Rising and falling tic
dangers to do
playing too clo
Always learn tide c
near the ocea

Do not turn your ba
a tsunami or o
event, you will
Leave the bea
evacuation sig
there is time, y
instructions ov
ers located thr

Sneaker waves. The
ocean change

FAX News Facts

Advance information for messengers and their methods

Use simple two column design for FAX newsletters

When preparing your newsletter for FAX

Be sure that the typography can survive the transmission process. Clear figures are important. 1234567890 Make certain that the type size is large enough to read if it becomes distorted. This is a 10 point Times serif type. San serif better than serif.

Be sure that the typography can survive the transmission process. Clear figures are important. 1234567890 Make certain that the type size is large enough to read if it becomes distorted. This is a 12 point Times serif type. Sans serif better than serif.

Be sure that the typography can survive the transmission process. Clear figures are important. 1234567890 Make certain that the type size is large enough to read if it becomes distorted. This is a 10 point Helvetic sans serif type.

Be sure that the typography can survive the transmission process. Clear figures are important. 1234567890 Make certain that the type size is large enough to read if it becomes distorted. This is a 12 point Helvetica sans serif type.

May, transmits 4 pages
• Save on phone bills – pg 2
• Wrong numbers – pg 3
• FAX forwarding – pg 4

Avoid photos and large solids.

This body copy set 11 pt on 13 for leading. Nehalem Bay State Park. The park has three camping sites in Loop A where tables, fire pits and ground cover facilitate access. The restroom and showers in Loop A meet access standards.

The dock at the boat ramp is accessible. The 1.5-mile bike pathwithin the park is paved. In addition to traversing the dunes,the path follows the west side of the bay for several hundred feet.

Oswald West State Park. The trail from the east parking lot to the picnic area offers one of Oregon's premier encounters with an old growth forest. The picnic area closely overlooks the beach.

Park near the restrooms and follow the trail that leads under Highway 101. Most of the trail is paved. The rest is relatively smooth, free from roots, and has a gentle grade. The steepest grade is the first hundred feet passing below the highway bridge. Daily in Seaside, morning, noon and evenings. Call 738-8310 for times and locations.

Antiques and collectibles. The area offers nine shops full of treasures. See also gifts. Wheeler and Antiques and Special Occasions.

Fish hatchery on Highway 53.Accessible fishing on the North Fork Nehalem River.Trails and ramps built in cooperation with Northwest steelheaders.

Following body copy set 12 on 13

This body copy is 12 pt on 13. Nehalem Bay Center offers step aerobic workouts as well as various machines for aerobic exercise. The pool program includes aqua aerobics. Air strip:Nehalem Bay State Park has a 2,400—foot air strip next to six fly—in campsites (map G15-16). No hookups. Fee for camping, but not for landing. Nearest phone at park registration booth. Parking lot and the picnic area are not designed for accessibility. The parking lot to the picnic area offers one of Oregon's premier encounters with an old growth forest. The picnic area itself closely overlooks the beach.

Type for speedy faxes

When designing a newsletter for faxing, follow these guidelines to ensure readability:

• choose sans serif type with big x-heights: Helvetica, Corona, Lucida or Courier
• set body copy in 11- or 12-point type
• emphasize with underlines, not boldface or italics
• add leading

• avoid photos
• bulk up rules to at least 2 point
• avoid large solids, tints or reverses that take a long time to transmit

Since each page of a faxed newsletter comes separately, use big, bold folios and make sure to repeat the newsletter name on each page.

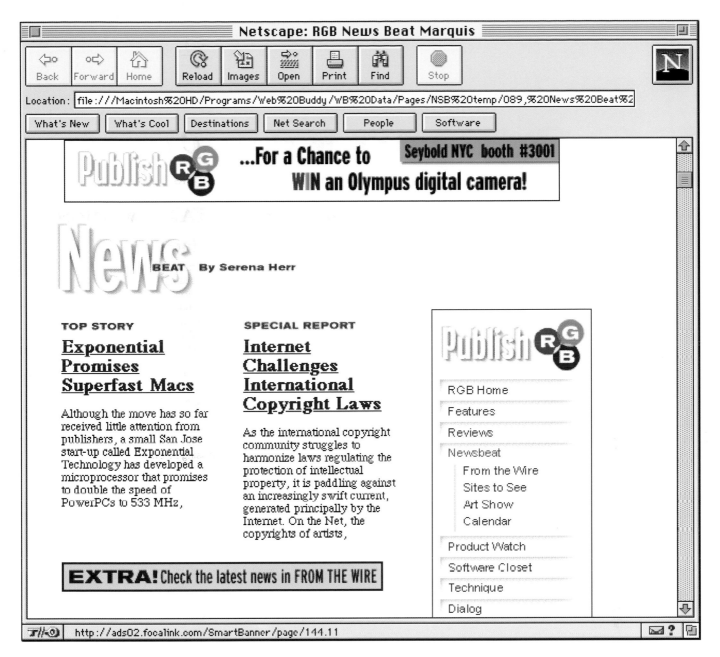

Type as text or graphic?

Once your newsletter hits the Web or goes to e-mail, your control over typeface, size and style is nonexistent. Users can set a Web browser to display type in whatever form a user chooses—with a screened background, Times or Courier, big or small. When the look of a headline or section of type is critical, Web designers set the type up as a graphic. The "News Beat" standing head, byline and kickers of *Publish* magazine's RGB website are set up as graphics. The headlines and text are controlled by the browser (in this case, Netscape). Because type that's set up as a graphic loads more slowly than type as text, consider this option carefully and use it appropriately.

NAME www.publish.com

PUBLISHER *Publish*, San Francisco, California

PURPOSE/AUDIENCE Service and marketing to customers

PRODUCTION/PRINTING Web

FORMAT Web

DESIGN Publish RGB Design Team

chapter four

ESSENTIALS

Successful newsletter designers use four visual elements to make their publications effective and distinctive: mailing panels, mastheads, calendars and contents boxes. In this chapter you'll find both creative and functional presentations of these elements.

Mailing panel

Make your mailing panel do double duty as space for messages as well as the address. Every mailing panel needs to include: your company or organization name and logo; your return address; and how to reach you (phone, fax and/or e-mail). Your mailing panel can also include your masthead or contents box, a location map, a teaser or a special notice.

Masthead

Every issue of your newsletter needs to tell the following business information in its masthead: name and address of your sponsoring organization; your name as editor; and how readers can reach you. Your masthead can also tell frequency of publication and subscription costs (if any), and give names of key officers and contributors. If your newsletter is copyrighted, the notice belongs in your masthead.

Calendar

Good calendar design begins with clear knowledge of what readers want to know. Calendars help readers by anticipating their questions and making the answers instantly available.

LOCATION. If you're announcing events at many stores, or a series of public hearings, readers only want to know about locations they find convenient. Put places first or in boldface type, and then tell dates and details.

ACTIVITY. If you're listing a variety of events, group them into categories that make sense to your readers. Don't make people who care only about one kind of event struggle through the entire list.

DATE. If you're presenting a variety of dates for the same event, such as a stage play, let your design highlight dates instead of the program or the performers. Repeating the name of the event for each performance isn't necessary.

Contents box

Newsletters that travel slowly to the recycle bin give readers information at a glance. Instant information starts with a list of articles in this issue. Highlight this list with bullets or boldface words, and put it on the mailing panel or page 1.

Autumn Calendar of

Cleveland Amory
the well-known critic, humorist, and bestselling author of **The Cat** Who Came for Christmas, has another clever book this season. It continues the true adventures of his feline friend, the incomparable Polar Bear. The chapter titles tell all: *Cat Power, You Ought to Be In Pictures, Romance a la Cat Blanche, First Dog, On the Cusp* and so on. We look forward to hosting America's favorite curmudgeon and his cat-loving fans for what could turn out to be a *purr*-fect afternoon.

Ivan Doig
grew up right here in the Rocky Mountains, where he worked as a ranch hand and a newspaperman. His first two novels, **Dancing at the Rascal Fair** and **English Creek**, began a trilogy about the McCaskill family, who came from Scotland to settle in the American West. **Ride With Me, Mariah Montana** completes that trilogy, bringing the story into the present, as it follows Jick McCaskill and his daughter Mariah back and forth across Montana in a Winnebago.

Jon Hassler
has been for years a solid storyteller, collecting rave reviews and inspiring the affection of readers. His novels, which include **Staggerford** and **The Love Hunter**, have reaped gratifying results, and now he has gone from solid to solid gold. Set in the Minnesota that he has made his own, his new novel, **North of Hope**, is an epic journey through the second half of this century — and the soul of one man. Frank Healey can love God or Libby Girard, but not both. He chooses the priesthood, only to have fate alter his plans. When he meets Libby twenty years later, her life is fraught with problems, but his own — and his search for its meaning — just begins.

Jill McCorkle
is a "born novelist," claims the *New York Times*. "She writes with an energy that makes her characters come to life," says *Newsday*. Jill McCorkle is a southern writer in the grand tradition. In her new novel, **Ferris Beach**, she lets loose a soaring imagination that would do her literary predecessors proud. The conflict is between manners and freedom of expression, between those who play by the rules and those who bend and twist them. Mo Rhodes is one of the defiant ones. She lives life at its white heat. She turns her yard into a Japanese rock garden; she's still in mourning for Buddy Holly. Her daughter's friend, Katie, wants to be just like her — until the day, in the dead of summer, when Mo ventures too far over the line.

Jean Auel
is one of the world's esteemed writers, having begun her career with the landmark novel, **Clan of the Cave Bear**. The books that followed in the *Earth's Children* series were **The Valley of Horses** and **The Mammoth Hunters**. Now, **The Plains of Passage**, her fourth book, continues Ayla's story as she and Jondalar set out on horseback across the windswept grasslands of Ice Age Europe in search of a place to call home. In the course of their odyssey, they encounter vast beauty, unknown dangers, friends, enemies and enlightenment.

Anne Rice
is the author of the extraordinary *Vampire Chronicles*. She now brings us **The Witching Hour**, a mesmerizing new novel of the occult played out over four centuries. It begins with a disaster at sea. The rescuer is a beautiful neurosurgeon who is aware of her strange and special powers but unaware that she is descended from a great dynasty of witches. The drowned man whom she brings back to life acquires in his brief interval of death a sensory power that both mystifies and frightens him. As the two set out to unlock the mysteries of their lives, the story moves backward and forward in time, through dramas of seduction and death.

Michael Hague
is an old friend and always a welcome guest at the Tattered Cover. He is one of today's most prolific and talented children's book illustrators, having worked his magic on classics such as **Aesop's Fables, Wind in the Willows, A Child's Book of Prayers**, and many others. This season, he delights us with a special autographing of his two holiday books, **Jingle Bells** and **We Wish You a Merry Christmas**.

Mickey Hart
is best known as the virtuoso percussionist for the Grateful Dead, one of the world's most enduring rock bands, but he is also a historian in his own right, serving on the board of directors of the Smithsonian Institution's Folkways Records. In this compelling new book, **Drumming at the Edge of Magic**, he documents ancient rhythmic traditions in an attempt to preserve the history of his instrument and the music that "contains the myths and dreams of all the people who came before." Through conversations with Joseph Campbell and encounters with drum masters from around the world, he paints a panoramic picture of a vibrant living tradition.

Oliver Sachs
is a professor of clinical neurology at Albert Einstein College of Medicine and the author of many fascinating books, including **The Man Who Mistook His Wife for a Hat** and **Awakenings**. His latest, **Seeing Voices: A Journey Into the World of the Deaf**, discusses the beautiful visual-gestural language of the deaf and raises important issues concerning a ne...

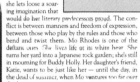

Calendar entries:

Friday, November 2, 4:30 p.m.
Cleveland Amory

Friday, November 2, 7:30 p.m.
*Ivan Doig**

Saturday, November 3, 2:00 p.m.
Michael Hague

Monday, November 5, 7:30 p.m.
*Oliver Sachs**

Wednesday, November 7, 7:30 p.m.
*Jill McCorkle**

Tuesday, November 13, 7:30 p.m.
Anne Rice

Tuesday, November 20, 7:30 p.m.
*Jon Hassler**

Wednesday, November 28, 7:00 p.m.
Jean Auel

Saturday, December 1, 6:00 p.m.
*Mickey Hart**

*reading and autographing

Real-world selling strategies and techniques from great salespeople

The Economics Press SalesMasterMind is published monthly by the Economics Press, Inc., 12 Daniel Road, Fairfield, NJ 07004-2565 USA. Editorial offices: Phone 201-227-1224. Fax: 201-227-3558. E-mail: edit@epinc.com

Copyright © 1996, The Economics Press, Inc. All rights reserved in all countries. Reproduction is prohibited without prior written permission.

For subscription information, call 1-800-526-2554 in the U.S. and Canada, 01727 844255 in the U.K., or (+1 201) 227-1224 worldwide. U.S. Fax (+1 201) 227-9742. E-mail: order@epinc.com

Editor: Jeffrey Gitomer, President of Business Marketing Services based in Charlotte, North Carolina, gives seminars, runs annual meetings, and conducts training programs on selling and customer service. His book *The Sales Bible* is available in bookstores. He can be reached at 704-333-1112.

"As a salesperson, you need answers to succeed. Fast answers. The value of those answers will drive your relationships with your customers into the 21st century—and make sales. Lots of sales. This newsletter is a mastermind of America's finest sales experts. They have the answers you need to differentiate yourself from the others . . . by creating and giving value—that leads to sales."

THE MASTHEAD

this is called

Newsletter Nameplate is published whenever we feel like it. Subscriptions are free and may be obtained with a simple phone call, brief note or fax message.

Printing: 80 lb. Beckett Cambric, text, marble
Black ink and Ruddle Rust inks (PMS 506).
Were we publishing this newsletter for a client, we would have charged $1,200 for the writing, artwork and photography (four pages at $300 per page). The printing was extra.

PRINTING: Oakmead Printing 408 739-4103

FILM WORK: ▶Digital Impressions

PARK LUCERNE EXECUTIVE CENTER ▪ 790 LUCERNE DRIVE ▪ SUITE 56
SUNNYVALE, CA 94086 ▪ TELEPHONE 408-737-8050 ▪ FAX 408-737-8014

Vital mastheads

Each issue of your newsletter needs a masthead that tells the name and address of the sponsoring organization, the editor's name and how readers can reach you. If applicable, list the names of graphic designers, photographers and other professionals who have contributed to the newsletter. Produce your masthead with the same content and in the same location from one issue to the next.

Depending on the goals of the newsletter, the masthead can also tell frequency of publication and subscription costs (if any), and give names of key officers and contributors. Potential contributors often look in your masthead to find out if you solicit articles and photographs.

If your newsletter is copyrighted, this notice also belongs in your masthead. You can include an International Standard Serial Number (ISSN). You should have an ISSN if you want librarians to catalog your publication. Newsletters mailed second class must display either an ISSN or a post office identification number in their nameplate, masthead or return address. The National Serials Data Program of the Library of Congress (Washington, DC 20540) assigns ISSNs at no fee.

About *Read Me*

Editor/Publisher: Cheryl Lockett Zubak
President, Work Write™
128 South Eastview Avenue
Feasterville, PA 19053
Phone: (215) 357-3453
Fax: (215) 357-0695
74654.1532@compuserve.com

ISSN: 1077-8845

Read Me is the quarterly newsletter of Work Write™, a corporate and technical communications consulting organization located in Bucks County, Pennsylvania. Work Write™ specializes in online and print user's guides, training materials, technical reports, and newsletters.

Read Me is offered free of charge to Work Write™ customers and contacts. Other interested persons may receive a yearly subscription (4 issues) by sending a check or money order for $29 made payable to Cheryl Lockett Zubak, Work Write™, 128 South Eastview Avenue, Feasterville, PA 19053.

© 1995 Cheryl Lockett Zubak. All rights reserved. You may reprint any article from *Read Me* provided you send a copy to the editor and include the following credits on the reprint: "This article was reprinted with permission from *Read Me*, a newsletter published by Cheryl Lockett Zubak. Cheryl is an independent consultant specializing in corporate and technical communication. You can reach her at (215) 357-3453." *STC editors may add: "Cheryl is a senior member of the Philadelphia Metro chapter."*

Colophon. *Nameplate, headlines:* Presidents type art (Image Glub Graphics); *Reverse Headings:* Centaur; *Body headings:* Stone Sans; *Body text:* Stone Serif.

Toolbox. Aldus PageMaker 5.0 on a 486/33 with 8MB of RAM and a 1.2GB hard drive. Proofs are output to a QMS 860 at 600 dpi; final copy is output to a Xerox DocuTech printing system (also at 600 dpi).

Print Shop: Graphic Reproductions, 1957 Pioneer Road, Building F, Huntingdon Valley, PA 19006. (215) 957-6120. Speak with Kim Ayling.

MUTUAL FUND DIGEST

47 Ridge Road, Glen Rock, NJ 07452
(201) 444-3583 • Fax (201) 444-6836

Regular subscriptions: $59 a year, $5 an issue

Editor: *Warren Boroson*
Senior editors: *Peter C. Hearne, Mark Howat*
First mate: *Rebecca Boroson*
Graphic artist: *Jerry Szubin*
Proofreader: *Matthew H. Boroson*
Interns: *Ira Rinn, Mitchell Rinn*

WARREN BOROSON won the 1996 award for excellence in financial writing, given by the Investment Company Institute and American University. Former staff writer for Money Magazine and Sylvia Porter's Personal Finance Magazine. Author of two best-selling books on mutual funds: *Keys to Investing in Mutual Funds* (third edition) and *The Ultimate Mutual Fund Guide* (second edition).

News & Views

is Published Bimonthly by the
Department of Patient Care Services

Robert H. Welton, RN, MSN
Editor

Direct inquiries and correspondence
to the Editor by phone
Office - 410-328-6257
Fax - 410-328-8258

or mail to

Office of Professional Development
Room S10B02
University of Maryland
Medical System
22 South Greene Street
Baltimore, MD 21201

*News for the next issue due
December 27, 1996*

Royal Trust *MoneyGuide* is published by:
Royal Trust Corporation of Canada, P.O. Box 7500, Station A, Toronto, Ontario M5W 1P9

The strategies and advice in this newsletter are provided for the general guidance and benefit of Royal Trust clients, based on information that is believed to be accurate at the time of writing. However, readers should consult their own Royal Trust office or personal financial advisor when planning to implement a strategy. This will ensure that their own circumstances have been considered properly, and that action is taken on the latest available information. Interest rates, market conditions, special offers, tax rulings, and other investment factors are subject to sometimes rapid change.

Royal Trust Mutual Funds are sold by Royal Mutual Funds Inc., a member of Royal Bank Financial Group, and are not insured by the Canada Deposit Insurance Corporation, the Régie de l'assurance-dépôts du Québec or any other deposit insurer nor guaranteed by Royal Bank or Royal Trust. Important information about the mutual funds is contained in the simplified prospectus, copies of which may be obtained in any branch of Royal Trust and which should be read carefully before investing. Unit values and investment returns will fluctuate.

 Printed on recyclable paper, using vegetable-based inks. **ISSN 0838-1283**

Keep contents boxes simple

Use the table of contents, sometimes called the index, to give readers a thumbnail review of what to expect inside the newsletter. Placed on the front page or on the mailing panel, the index lists articles and page numbers.

The goal of the contents box is to help readers find articles in longer newsletters. Keep the information short and simple. Consider adding a summary line with the article's headline, and repeating graphics used on the page with the article. Separate the contents box from the rest of the page by using rules, a screen tint or a reverse.

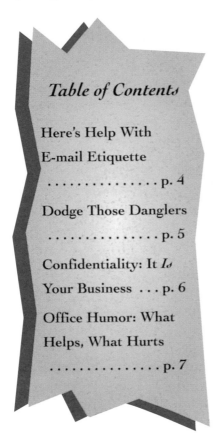

Table of Contents

Here's Help With
E-mail Etiquette
.... p. 4

Dodge Those Danglers
.... p. 5

Confidentiality: It *Is*
Your Business ... p. 6

Office Humor: What
Helps, What Hurts
.... p. 7

Inside this issue . . .

World's largest car wash 2

New train station 3

Golf tourney recaps 4

American Express shares 5

Bozo grants wish 6

Letters from families 7

GKTW

210 S. Bass Rd.
Kissimmee,
Florida 34746
(407) 396-1114
Fax (407) 396-1207

Give Kids The World® is a nonprofit organization that provides a memorable six-day, Central Florida vacation experience for children with terminal illnesses and their families, at no cost to them. It serves qualified children from around the world whose last wish is to meet Mickey Mouse and visit the Walt Disney World Resort® and Central Florida attractions.

Hot Tip

Next time you need to inform your suppliers with specific details about a project, tape it on a microcassette recorder. This recording will slash the time you spend on instructions by as much as 90% plus you can stress important points with the inflection of your voice. Cost of the recorder... $29 and up from your local business supercenter. Replacement tapes are cheap! Best of all, you're helping to reduce paper waste.

Inside this issue...

Questions & Answers
Return addresses, good response rates & when to mail
page 2

DM Resources
Complete listing of direct-mail suppliers
page 3

DM NewsBriefs
FileMaker relational & improved bulk mail stamps
page 6

Saving money when rates & costs go up
by Vincent F. Safuto
page 7

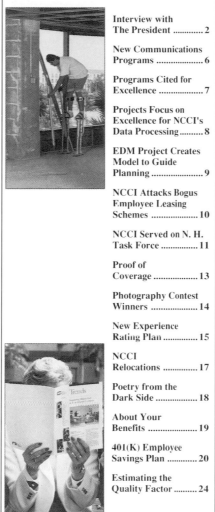

In this issue

COVER STORY
Today there are more treatment options for people with Parkinson's disease.

Lifestyle changes 3
If you can't live by yourself, should you move in with your kids?

Chest surgery 4
New video technique reduces hospital time, recovery and cost.

Alcohol and your heart 6
Moderate drinking may help protect you from heart disease. We'll show you how to weigh the benefits and hazards of alcohol.

Update '91 7
Exercise: A little can mean a lot.
Television: How much you watch may affect what you weigh.

Second opinion 8
Is dried, flaked **coconut** high in saturated fat? Can **stretch marks** disappear? What is **Schamberg's disease**?

Coming in January

How much do you weigh? How much would you like to weigh? How much should you weigh? With holidays past and resolutions still intact, our article on **healthy weight** explains why you shouldn't take weight charts too seriously. **Burning feet** is a common complaint. We'll address causes and offer self-help measures.

mayo

FROM THE
FIELD

Crested Butte Wildflower F[...]
July 12-17, Crested Butte, CO. [...]
Contact: Crested Butte Cham[...]
Commerce, P.O. Box 216, Cr[...]
Butte, CO 81224.

Landscaping with Native Pl[...]
(Cullowhee Conference), Ju[...]
24, *Cullowhee, NC.* **Contact:** [...]
tration Office, Western Caro[...]
University, Cullowhee, NC 2[...]
(704) 227-7397.

Rhode Island Highway Plan[...]
Practice & Policy, *July 27, R[...]
Island.* **Contact:** Rhode Island [...]
Plant Society, 12 Sanderson [...]
Smithfield RI 02917, (401) 94[...]

Ecology and Global Sustain[...]
July 31-Aug. 4, Madison, WI. [...]
meeting of the Ecological Society of
America. **Contact:** Dennis
Whigham, Smithsonian Environ-
mental Research Center, Box 28,
Edgewater, MD 21037, (410) 798-
4424.

Grasslands, *Aug. 1-5, Ames, IA.*[...]
Annual meeting of the Americ[...]
Institute of Biological Sciences. [...]
Contact: Louise Salmon, AIBS, [...]
11th St. NW, Washington, DC [...]
20001, (202) 685-1500.

Ecology, Restoration, and Ma[...]
ment of Prairie Wetlands, *Aug[...]*
13, *Jamestown, ND.* **Contact:** Dr[...]
Ned H. Euliss Jr., U.S. Fish and [...]
Wildlife Service, Northern Prai[...]
Wildlife Research Center, Rout[...]
Box 96C, Jamestown, ND 5840[...]
9736, (701) 252-5363.

Invasive Exotic Plants, *Aug. 12[...]*
Blacksburg, VA. Co-sponsored b[...]
the Virginia Native Plant Society,
Dept. of Conservation and Recre-
ation—Division of Natural Heri-
tage, Virginia Polytechnic Institute
& State University's Dept. of
Horticulture. **Contact:** VNPS, P.O.
Box 844, Annandale, VA 22003,
(703) 231-5783.

Return of the Natives, *Aug. 26,*
Stevenson, MD. Native plant sym-
posium. **Contact:** Irvine Natural
Science Center (410) 484-2413.

ATLANTA HISTORY CENTER
PROGRAMS
May through August 1993

MAY

Spring and summer at the Atlanta History Center bring two of our most popular events. The Atlanta Storytelling Festival in May features dozens of professional storytellers sharing stories from cultures and traditions the world over, plus music, children's activities, and workshops. Civil War Encampment 1993 in July offers a fascinating look at the life of 1860s soldiers, women, and children, and includes infantry and cavalry drills, artillery firing, films, music, and much more.

5 • *Wednesday*
"Culture Wars"
John Freikamayer
Alston Lecture
Noon GPC

6 • *Thursday*
"Praying for Sheetrock"
Melissa Fay Greene
Livingston Lecture
8:00 p.m.

14 • *Friday*
Atlanta Storytelling Festival
Terry Kay
7:30 p.m.

15 • *Saturday*
Atlanta Storytelling Festival
10:00 a.m.-8:00 p.m.

Storyteller Kathryn Windham
7:30 p.m.

16 • *Sunday*
Atlanta Storytelling Festival
10:00 a.m.-8:00 p.m.

19 • *Wednesday*
"Covering the Bases"
Furman Bisher and Skip Caray
Noon GPC

"American Stories"
Calvin Trillin
Livingston Lecture
8:00 p.m.

23 • *Sunday*
World War II Remembered series
"The Holocaust and Atlanta's Jewish Community"
2:00 p.m.

Author, columnist, and humorist Calvin Trillin speaks May 19.

CALENDAR CORNER

May
4 - Concert & Art Show - 7:30 p.m. - PCHS
5 - Incoming Kindergarten Parents' Night -
   7:30 p.m. - King St.
13 - Spring Concert - Gr. 7&8 - 7:30 p.m. - PCMS
17 - Spring Concert - Gr. 5&6 - 7:30 p.m. - PCMS
18 - Incoming Kindergarten Parents' Night -
   7:30 p.m. - Park Ave.
19 - Vote for '93 - '94 Budget and Board of Ed
20 - Senior Awards Assembly - 7:30 p.m. - PCHS
25 - Incoming Kindergarten Parents' Night -
   7:30 p.m. - Edison
26 - Planetarium Skyshow - 7:30 p.m. - PCMS
31 - Memorial Day - schools closed

June
7 - Performing Arts Awards - 7:30 p.m. - PCMS
8 - Band Night - 7 p.m. - PCHS
17 - Regents Exams begin
   [...]ams begin
   [...]of school
   [...]n - 2 p.m. - PCHS

OCTOBER
CALENDAR

1 SOCIAL SERVICE LEAVE APPLICATIONS ACCEPTED
For a Social Service Leave application, call VP Diane Ignizian, Corporate Responsibility Department, Bankmet 396-4365. Complete and return it by Nov. 15.

3 AIDSWALK, SAN DIEGO
Join the 10K walk at the County Administration Building. Registration is at 9.

5 CAREER EXPO, SAN DIEGO
Prospect your next career at Wells Fargo. 4-8 p.m., Town & Country Hotel.

9 HEALDSBURG OFFICE GRAND REOPENING AS SUPERMARKET BRANCH
Visit Safeway for refreshments, prizes and giveaways. Ride a stagecoach from 11-2. Call Julie Jakek, Bankmet 440-4109.

11 COLUMBUS DAY, BANK HOLIDAY

It's Community Support Campaign Season
The "Thanks to You" campaign winds down **Oct. 15**, although contributions will be accepted until **Nov. 30**. The goal is for at least 85 percent of employees to help raise at least $2.2 million.

Thinking of Retiring?
Register for one of three retirement seminars coming to: **San Diego**, Oct. 14, 1-5 p.m., 401 West 24th St., Rooms A&B; **Los Angeles**, Oct. 15, 9 a.m.-1 p.m., 333 South Grand, History Room; or **San Jose**, Oct. 27, 1-5 p.m., 2331 Zanker Road, new training room. To reserve, call Michael Richards, Bankmet 396-0237.

16-17 FESTIVAL OF MASKS, LOS ANGELES
Celebrate Los Angeles' diverse ethnic heritage. Call the Wells Team, Bankmet 396-4366.

24 BOO AT THE ZOO, SANTA ANA ZOO
Treat Orange County kids to a safe Halloween by manning a trick-or-treat station at the zoo. Call the Wells Team, Bankmet 396-4366.

31 HALLOWEEN

Do you have a deadline or an event coming up? Submit calendar entries by Oct. 8 for the November issue. (Items for further in the future are welcome, too, and may serve as story tips.) Address below.

1993

Meetings with Bankers in Southeastern Ohio and West Virginia, Wheeling, West Virginia	November 2
Meetings with Bankers in Western Pennsylvania, Mars and Greensburg, Pennsylvania	November 3
Veterans Day (Bank Holiday)	November 11
Small Bank Advisory Council Meeting, Cleveland, Ohio	November 20
Thanksgiving Day (Bank Holiday)	November 26

1997 Educational Calendar

Standing Nursing Education

PROGRAM	JAN	FEB	MAR	APR	MAY	JUNE	JULY	AUG	SEPT	OCT	NOV	DEC
H. R. Orientation[1]	27	24	31	28	19	30	28	25	29	27	24	15
Patient Care Services Orientation[1]	28	25		1&9	20		1&29	26	30	28	25	16
Preceptor Workshop[2]			19		14						19	
Special Topics in Med/Surg Practice						24 HIV/AIDS				21 Med/Surg		
Developing Presentation Skills					1							
EKG Interpretation Course[2]		3&6				2&5			22&25			
Basic Critical Care Nursing Course[2]		11-13 18&19				10-12 17&18				7-9 14&15		
Advanced Concepts in Critical Care				22						10		
Trauma Theory (STC)[3]			4, 5 11, 12				8, 9 15, 16				4, 5 11, 12	
Critical Care Concepts (STC)[3]			18-19				22, 23				18, 19	

Cardiac Education

PROGRAM	JAN	FEB	MAR	APR	MAY	JUNE	JULY	AUG	SEPT	OCT	NOV	DEC
ACLS Provider Course[4]	5&6	8&9 20&21	7&8	3&4 26&27	3&4 23&24	18&19 20&21	12&13 26&27	7&8	6&7	3&4 24&25	7&8	6&7
ACLS Renewal Course[4]	4			6			11			6		8
ACLS Instructor Course[5]	3			7						5		
BLS Provider Renewal Course[6]	13	10	10	14	5	2	14	11	8	13	3	1
BLS Instructor Course[7]			14&15									

Calendars that work

Make calendars easy to assemble and proofread, efficient to read and conservative of space. Rules and the strategic use of boldface typography keep information organized and complete. Place the calendar in the same spot each issue, and watch out for items placed on the back of the calendar—it might be cut out and saved and important information could be removed from the body of the newsletter.

Good calendar design begins with clear knowledge of what readers want to know. Make the calendar design help to answer readers' questions. For example, the calendar for *News and Views* helps busy professionals with planning by showing the entire year organized by topic.

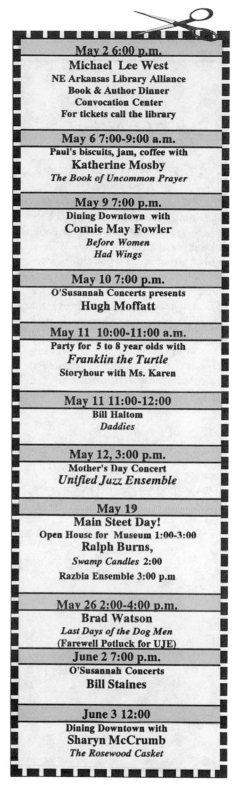

May 2 6:00 p.m.
Michael Lee West
NE Arkansas Library Alliance
Book & Author Dinner
Convocation Center
For tickets call the library

May 6 7:00-9:00 a.m.
Paul's biscuits, jam, coffee with
Katherine Mosby
The Book of Uncommon Prayer

May 9 7:00 p.m.
Dining Downtown with
Connie May Fowler
Before Women Had Wings

May 10 7:00 p.m.
O'Susannah Concerts presents
Hugh Moffatt

May 11 10:00-11:00 a.m.
Party for 5 to 8 year olds with
Franklin the Turtle
Storyhour with Ms. Karen

May 11 11:00-12:00
Bill Haltom
Daddies

May 12, 3:00 p.m.
Mother's Day Concert
Unified Jazz Ensemble

May 19
Main Steet Day!
Open House for Museum 1:00-3:00
Ralph Burns,
Swamp Candles 2:00
Razbia Ensemble 3:00 p.m

May 26 2:00-4:00 p.m.
Brad Watson
Last Days of the Dog Men
(Farewell Potluck for UJE)

June 2 7:00 p.m.
O'Susannah Concerts
Bill Staines

June 3 12:00
Dining Downtown with
Sharyn McCrumb
The Rosewood Casket

Organizing by interest

Because Christie's buyers are interested in specific kinds of art, the calendar is organized first by genre, next by topic and finally by date. The eye of the reader can go immediately to events of interest.

NAME *Auction News*

PUBLISHER Christie, Manson and Woods

International, Inc., New York, New York

PURPOSE/AUDIENCE Service and marketing to

customers

PRODUCTION/PRINTING Four-color process

plus fifth color on white gloss-coated

FORMAT 9" x 12"; twelve pages

DESIGN Stillman Designs/Linda Stillman and

Connie Circosta

Calendar of Future Sales

Park: 502 Park Avenue, 212/546-1000   **East:** 219 East 67th Street, 212/606-0400

AMERICAN DECORATIVE ARTS

Fine American Furniture, Silver, Folk Art & Decorative Arts	June 25, 2 p.m.	Viewing from June 20-24 at Park

BOOKS

The Stuart B. Schimmel Collection of the Book Arts	May 17, 10 a.m.	Viewing from May 10-16 at Park
Printed Books & Manuscripts including Americana	May 17, 2 p.m. & May 18, 10 a.m.	Viewing from May 10-16 at Park

CARS

Important Motor Cars & Automobilia	May 20, 2 p.m.	at the Vintage Car Store, Nyack, NY

CHINESE ART

Fine Chinese Paintings & Calligraphy	May 29, 10 a.m.	Viewing from May 25-28 at Park
Fine Chinese Ceramics & Works of Art	May 30, 10 a.m. & 2 p.m.	Viewing from May 25-29 at Park

COINS

Ancient, Foreign & United States Coins & Important World Banknotes from the Archives of The American Banknote Company	June 5, 10 a.m., 2:00 p.m. & 6 p.m.	Viewing from June 1-4 at Park

EUROPEAN FURNITURE

Important French Furniture, Porcelain, Sculpture, Clocks & Tapestries	May 8, 10 a.m.	Viewing from May 4-7 at Park

GENERAL SALES

Nineteenth-Century English & Continental Furniture, Decorations & Porcelain	May 14, 10 a.m.	Viewing from May 10-13 at East
English & Continental Furniture, Decorations, Porcelain, Paintings & Oriental Works of Art	June 11, 10 a.m.	Viewing from June 7-10 at East

JEWELRY

Important Jewels	June 11, 10 a.m. & 2 p.m.	Viewing from June 7-10 at Park
Antique & Fine Jewelry	June 13, 10 a.m. & 2 p.m.	Viewing from June 8-12 at East

PAINTINGS, DRAWINGS & PRINTS

Contemporary Art (Part I)	May 1, 7 p.m.	Viewing from April 26-May 1 at Park
Contemporary Art (Part II)	May 2, 10 a.m.	Viewing from April 26-May 1 at Park
Modern and Contemporary Paintings, Watercolors, Drawings & Sculpture	May 7, 10 a.m.	Viewing from May 3-6 at East
Impressionist & Modern Paintings & Sculpture (Part I)	May 8, 7 p.m.	Viewing from May 3-8 at Park
Impressionist & Modern Paintings & Sculpture (Part II)	May 9, 2 p.m.	Viewing from May 3-8 at Park
Impressionist & Modern Drawings & Watercolors	May 9, 10 a.m.	Viewing from May 3-8 at Park
Old Master, American, Modern & Contemporary Prints	May 14, 10 a.m. & 2 p.m. May 15, 10 a.m. & 2 p.m.	Viewing from May 10-13 at Park
Haitian Paintings from the Collection of Angela Gross & Latin American Paintings, Drawings & Sculpture	May 15, 10 a.m.	Viewing from May 11-14 at East
Latin American Paintings, Drawings & Sculpture	May 15, 7 p.m. May 16, 10 a.m.	Viewing from May 11-15 at Park
Nineteenth-Century European & American Paintings, Watercolors, Drawings & Sculpture	May 21, 10 a.m. & 2 p.m.	Viewing from May 17-20 at East
Important American Paintings, Drawings & Sculpture of the 19th & 20th Centuries including Paintings from the Collection of Mrs. George Arden, Part I	May 22, 10 a.m. & 2 p.m.	Viewing from May 17-21 at Park
Barbizon, Realist & French Landscape Painting	May 23, 10 a.m.	Viewing from May 18-22 at Park
Nineteenth-Century European Paintings, Drawings, Watercolors & Sculpture	May 23, 10 a.m.	Viewing from May 18-22 at Park
Important Paintings by Old Masters	May 31, 10 a.m.	Viewing from May 25-30 at Park
Old Master Paintings	May 31, 2 p.m.	Viewing from May 25-30 at Park

STAMPS

Important United States Stamps & Covers	June 12, 10 a.m. & 2 p.m. June 13, 10 a.m. & 2 p.m.	Viewing from June 7-11 at Park

TWENTIETH-CENTURY DECORATIVE ARTS

Art Nouveau, Art Deco & Arts & Crafts	June 6, 10 a.m. & 2 p.m.	Viewing from June 1-5 at East
Important Twentieth-Century Decorative Arts, including works by the Tiffany Studios, American Arts & Crafts, & Architectural Designs and Commissions	June 8, 10 a.m. & 2 p.m.	Viewing from June 1-7 at Park

WINE

Fine & Rare Wines	June 15, 10:30 a.m.	in Chicago

Viewing: Tuesday–Saturday, 10 a.m.–5 p.m.; Sunday, 1 p.m.–5 p.m.; day preceding a sale, 10 a.m.–2 p.m.; Monday, 10 a.m.–5 p.m.; by appointment. Schedule subject to change–refer to catalogue. Call 212/371-5438 for more information.

Catalogue information: To order a catalogue or to obtain a subscription, please call 718/784-1480 or write to Christie's Publications Department, 21-24 44th Avenue, Long Island City, NY 11101

11

Join us in a Celebration of
Our Ten Years *October 1-9*

1984

Upcoming Events at Politics & Prose

15 Fall 1994

7 SEPTEMBER
Wednesday, 6:30pm
Patricia O'Brien,
Ladies' Lunch

8 SEPTEMBER
Thursday, 6:30pm
**Carol Anderson
& Susan Stewart,**
*Flying Solo: Single
Women in Midlife*

9 SEPTEMBER
Friday, 7:30pm
Howard Norman,
The Bird Artist

12 SEPTEMBER
Monday, 6:30pm
Richard Bernstein,
*The Dictatorship
of Virtue*

13 SEPTEMBER
Tuesday, 6:30pm
William Gildea,
*When the
Colts Belonged
to Baltimore*

16 SEPTEMBER
Friday, 6:30pm
Karen Armstrong,
A History of God

20 SEPTEMBER
Tuesday, 6:30pm
Anne Meadows,
*Digging up Butch
and Sundance*

21 SEPTEMBER
Wednesday, 6:30pm
Mark Olshaker,
The Edge

22 SEPTEMBER
Thursday, 6:30pm
Kevin Phillips,
Arrogant Capital

26 SEPTEMBER
Monday, 6:30pm
William Kunstler,
*My Life as a
Radical Lawyer*

27 SEPTEMBER
Tuesday, 7:00pm
Ivan Doig,
Heart Earth

28 SEPTEMBER
Wednesday, 6:30pm
Terry Kay,
*Shadow Song and
Sundance*

3 OCTOBER
Monday, 6:30pm
David Grossman,
*The Intimate Book
of Grammar*

4 OCTOBER CANCELLED
Tuesday, 7:30pm
Nadine Gordimer,
*None To
Accompany Me*

8 OCTOBER
Saturday, 7-9pm
**Washington Writers
party with Faye
Moskowitz,** *Her
Face in the Mirror*

17 OCTOBER
Monday, 6:30pm
Deborah Tannen,
*Gender and
Discourse*

18 OCTOBER
Tuesday, 6:30pm
Joyce Carol Oates,
What I Lived For

19 OCTOBER
Wednesday, 6:30pm
Juliet Wittman,
*Breast Cancer
Journal: A Century
of Petals*

26 OCTOBER
Wednesday, 6:30pm
Neil Gabler,
*Winchell: Gossip,
Power, and the
Culture of Celebrity*

28 OCTOBER
Friday, 6:30pm
Molly Ivins,
*Nothin But Good
Times Ahead*

Photos highlight calendars

Authors personally invite readers to their events with this calendar design from *Politics & Prose*. This newsletter lets readers know at a glance when their favorite authors are in town.

NAME *Politics & Prose*

PUBLISHER Politics & Prose, Washington, DC

PURPOSE/AUDIENCE Service and marketing to customers

PRODUCTION/PRINTING Two-color on white 60# offset

FORMAT 8½" x 11"; sixteen pages

DESIGN Hannah Smotrich

FOCUS

How you can help save energy at MU - see page 2

Facilities Focus is published quarterly by Campus Facilities
to keep the MU community informed
of our activities and facilities news and information.

Editor: **Marcia K. Lindberg**
phone: (573) 882-3552, fax: (573) 884-5603, mail: E103 GSB
email: Marcia_K._Lindberg@muccmail.missouri.edu
Contributing Writer: Leilani Haywood

Campus
Facilities

University of Missouri-Columbia
Columbia, MO 65211

Highlights

Highlights is published monthly by
Campus Facilities to share news and
showcase the activities of our
employees.

EDITOR: Marcia K. Lindberg
phone: (573) 882-3552
fax: (573) 884-5603
mail: E103 GSB
University of Missouri-Columbia
Columbia, MO 65211

REPORTERS:
Gene Nelson, grounds
Shelly Ennis, maintenance
Thelma Crane, PD&C
Dilauna Breedlove, PD&C
Nancy Wawrzyniak, PD&C
Sandy Short, energy management
Judy Stock, energy management
DaLana Clay, building services

Campus
Facilities

**GREATER AUSTIN CHAMBER OF COMMERCE
ECONOMIC DEVELOPMENT DIVISION**

111 CONGRESS AVE., PLAZA LEVEL
P.O. BOX 1967
AUSTIN, TX 78767

If you have any questions please call **512-322-5608**
or visit our website at **http://www.austin-chamber.org**

Give Kids The World
210 South Bass Road
Kissimmee, FL 34746
phone (407) 396-1114
fax (407) 396-1207

*"We make a living by
what we get, but we make
a life by what we give."*
Winston Churchill

Mailing Label Changes
*Please check the appropriate box below,
correct the label, then return to GKTW.*
❏ *Name change or misspelled*
❏ *Address change*
❏ *Remove from mailing list*

Mark your
calendar now!
MAY 3 • GALA

New Name. New Look.
Give Kids The World
Miracles & Memories
Newsletter

*Watch for your issue to
arrive each quarter and
be sure to pass it on!*
**We'd also like your
input on this issue and
what you'd like to hear
about in the future.**
Contact Chris Magness.

Earth's Best® Baby Food
4840 Pearl East Circle Suite 201E
Boulder, CO 80301

Free bib, newsletters
& coupons.
Details inside.

Arrive in style

When your newsletter arrives in the mail, the first words most readers see are
their name on the address label and your name in the return address. Place
colorful graphics, your masthead, a welcome message, an inspirational quote,
event notices, a contents box or other news that invites readers into your
newsletter in the area under your return address.

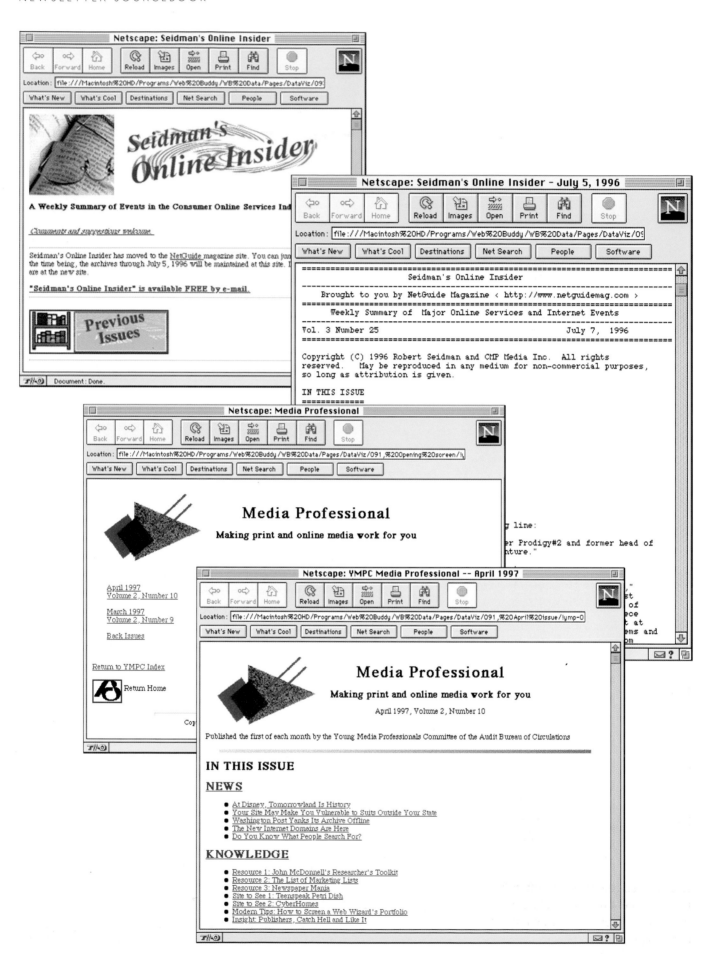

Electronic essentials

Calendars, contents boxes and mast-heads are essential for electronic newsletters, as well as for print ones. Most Web publications use indexes at the beginning of the news site and icons to aid navigation through the publication. Because the reader can't tell how long an e-mail newsletter is or what's in it, contents boxes or indexes are vital for clear communication. Web calendars are often used to supplement or update changing dates after a newsletter calendar has gone to print.

COLOR

When you think about UPS trucks or ads for Coca Cola, distinctive colors come to mind. You can use color as part of your corporate identity, just as these companies do.

Using color successfully requires care and discipline. Care involves matching hues to your audience; discipline calls for sticking with your choice issue after issue. Readers are only confused by constant changes of inks or papers.

Readers expect color. Designers who use it most effectively apply it to the following purposes:

- identity, as in logos and nameplates
- organization, as with bullets or standing headlines
- highlights, as for pull quotes
- explanation, as in charts and graphs

While adding emphasis, color detracts from readability. Type—even headlines—printed in color slows reading and reduces understanding. Use color type carefully.

Although many newsletters include color, very few are printed using four-color process: Most use only one ink color, in addition to black, to achieve their colorful effects. Many achieve the effect of several colors by using both black and a second ink in a variety of screen tints, as well as printing them at 100 percent.

Paper influences color as much as ink. Bright ink colors work best on coated stock; soft colors work best on uncoated sheets. Unfortunately, photographic reproductions of colors (such as those used in this book) cannot fully convey the impact of ink on paper.

Newsletters appeal to the full range of human interests, so invite the full range of color possibilities. The newsletters shown in this chapter include pastels, metallics, primaries and many other color possibilities.

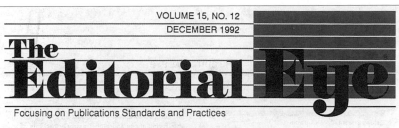

VOLUME 15, NO. 12

DECEMBER 1992

The Editorial Eye

Focusing on Publications Standards and Practices

When Writers Have Trouble Getting Started

You can beat writer's block if you know what you're up against.

by Dianne Snyder

How do *you* get started on a piece of writing?

- Wait for inspiration to strike.
- Wait for the deadline to force your hand.
- Wait for the perfect first sentence to appear.
- Water the begonias.

Getting started does not have to be a hit-or-miss enterprise or an exercise in procrastination. Speaking as a professional writer who has tried all of the above, I have wasted days searching for a magic combination to start the flow of words. What follows are insights I've wrested from my bouts with the problem, from working with fellow sufferers, and from the research of others—notably Linda Flower of Carnegie-Mellon University—into the writing process itself.

What Are Writers Made Of?

All writers (defined here as anyone called upon to write) are inhabited by three selves: a **creator**, a **critic**, and a **scribe**. The first two are natural rivals

who spend much of the time contradicting each other's dictates to the third.

I think of the creative self as a demon in the

Inside

1992 APEX Awards for Publications Excellence; Winner, 1991 E 1990 Washington Edpress Excellence in Print Awa

© 1992 *The E*

From rowdy red to relaxing blue

The editorial experts of *The Editorial Eye* changed the spot color of their newsletter from red to a periwinkle blue to better reach their target audience of mostly women. After the redesign, focus groups revealed that men also preferred blue to red.

NAME *The Editorial Eye*

PUBLISHER EEI Communications, Alexandria, Virginia

PURPOSE/AUDIENCE Service to subscribers

PRODUCTION/PRINTING Two-color on 50# offset

FORMAT 8½" × 11"; twelve pages

DESIGN EEI Communications

The Editorial Eye

Volume 19, No. 5
May 1996

Focusing on Publications Standards and Practices

Using Other People's Words: The Art of Quotation

by Arthur Plotnik

True wit is nature to advantage dress'd, / What oft was thought, but ne'er so well express'd.

—Alexander Pope
Essay on Criticism, II

When you encounter exemplary expression—words producing the very effect you long to achieve—you can do two things: (1) emulate it, fashioning your own expression after the model; or (2) quote it; that is, borrow someone else's words to dress up your messages.

Everyone borrows words; some do so more nimbly than others. Expression would be insufferably bleak without the charms and treasures of utterances past. Borrowed words connect us to one another, across periods, across cultures. They affirm the universality of human thought and emotions. And for "one brief shining moment" (*Camelot*) at a time, they make us look good.

"Freedom is like a blanket which, pulled up to the chin, uncovers the feet," I've often said to nods of approval. It so happens that John Updike said these words previously in his novel *The Coup*. But they passed my simple tests of quotabil-

ity—*I wish I'd said them, and I'd love to use them*. So into my notebook they went and out they come at appropriate times, usually with credit to Mr. Updike.

Not every well-turned phrase you encounter can be vacuumed into your prose; but those that resonate, those relating to the things you need to talk about, and those not likely to appear in popular quotation books are good bets for your repertoire of expressiveness. The more arcane or private the source, the better; the words will be fresh to your audience. A friend given to quirky outbursts once announced, "I enjoy life through the medium of dread." It's in my notebook.

What we think of as familiar or "best-loved" quotes may lack freshness but usually bear selective use. They are best-loved for good reasons:

Sound and rhythm: "'Twas brillig, and the slithy toves, / Did gyre and gimble in the wabe;..." (Lewis Carroll)

Concise wisdom (economy): "...to thine own self be true,..." (William Shakespeare)

Comfort: "After all, tomorrow is another day." (Margaret Mitchell)

Precision: "They shall beat their swords into plowshares,...." (Isaiah 1:18)

Humanity: "Give me your tired, your poor, / Your huddled masses yearning to breathe free." (Emma Lazarus)

Wit: "I never forget a face, but in your case I'll make an exception." (Groucho Marx)

Application to one's purpose: "Rise up, my love, my fair one, and come away," (Song of Solomon, 2:10)

Such standbys are durable over the long term but cloying when they come thick and fast. As "brevity is the soul of wit" (Shakespeare),

To page 2 ▶

Inside

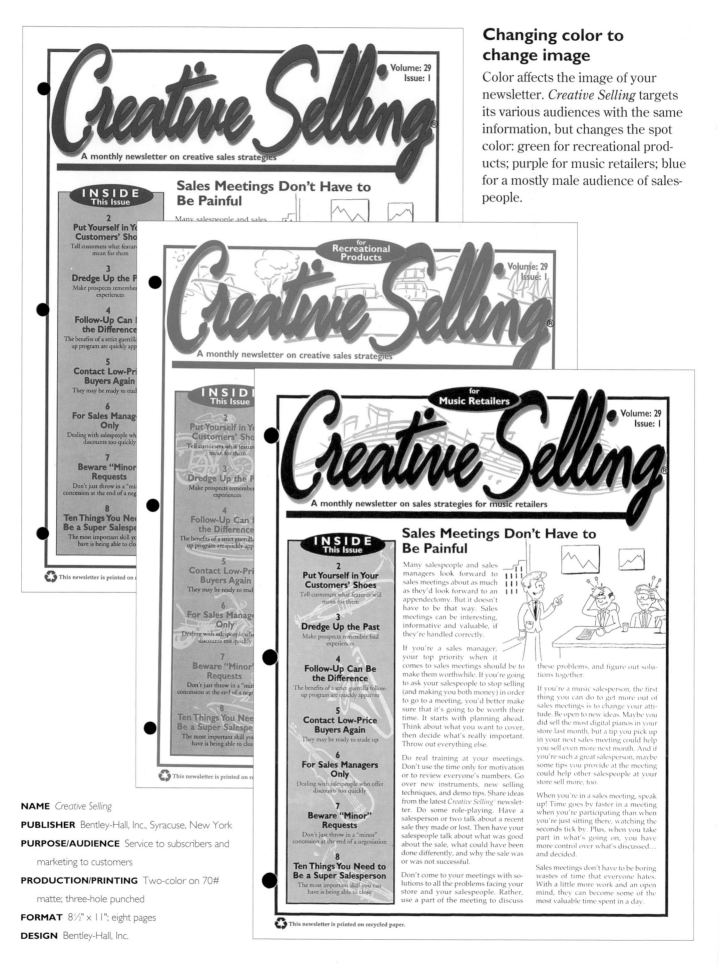

Changing color to change image

Color affects the image of your newsletter. *Creative Selling* targets its various audiences with the same information, but changes the spot color: green for recreational products; purple for music retailers; blue for a mostly male audience of salespeople.

NAME *Creative Selling*

PUBLISHER Bentley-Hall, Inc., Syracuse, New York

PURPOSE/AUDIENCE Service to subscribers and marketing to customers

PRODUCTION/PRINTING Two-color on 70# matte; three-hole punched

FORMAT 8½" x 11"; eight pages

DESIGN Bentley-Hall, Inc.

Always dependable

The cream paper and golden ink of this investment newsletter convey a solid and reliable image. These comforting colors never go out of fashion.

NAME *Investment Watch*

PUBLISHER Phoenix Funds, Boston, Massachusetts

PURPOSE/AUDIENCE Service and marketing to customers

PRODUCTION/PRINTING Four-color process on cream 70# coated

FORMAT 8½" x 11"; four pages

DESIGN Phoenix Funds

Investment Watch

Fall 1995

A Timely Look at Phoenix and Your Investments

Phoenix Philosophies

Philip R. McLoughlin
President,
Phoenix Funds

As 1995 draws to a close, your thoughts may turn to wrapping up year-end finances. This issue of *Investment Watch* is devoted to strategies for taking the sting out of the annual tax bite while keeping your long-term financial goals in mind.

For an overview of tax strategies you can use right now, read the accompanying "Take Some Tax-Saving Steps Into 1996." On the following pages you'll find a wealth of specific information on the world of investments and taxes. We also provide a close-up look at how tax-exempt bond funds can help trim your tax bill both now and in future years.* In addition, you can learn about how to make long-term investing more tax-wise.

After reading this issue, don't hesitate to contact your financial advisor with questions about your investment strategy. Or call Phoenix at (800) 243-4361 for more information about our products and services. We hope you turn to Phoenix to help meet your financial goals — and to make the coming tax season easier.

Sincerely,

Philip R. McLoughlin
President, Phoenix Funds

Some of these funds' holdings may be subject to the federal alternative minimum tax. Capital gains (if any) are taxable for federal and, in most cases, state purposes.

Inside This Issue

2
10 Minutes With a Fund Manager

3
Travel the Tax-Exempt Route
to Potential Savings

3
Retirement Savings Can Be Tax-Wise, Too

4
At Your Service

Phoenix Investments

Take Some Tax-Saving Steps Into 1996

With few exceptions, the steps you take this year could affect the taxes you pay next April 15. Here are some ways to keep your long-term investment strategies in sight while helping reduce taxes in 1995 and beyond.

Look Carefully at Capital Gains

Holding an investment at least a year may make good tax sense. That's because short-term capital gains on shares held less than a year are taxed at ordinary income tax rates. Long-term capital gains on investments held longer than a year are also taxed at ordinary income tax rates, but only up to 28%. This is significant, considering that ordinary income rates run as high as 39.6% at the federal level.

For example, if you're in the 39.6% tax bracket, on a short-term capital gain of $1,000 you would pay $396 in taxes. If that $1,000 were a long-term gain, your tax bill would fall to $280.

Know Your Distributions

Be careful to treat any periodic dividend or capital gains distributions made by your fund (often at year-end) separately from gains or losses from selling shares. Dividend distributions are taxed at your top income tax bracket. But capital gains distributions are taxed as long-term gains — only up to 28% — regardless of how long you have owned the shares. This is also why some aggressive stock funds — which may generate more capital gains than income — may be worth considering for many investors in higher tax brackets.

For Phoenix Funds that make year-end distributions, you will receive a 1995 income and capital gain check or statement in early January. Later in the month you will receive Form 1099-DIV,

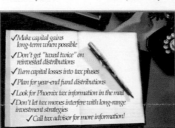
Year-end is a good time to look at how you can possibly trim your investment tax bill.

✓ Make capital gains long-term when possible
✓ Don't get "taxed twice" on reinvested distributions
✓ Turn capital losses into tax pluses
✓ Plan for year-end fund distributions
✓ Look for Phoenix tax information in the mail
✓ Don't let tax moves interfere with long-range investment strategies
✓ Call tax advisor for more information!

(continued on page 2)

investment management

VIEWS

Winter 1997

Investment Commentary

Outlook mostly positive for markets in 1997

 RT INVESTMENT COUNSEL INC.

affiliated with Royal Trust

THE HEALTHY, YET UNSPECTACULAR, level of growth seen in most areas of the world in 1996 provided just the fuel financial markets needed for a record-breaking ascent. Prolonged low inflation and low interest rates have propelled bond and equity markets forward. Considerable volatility notwithstanding, markets in North America, Europe, and some parts of Asia left investors with solid returns. The ever-present fear of a resurgence in inflation was the only factor to dampen spirits, albeit only slightly.

Economic overview

Economic growth improved in Canada, the United Kingdom, and Germany, while the U.S. experienced a slowdown and Japan struggled to get its recovery off the ground.

Meanwhile, growth in Asian economies slowed significantly. This was largely the aftershock of tighter monetary policies, which were a response to the economic overheating experienced in the region earlier this decade.

Yet there was nothing slow about financial markets. Equity and bond prices gathered steam with every indication that moderate economic growth posed no threat of inflation, and that interest rates would remain low.

North American and European equity markets shrugged off frequent bouts of insecurity over the economic outlook to produce healthy returns for the year. They were joined by the Hong Kong stock market, which soared largely on the strength of low interest rates.

There were laggards, however. For example, Japanese stocks had difficulty maintaining momentum as the country's economic prospects remained cloudy. Poor economic prospects combined with political uncertainties held back Southeast Asian markets such as South Korea and Thailand.

Bond markets have strong run

Bond markets were also beneficiaries of a benign economic environment, leading the way to lower yields and higher prices.

We expect interest rates to rise modestly during the second half of 1997.

Continued on Page 2

Investment Commentary
A review of the capital markets in 1996 and the outlook for '97.

Other Views
A look at credit card use in the West.

Inside Views
A brief history of RT Investment Counsel.

Rich gold, stable blue

Cream-colored paper helps *Investment Management Views* build trust.

NAME *Investment Management Views*

PUBLISHER RT Investment Counsel Inc., Toronto Ontario, Canada

PURPOSE/AUDIENCE Service and marketing to customers

PRODUCTION/PRINTING Three-color on natural 60# offset

FORMAT 8½" x 11"; four pages

DESIGN Ariad Custom Publishing

ROYAL TRUST

January 1997

MONEYGUIDE™

Canada's newsletter on preserving and building wealth

Retirement in the 21st century

In this exclusive *MoneyGuide* article, John McCallum, Chief Economist of the Royal Bank of Canada, offers some specific advice on the future of retirement in Canada. He suggests how Canadians in every age group can prepare for retirement going into the 21st century.

By John McCallum

Until recently, Canadians have more or less taken for granted that a combination of government programs and employer pension plans would guarantee their retirement income.

Today those guarantees are in question. Planning for retirement has become more complicated because of a number of new, unknown variables: What will happen to the Canada Pension Plan (CPP) and Quebec Pension Plan (QPP)? Will the federal government's proposed Seniors Benefit go forward? Are defined-benefit pension plans on the way out? Will younger taxpayers stage a revolt as they're asked to shoulder more of the cost of caring for an aging population?

No one knows all the answers. But certain trends are emerging that offer insight into what we can expect in the years ahead. Here's what we see happening.

Government programs

The CPP will survive. The federal government and the provinces are currently locked

Retirement in the future will look quite different than it does today. This article examines what may change and how to prepare for it.

in debate over the future of the CPP. But it is clear that there is a political will on all sides to retain the CPP in something resembling its current form.

There may be changes to certain aspects, such as raising the retirement age and reducing some benefits. And there will certainly be increases in premiums.

We expect premiums will eventually level off at around 10% of contributable earnings (the 1996 figure was 5.6%, divided equally between employer and employee).

Whatever changes are made to the plan, it is clear that CPP payments will not be adequate to support the average person in retirement. The 1996 maximum payment for a 65-year-old was just over $8,700. It's unlikely to rise above that in inflation-

Continued on Page 2

The Ideal RRSP

Rousing red

On white, matte-coated paper, the blue in the *Royal Trust Money Guide* says stable, while the red says energetic. The color combination here could mean "willing to take some risk"; the upbeat art, with its multi-use of color, could mean "we are innovative and willing to believe in future opportunity."

NAME *Royal Trust Money Guide*

PUBLISHER Royal Trust, Inc., Toronto, Ontario, Canada

PURPOSE/AUDIENCE Service and marketing to customers

PRODUCTION/PRINTING Four-color process on 50# matte

FORMAT 8½" x 11"; twelve pages

DESIGN Ariad Custom Publishing

Newsletter Communications

News & information to help professionals use newsletters for effective communications

Does Your Means of Newsletter Distribution Fit Your Newsletter's Purpose?

Instead of viewing distribution as a means to an end (getting your newsletter into your audience's hands), think of distribution as a part of the whole package. Like every other aspect of newsletter production, you should select your distribution mode with your audience and your newsletter goals in mind.

If you produce a newsletter for employees, hand distribution probably offers the least costly method. Why spend money on postage when you can simply place a newsletter in everyone's box or at his or her workstation? Or place stacks of newsletters in the breakroom and other places where employees congregate. For association/membership newsletters, handing out issues at meetings or stacking them near entrances and exits will afford you similar savings.

Please see NEWSLETTER DISTRIBUTION, page 2

What Should I Do About Protecting Newsletter Copyrights Abroad and Obtaining U.S. Registrations?

*There's often a great deal of confusion about the provisions of the copyright law, particularly since the changes that occurred when the Berne Convention became law on March 1, 1989. To help reduce some of the confusion, here are excerpts from the copyright law of the United States of America, preceded by questions to organize the information. The text in italics is produced by Newsletter Communications. Non-italic text is from the law itself. An ellipsis (…) indicates that part of the law text has been omitted, and in a few places long paragraphs have been broken up to make the text more readable. If you have any questions, consult an attorney. This informa-*tion is not presented as legal advice, but purely for informational purposes.*

HOW CAN I HAVE MY NEWSLETTER PROTECTED IN OTHER COUNTRIES?

There is no such thing as an "international copyright" that will automatically protect an author's writings throughout the entire world. Protection against unauthorized use in a particular country depends, basically, on the national laws of that country. However, most countries do offer pro-

Please see COPYRIGHTS, page 10

Radius, Power Computing, and Cutting Edge have already signed licensing agreements with Apple and each has charted radically different courses in these new waters:

• **Radius,** a longtime vendor of Mac displays, video adapters, and digital-video equipment, will use that expertise to devise a high-end digital-video-editing system. However, this system, which the company is thinking of calling the VideoVision Workstation, will be more of a value-added design than a true clone. Radius plans to combine its present digital-video products with a Power Mac 8100 motherboard, bundle it with Radius Edit software, a new digital-video-editing package that mimics analog editing systems that video professionals use. Radius has proposed that the $30,000-or-so system will be part of a product line including both low-end and high-end systems. *Radius (408) 541-6100*

• **Cutting Edge** will base its Quatro 850 on a Mac Quadra 650 68040-based logic board purchased from Apple, enabling these systems to run the Mac OS. The first model released will be 25-MHz, with 33-MHz models following. While very basic, these systems will retail for less than $1,000 (includes mouse and keyboard, but no monitor). Slated for shipment very soon, Quatro 850s will probably be the first Mac clones available to the public. *Cutting Edge (619) 441-6991*

• **Power Computing** will produce models that are more like traditional clones, with off-the-shelf modular designs, flexible configurations, and lower cost. Also, unlike Radius and Cutting Edge, Power Computing, which was created specifically to produce Mac clones, will design its own motherboards for its clones, though the systems will use Apple ROMs and other Apple products. The first two models, which are roughly equal to the 7100- and 8100-based Power Macs, were scheduled to ship in April, and Power Computing assures they will be completely compatible with Macs. And though priced comparably to baseline Macs, the new models reportedly have more RAM, more storage bays, more slots, and larger-capacity hard drives. They may even be available with bundled software and CD-ROM drives. *Power Computing (408) 526-0500*

If the Mac's simplicity always appealed to you but the price did not, now's your chance to jump on the Mac clone wagon. After years of PC vs. Mac, the release of the Power Mac and now Mac clones has opened up a whole new world in personal computing. ●

Newsletter Communications

is published 10 times a year by The Newsletter Factory® to help acquaint our clients with innovations and opportunities in the area of newsletter design, production, and writing.

Thomas Hartmann
Publisher

Dave Mullinax
Editor-in-Chief

G.W. Hall
Managing Editor

Ellen Mathis
Senior Editor

J.C. Justice
Art Director

Shinn Uehara
Graphic Designer

Keith Caruso
Production Manager

April 1995• Newsletter Communications **3**

HARDWARE

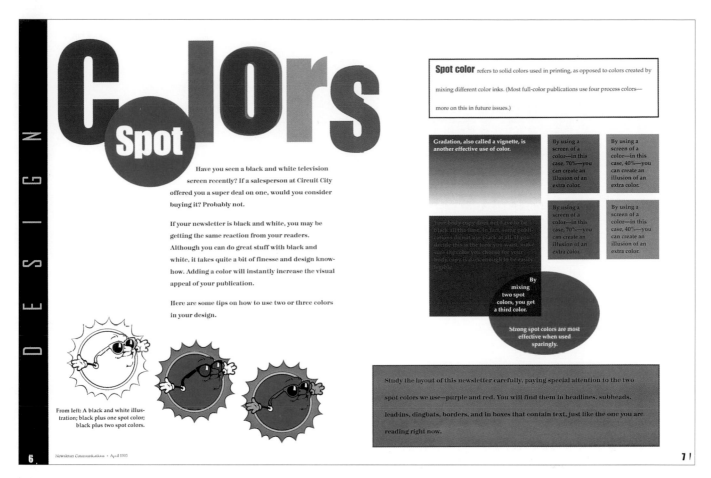

Electric colors

The results of overlapping screens and butting inks can look dazzling or dangerous, but there is no doubt that color influences your reader. The examples shown here help readers visualize the effects of screen tints, reverses and overprints.

NAME *Newsletter Communications*

PUBLISHER The Newsletter Factory, Atlanta, Georgia

PURPOSE/AUDIENCE Service and marketing to customers

PRODUCTION/PRINTING Three-color on white 100# dull-coated

FORMAT 8½" × 11"; twelve pages

DESIGN The Newsletter Factory

The Art of SELF ◆ PROMOTION

Nuts 'n bolts for manageable marketing

Number 14
Winter 1995

this issue

The Do-able Marketing Plan

HOW MANY TIMES HAVE YOU WANTED TO CREATE A MARKETING PLAN...

...but just didn't take the time to sit down and do it? Or maybe you've started the process but never finished it?

The truth is, you don't have to have a plan. It is possible to run, and even grow, your business without one - most people do.

Plans may be useless but the planning process is indispensable

OPTION 1

However, without a plan, your marketing is probably haphazard, scattered and slapshot. A marketing opportunity pops up, maybe an ad in a special section of the local paper or a trade show you weren't planning to exhibit at, and you jump at it because you've been meaning to do some marketing.

So you create that ad or slap together a promo piece to hand out at your booth. But because it's last minute, you don't have the time to proofread, so there a few typographical errors, or maybe you forget to put your phone number on it. But at least it's done - and you go back to doing your work and wait for the new clients to come knocking on your door , which could happen, I suppose. That's one option.

OPTION 2

If, on the other hand, you have a marketing plan into which you fit that ad or trade show, you can make time for the necessary preparation, execution and follow through in a methodical way. A marketing plan doesn't have to be an overwhelming task - a 100-page manuscript that you slave over and then put on your shelf to gather dust. It can fit on one page. It can be simple to write and easy to use. Anyone, with or without marketing experience, can create one.

DO WHATEVER IT TAKES

...to step away from your work to plan the short and long-term futures of your business. One morning a month, try shutting your office door or going out for breakfast, alone or with a colleague, to focus on planning, to focus on the future. If taking time out of your workday seems impossible, see if you can spend one weekend morning per month on it. Because if you don't, you'll be chasing your business from behind, rather than being the driving force behind it.

Dear Self Promoter:

This issue's theme comes directly from recent experience. I find that my business is cyclical and right now I'm in a Marketing Plan cycle. I've spent the last three months doing what I call "marketing liaison" projects, where I actually serve as the part-time, off- site marketing director for a handful of small businesses, creating marketing plans and then implementing them for my clients.

In addition, my consultation clients are using our 2 hours together to create a basic, single objective marketing plan.

Often, the role I play. is to bring structure. When my clients schedule an appointment with me, they are making a commitment to me - but more importantly, to themselves. Paying me for my time forces them to take their marketing seriously, to focus their attention on it.

If you can't do your marketing on your own, get help. Call me or someone else. But do it! It's not as big a deal as you imagine.

Ilise Benun

...201-653-0783

→ MORE INSIDE

INSIDE:
→ Format for Your One-Page Marketing Plan
→ Subscriber Profile: Top Design

Controlled red

The red spot color here adds life to the page without being overwhelming. The designer uses screened black to add dimension to the page. The deep cream-colored paper gives the illusion of yet more color in the reversed type. This design gets ample mileage out of the minimal extra costs for the red ink.

NAME *The Art of Self Promotion*

PUBLISHER Ilise Benun, Hoboken, New Jersey

PURPOSE/AUDIENCE Service to subscribers and customers

PRODUCTION/PRINTING Two-color on cream 70# offset

FORMAT 8½" x11"; six pages (with insert)

DESIGN June Evers, graphic designer

Here's What Abe Lincoln Taught Us About Direct Mail

Someone once asked Abraham Lincoln how long a man's legs should be. As the story goes, he responded, "Long enough to reach the ground."

Inadvertently, in responding to this question, Mr. Lincoln may also have stumbled onto the First Law of Direct Mail Copywriting.

So, let's put Mr. Lincoln's extremely intuitive answer into its proper context. "How long should direct mail copy be?"

Well, the answer wouldn't be, "Long enough to reach the ground." But it would be, "Long enough to say exactly what you need to say. Not more, not less."

When preconceived notions about the length of copy — say for a sales letter — come into play, it seems to work against the total effectiveness of the direct mail effort.

That means you probably *don't* want to start your creative planning meeting by saying "let's use a six-page sales letter."

Instead, sit down and start writing. Say what you need to say. Then, when you've said all that needs to be said, stop writing. Like magic, your copy tells *you* how long it needs to be.

Believe it or not, it's harder to write short than long. So, if you start with a preconceived notion of a two-page letter, for example, you may miss the mark.

Not allocating the right amount of space can work against you just as much as trying to fill an extra page-and-a-half in your six-page letter. Not only is writing-to-fill-space not much fun, but it somehow always turns out flat.

Who's Handing You This Bull?

Bullseye is brought to you by **Direct Mail Productions, Inc.** — a national full-service printing and direct-mail processing company.

At Direct Mail Productions, we're organized and structured to handle large and frequent mailings, where requirements reach into the millions.

And we're CASS Certified by the U.S. Postal Service. That means we know every trick in the book to help you take advantage of every allowable postal discount.

Take the bull by the horns and put us to a test on your next mailing.

Write to us at 340 Scarlet Boulevard, Oldsmar, FL 34677. Or call our Customer Service Department at **(813) 854-5700**, toll-free **1-800-771-9898**. Our fax is (813) 854-2693.

Handwritten margin notes:

Think about this:
- Bullseye makes you the expert.
- Bullseye can now be yours in your market Exclusively!

Your name goes in the callout.

"
At Direct Mail Productions we're organized and structured to handle large and frequent mailings.
"

This story is all about You. It focuses on your special strengths. You tell us. We write it. You see a proof!

We share the copyright. So, Bullseye looks like it belongs to you!

You!   Us!

CALL NOW
1-800-226-2428

Write me a letter

Handwriting in the margin outside of the body copy conveys a personal afterthought from the editor directly to the reader. Because it deviates stylistically from typical typestyles, readers notice it. Use of the red spot color also makes sure it's read.

NAME *Bullseye*

PUBLISHER Strategies for Growth, Inc., Dunedin, Florida

PURPOSE/AUDIENCE Service and marketing to customers

PRODUCTION/PRINTING Four-color process on white 70# matte-coated

FORMAT 8½" × 11"; four pages

DESIGN Strategies for Growth, Inc.

The following is the reproduced newsletter spread:

Aggressive Russian olives invading Midwest and Plains

The Russians are here!

The Russians I'm referring to are Russian olives (*Eleagnus angustifolia*) and they are fast becoming an enemy in the Midwest and Plains.

When I moved to Minnesota in 1969, I saw my first Russian olive in Hastings Park. I still remember its attractive silvery foliage, dark bark, and almost sculpture-like form.

As a landscape designer in the 1970s, I installed many Russian olives in my landscape plans, although we worried then about the verticillium wilt that besieged the plant, rendering it wilted, brown, and partially dead. (Wisconsin nurseries actually stopped producing and selling it for awhile.) But the wilt passed and we continued planting the Russian olive, which is a native of Europe. After all, besides its aesthetic strengths, the plant also tolerates a wide range of soils, droughty conditions and a cold climate. We all planted a large number of the plants for screens and windbreaks.

But the Russian olive's broad range of tolerance is making it an enemy! When birds carry the tasty berries across the landscape, the dropped seeds have no problem

Aggressive Russian olives are a menace to the Midwest region of the United States.

establishing anywhere, and the plants quickly take advantage of each new opportunity.

On a recent cross-country trip through Iowa, Nebraska, Colorado, and New Mexico, I saw Russian olives growing in pastures and river valleys, displacing prized grazing land and replacing valuable lowland wildlife habitat. The trees can be as much of a problem as red cedar in the Midwest and mesquite in the Southwest. Because all these plants are easier to establish than to eliminate, severe vegetation management techniques are used, further disrupting and degrading the land.

For example, in Texas, native juniper and mesquite trees are "chained off" by bulldozers dragging chains to uproot the trees. But that method further degrades the pastures, allowing pioneer weeds to quickly take advantage of the disruption.

I have no easy solution for stopping any of these aggressive plants.

But, based on my observations during my driving trip, I will no longer plant or recommend planting Russian olives. If you need to see for yourself, you also can take a driving trip — not cross-country — but simply along T.H. 169 south of Shakopee, Minn. You will see pasture land dotted with Russian olives spreading across the landscape.

Birds aid the Russian olive's movement, and its broad range of tolerance allows its easy establishment. Believe what you see — we have a problem with this Russian!

Bonnie Harper-Lore
Midwest Office
Program Coordinator

Bonnie Harper-Lore, program coordinator of the Wildflower Center's Midwest Regional Office, spoke this spring at the University of Wisconsin Arboretum in Madison and at the Michigan Wildflower Association's annual conference in Detroit.

Midwest Office information officer Maria Urice and Bonnie presented a number of talks at local workshops, conferences, and garden club meetings this spring. The staff also appeared on a call-in talk show on radio station KUOM in Minneapolis to discuss "Native Plants for Residential Use."

Bonnie has met with Bloomington,

MIDWEST UPDATE

Minn., city officials to discuss changes in the city's lawn ordinance. The city is interested in making changes that will allow the use of native vegetation in planned landscapes.

This spring, the Minnesota-based environmental group "Kids for Saving Earth" distributed packets of wildflower seeds through Target stores to kids across the United States. The regional office was part of

the initial planning stages of the project, defining species lists, locating seed sources, and advising the project coordinators about the importance of using native plants.

A traveling display for the regional office is now available.

The book *Vascular Plants of Minnesota: A Checklist and Atlas*, by University of Minnesota emeritus professors Gerald Ownbey and Thomas Morley, is now available. The regional office is co-sponsoring a book-signing with the Minnesota Native Plant Society to honor the authors.

Membership Department makes sure you belong

The thousands of National Wildflower Research Center members have one thing in common: their interest in wildflowers and native plants.

When Wildflower Center staffers meet members, they're always impressed with the members' knowledge of native flora.

"We're always amazed and delighted to learn how knowledgeable and enthusiastic members are about native plants. It's always a treat to discover," says Mae Daniller, director of development.

The Center's membership program started in 1984 with 1,700 members at year's end. Now, more than 15,000 people are members of the Wildflower Center.

Mae says the staff is always eager to serve Wildflower Center members better. "We want you to tell us what you like and don't like."

Besides Mae, two other Wildflower Center staff deal directly with members' concerns. Tony Martinez processes and maintains the Center's membership records, and Marianne Pfeil deals personally with member correspondence.

Wildflower Center members receive the newsletter and the journal as part of their membership benefits package. Both award-winning publications were developed to respond to members' requests for native plant information.

Other membership benefits in the Center include free, priority handling of information requests from the Clearinghouse, a 10-percent discount on purchases through the gift shop and catalog, plus invitations to seminars, tours, and a special membership open house each year.

Sometimes members forget that the Clearinghouse can provide free native plant information; Mae wants to encourage you to take advantage of the service.

"Even if you live in Oregon, or North Carolina, or New York, or anywhere else, members can write to us and get free information on wildflowers and native plants," she says.

The seminars, tours, and open house allow Wildflower Center staff members to meet their "constituents."

"We know we can't meet each and every one of our members, but we want to meet as many of them as we can," Mae says.

Mae says the Center's goal is to grow to 35,000 members by 1994. Even when membership becomes that large, she says, the Membership Department will still be eager to serve members with the same prompt and caring attitude.

"The greatest compliment a current member can give us is to give a gift of Center membership to a friend! Then we know that you appreciate our programs and benefits so much that you wish to share them with others," Mae says. "It makes us all feel good!"

Membership Growth 1984 to 1990

Year	Members
1984	1700
1985	4229
1986	7631
1987	7712
1988	14398
1989	15902
1990	15396

New book offers "wildflowers all year long"

Wildflower Center trustee Bette W. Castro has published a book of poetry celebrating the beauty of American wildflowers.

The hard-bound 5-inch by 7-1/2 inch book, with 48 pages and illustrated with watercolors by Marjorie Stodgell, features an introduction by Lady Bird Johnson and a foreword by Helen Hayes — co-chairs of the Wildflower Center.

Miss Hayes says the book has given her "spring on the coldest, darkest, winter days and wildflowers all year long."

A portion of the book's proceeds benefits the Wildflower Center.

Mrs. Johnson says the book "speaks to the heart. (Bette Castro) has captured the essence of wildflowers, giving us a heightened sense of community with the natural world."

Copies of *The Wildflower* are available from the Wildflower Center for $9.95, plus $3 shipping for each book. Please use the order form in the enclosed catalog, or write to "Books," at the address listed on the newsletter's back page.

Type enhances color

Elegant, willowy type reinforces the pastel graphics and botanical illustrations in *Wildflower*. Dark green, the theme color, is used for type as well as tint blocks and drawings. Tints of burgundy create a lilac hue. The total effect is delicate color that unites readers in their affection for wildflowers—a fine example of matching technique to message.

NAME *Wildflower*

PUBLISHER National Wildflower Research Center, Austin, Texas

PURPOSE/AUDIENCE Service to members and friends of the center

PRODUCTION/PRINTING Three-color on light-green 60# offset

FORMAT 8½" × 11"; six pages (six-panel foldout)

DESIGN Patty Alvey and Elaine Walker

2-COLOR DESIGN

How to milk black + a color

*I*n last month's story about newsletter-design-contest winners, we didn't have the space (or the original artwork) to show *Free Spirit* newsletter's full-color, full-sized version of two-color cartoons that look like at least three-color.

We thought you'd like to see them (and we're in a recycling mood), so we got the artwork and the color breaks to show you how you can "paint" with black plus one color. Rick Korab of Punch Design, Minneapolis, designed the color for the cartoons by Harry Pulver, Jr. The cartoons illustrated articles on "Ways to Make a Difference in the World."

Korab used orange ink (PANTONE #151) as a second color on white paper, and we use red (#185) on ivory, so he came up with new color breaks to give our combination the same effect as his. See the color breaks at lower right.

The color breaks
All of this color comes from only one color (#185-red) plus black — in solids, and screens of 20% and 40%. Color breaks from Rick Korab, a smart designer who knows the benefits of a screen style sheet. Cartoons by Harry Pulver, Jr.

- 100% #185
- 40% #185 / 20% black
- 40% black / 20% #185
- 20% black
- 20% #185

IN HOUSE GRAPHICS • 5

Maximize two ink colors

Two-color illustrations, which are produced by overlapping screen tints, seem to be printed in many colors. The illustrator and designer for the art reproduced in the above example are the same as for *Free Spirit*, reproduced on pages 100 and 101.

NAME *In House Graphics*

PUBLISHER United Communications Group, Rockville, Maryland

PURPOSE/AUDIENCE Service to subscribers

PRODUCTION/PRINTING Two-color on natural 70# offset

FORMAT 8½" x 11"; eight pages

DESIGN Ronnie Lipton

Current Topics in Food Safety and Nutrition

TOTAL QUALITY

SOLUTIONS

 NEWS

Preprinting color

Cost-conscious designers use preprinting to add a second color to newsletters. Preprinting calls for printing the second color for many monthly issues at once, and then printing individual monthly issues using black ink only.

For example, a newsletter needing 1,000 copies per month would preprint 12,000 copies—a supply for one year—and then produce each monthly press run in black.

These examples show the use of preprinting in name

Food Insight®

Current Topics in Food Safety and Nutrition

The Inside Report
on America's New Competitiveness

TOTAL QUALITY®
N E W S L E T T E R

SOLUTIONS
BBB

A PUBLICATION OF THE ALTERNATIVE DISPUTE RESOLUTION DIVISION · COUNCIL OF BETTER BUSINESS BUREAUS

plates. The technique is also used to produce colorful rules, tints, standing headlines and other elements that remain the same issue after issue. Carefully planning preprinting can also yield simulated third and fourth colors.

Future Color:
New Markets/New Technology

Michael H. Bruno's contributions to the graphic arts industry span over 5 decades. His bio is two pages of single spaced achievements, illustrating he is indeed the "Babe Ruth" of the printing industry. Mike received his degree in chemistry from Yale in 1931. His professional career has included research management, technical services, troubleshooting, conference planning, lecturing, teaching, writing, editing, publishing and consulting. Mike is also the editor of the Pocket Pal, *published by International Paper Company since 1934.* Pocket Pal *is the standard industry reference for anyone connected with graphic arts. Currently, Mr. Bruno publishes a newsletter, provides consulting services, and writes an annual report on the status of printing.*

When we spoke with Mike, we asked about recent developments in short run, four color printing using Postscript files — more specifically, we asked him about Presstek (Refer to our Summer 1990 issue of Ligature) and their direct-to-plate imaging technology.

Bruno: One of the things that has really fascinated me about Presstek is the fact that they can run without water. It's the ink/water balance that separates the men from the boys (or the girls from the women) in the printing industry. An awful lot of experience and skill is required to establish the correct ink/water balance and maintain it during printing.

Lg: And without the ink/water balance, the skill level required is decreased. . .

Bruno: Yes, it's just like letter press then, where you have only the ink, the paper and the plate. So not only is the required skill level lower, but the consistency is much greater. The trouble with using an ink/water balance is that once you stop the press, the balance is destroyed. When you restart the press, you have to re-establish the ink/water balance and it is usually not the same as when you first stopped the press, giving inconsistent results.

Lg: Do you feel the most significant feature of the Presstek press is the fact that it uses no water?

Bruno: Well, that's one. The other is, of course, the character of the plate itself — the fact that lasers aren't used to make the plate.

Lg: Why is that significant?

Bruno: It's different. It's important because the mechanism

for making the plate is a lot less complicated than a laser. It's more mechanical and easier to control.

Lg: What do you think about the quality produced by this new, "waterless" process?

Bruno: It far exceeds my expectations. I have three levels of quality standards: 1) is annual report quality, 2) is magazine, and 3) is newspaper quality. The goal I had set for Presstek is magazine quality and I think it is already beyond that.

Lg: Let's talk about the color market in general. What are your predictions for the color market by the year 1995?

Bruno: Dr. Thomas Dunn (of Dunn Technology, San Diego) has stated that the capacity for color by the year 1995 will be about 5 times what it was in 1990 and that the color market, if it continues as it is now, will only be twice the size of today's market. So, it appears, we're going to have a tremendous over-capacity to produce color.

Lg: Do you agree with Mr. Dunn's figures?

Bruno: I think he may be very close. This is another reason why

Summer 1991

No Film!

This issue of "Ligature" was produced completely electronically all the way to the printing press — a milestone in graphic reproduction! The text was generated using WordPerfect 5.0 on an IBM compatible computer. Photographs were scanned with a Nikon LS-3500 slide scanner, corrected and manipulated with Adobe PhotoShop on a Macintosh computer. Our Flying Colorities logo was created in Adobe Illustrator and the pages were electronically assembled in QuarkXpress. Color proofs were generated on a QMS Colorscript 100. The final file was sent to Digital Quickcolor, Inc. in Laguna Hills, California where it was ripped into CMYK and directly imaged to plate on their Heidelberg-Presstek digital printing press. The major significance here —no film!

Industry Guru Describes Color Breakthrough on the Desktop Horizon

For this issue of Ligature, we talked with Efraim Arazi, the founder of Scitex Corporation, Ltd. and now president and CEO of Electronics For Imaging, Inc. He is an industry pioneer and visionary—a scientist, inventor, and marketeer who specializes in electronic image processing.

Scitex pioneered electronic color imaging in 1968. It is the world leader and innovator of computerized color pre-press for high-quality conventional "long-run" printing.

Arazi's present company, EFI, is developing software and hardware that will enable individuals, businesses, and professional publishers to author, design and print photographic-quality color in text documents. EFI's products are targeted to lower the cost and to lower the skill level required to produce professional-quality color print material, giving desktop publishers access to widespread use of color.

Arazi is aiming at a new market: desktop publishers who are eager for color, but do not now have access to it. His central thrust is

three going to beta testing the first half of '91.

Lg: How long will Post-Script remain a standard?

Arazi: I don't have an answer to that question. PostScript has delivered a solution that the market needed and enabled device-independent black-and-white printing. At EFI we are adding the additional technology that will enable color device-independent printing. We're consistent

copies, because the first page out cost, with just setting up the prepress, makes the page cost too high to get 50 or 100 copies from a commercial printer.

Lg: What about electronic 4-color printing presses—like Presstek?

Arazi: Those are very important releases because they will be very useful to bridge the gap between the electrophotographic and what is known as color xerography and the 10-page-per-minute printers, to offset runs with 2,000-page-per-minute capacity. So we are very excited about that technology and how we can also work with it.

Lg: When will the 40-inch 4-color presses start to convert to electronic?

Autumn 1990

NAME *Ligature*

PUBLISHER L. Grafix, Portland, Oregon

PURPOSE/AUDIENCE Service and marketing to customers

PRODUCTION/PRINTING Four-color process on coated or uncoated paper, depending on the style of illustrations

FORMAT 8½" x 11"; four pages

DESIGN Rich Sanders, Judith Quinn and Terri Thompson

Getting color fancy

The designers of *Ligature*, published by a service bureau, have fun with colors in the vertical nameplate, which changes from issue to issue. The huge letter *L* always forms a background for fanciful images that test the limits of artistic vision and showcase the company's production skills.

Color that hits the slopes

The *Summit Express* nameplate and graphics invite readers to join the colorful world of skiing. Using vibrant colors, the designer captures the freedom and energy that skiers feel on the slopes, and helps readers imagine which trail to hop on and which trees to look out for. Printed on sturdy offset paper, the piece can take abuse either in the mail or as an insert without the images scratching or fading.

NAME *Summit Express*

PUBLISHER Mt. Bachelor Ski Area, Bend, Oregon

PURPOSE/AUDIENCE Service and marketing to customers and the media

PRODUCTION/PRINTING Four-color process on white offset

FORMAT 11" × 17"; four pages

DESIGN Mandala Communications

Compact, simplify and clarify

Readers see the "Asset mix recommendations" graph from several points of view, so the three-dimensional quality of the stacked order lets readers see exactly what applies to them personally. In *Trend Alert*, the large arrows pull readers in quickly to let them know which stocks are hottest. Note how a multicolored newsletter helps the reader make sense of graphs. Timeline graphs are most effective as horizontals, but they make layout tricky when they cross to another page: Always run them on a center spread.

NAME *Royal Trust Money Guide*

PUBLISHER Royal Trust, Toronto, Ontario, Canada

PURPOSE/AUDIENCE Service and marketing to customers

PRODUCTION/PRINTING Four-color process on 50# matte

FORMAT 8½" × 11"; twelve pages

DESIGN Ariad Custom Publishing

NAME *US West Today*

PUBLISHER US West, Englewood, Colorado

PURPOSE/AUDIENCE Service to employees

PRODUCTION/PRINTING Three-color

FORMAT 11" × 17"; four pages

DESIGN US West Communications

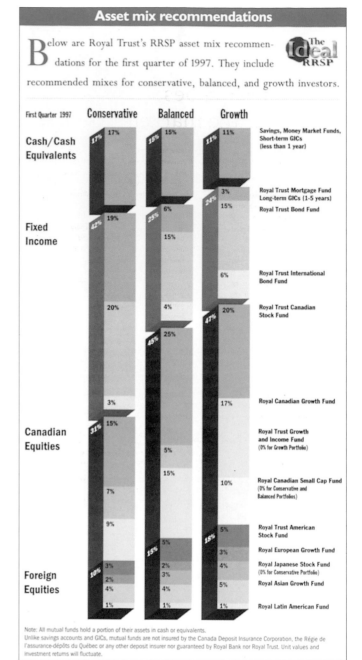

Asset mix recommendations

Below are Royal Trust's RRSP asset mix recommendations for the first quarter of 1997. They include recommended mixes for conservative, balanced, and growth investors.

The Ideal RRSP

First Quarter 1997

	Conservative	Balanced	Growth	
Cash/Cash Equivalents	17%	15%	11%	Savings, Money Market Funds, Short-term GICs (less than 1 year)
Fixed Income	42% / 19%	25% / 6% / 15%	24% / 3% / 15% / 6%	Royal Trust Mortgage Fund / Long-term GICs (1-5 years) / Royal Trust Bond Fund / Royal Trust International Bond Fund
Canadian Equities	31% / 20% / 3% / 15% / 7% / 9%	45% / 4% / 25% / 5% / 15%	47% / 20% / 17% / 10%	Royal Trust Canadian Stock Fund / Royal Canadian Growth Fund / Royal Trust Growth and Income Fund (0% for Growth Portfolio) / Royal Canadian Small Cap Fund (0% for Conservative and Balanced Portfolios)
Foreign Equities	10% / 3% / 2% / 4% / 1%	15% / 5% / 2% / 3% / 4% / 1%	18% / 5% / 3% / 4% / 5% / 1%	Royal Trust American Stock Fund / Royal European Growth Fund / Royal Japanese Stock Fund (0% for Conservative Portfolio) / Royal Asian Growth Fund / Royal Latin American Fund

Note: All mutual funds hold a portion of their assets in cash or equivalents. Unlike savings accounts and GICs, mutual funds are not insured by the Canada Deposit Insurance Corporation, the Régie de l'assurance-dépôts du Québec or any other deposit insurer nor guaranteed by Royal Bank nor Royal Trust. Unit values and investment returns will fluctuate.

TIMELINE TO TEL

1974
Bell System went to Congress with the Consumer Communications Reform Act to try to get new rules written for the industry. The strategy failed to get new rules, but succeeded in drawing attention to the need for new national policy.

From 1984 on, there were legislative efforts r restrictions imposed on the Bell companies. believed that Congress had to set new nation

1975   1980   1985

1984
Divestiture and the business restrictions imposed on the Bell companies b Modified Final Judgment (MFJ) triggered more focus on the industry and r attempts to rewrite the laws.

 Investment Roadmap

TREND ALERT

When is the best time to enter the markets?

By T.A.L. Investment Counsel Ltd.,
Investment Manager of CIBC Mutual Funds

In recent years, capital markets have been booming, while interest rates have relentlessly headed downward. Accordingly, many investors are questioning whether now is a good time to enter the capital markets. Have equities (stocks) and bonds reached their peak? Or is there room for even greater growth?

One school of thought suggests that now is not a good time to invest. Strong equity returns in 1995 and 1996 are seen as the calm before the storm. These theorists argue that interest rates generally move in cycles, so it's only a matter of time before they begin to rise again. Investing in this environment, they say, is the equivalent of getting in at the top, with nowhere to go but down.

Predicting the short-term or medium-term direction of the capital markets with any accuracy is extremely difficult.

Even highly trained economists seldom forecast the short-term direction of the capital markets and the magnitude of the change correctly.

The only thing that can be predicted with any certainty is that, based on historical performance, the long-term direction of the capital markets should be up (see chart below). Disciplined investors who avoid the temptation to time the market see their net worth rise over time.

Your roadmap: The best way to participate in the upside of the capital markets is to hold a balanced mix of investments in the three asset classes — short-term (savings), fixed-income (income), and equities (growth) — in keeping with your investment style. The downside of investing in an asset class that may do poorly in a given year is offset by the possibility that another asset class may do well. Over time, the volatility of your returns eases and you are left with steady, long-term growth.

Interest rates
Yields on 91-day Canada T-bills closed at the end of November at 2.71%, as the Canadian dollar closed strongly at $0.74 U.S. **Forecast:** We expect short-term interest rates to stabilize. There is little room for further declines.

Canadian bonds
Brisk U.S. buying has driven long bond yields down. Thirty-year Government of Canada bonds are on the verge of moving below 6.7%. **Forecast:** We anticipate any movement in bond yields will be sideways from current levels.

Canadian stocks
The TSE 300 has emerged as one of the world's strongest equity markets this year, rising approximately 27.0%. Strong foreign buying has been a large contributing factor. **Forecast:** As long as Canadian interest rates remain subdued, the TSE 300 should continue to outpace the U.S. market.

U.S. stocks
A stable interest rate environment has enabled the Dow Jones Industrial Average to stay in the 6,200-6,500 range. **Forecast:** The current levels can be maintained only if interest rates remain in check.

International stocks
So far, 1996 has seen mixed results from non-North American stocks. European stocks (MSCI-Europe Index) are up 16.5%, while Asian stocks (MSCI-Pacific Index) are down 2.7%. **Forecast:** U.S. interest rate stability will aid foreign markets. Political concerns aside, Hong Kong, in particular, will benefit from the stable U.S. dollar.

Long-term direction of the markets has been up

- TSE 300 Total Return Index $10,437
- ScotiaMcLeod Long-Term Bond Index $2,411
- 91-day Canada Treasury Bills $1,844
- C.P.I. $719

$10,000 / $1,000 / $100
1950 1960 1970 1980 1990 1995

Source: Andex Associates

This chart shows how $100 invested in Treasury bills, long-term bonds, and equities would have grown over the past 25 years. While the returns of the capital markets are volatile, based on historical performance, the long-term trend should be up.

Winter 1997

CIBC NetWorth • 3

NAME *CIBC NetWorth*

PUBLISHER Investors Group, Toronto, Ontario, Canada

PURPOSE/AUDIENCE Service and marketing to customers

PRODUCTION/PRINTING Four-color process on 45# matte

FORMAT 8½" × 11"; four pages, paste binding

DESIGN Ariad Custom Publishing

...ICATIONS REFORM

...e of the ...th parties

1994:
Congress proposed letting all communications companies into all segments of the industry. The House had passed a telecom reform bill by a wide margin and similar legislation was heading to the Senate, but was withdrawn after strong opposition.

1990   **1995**   **1996**

...3-94:
...mission proceedings in some states had opened the local loop to ...petition. U S WEST invested $2.5 billion in Time Warner Entertain-...t. Other mergers began shaping the telecommunications landscape.

1995:
Congress elected in November 1994 introduced bills which win favor of U S WEST and other baby Bells.

Feb. 8, 1996:
President Clinton signed the Telecommunications Act of 1996 into law.

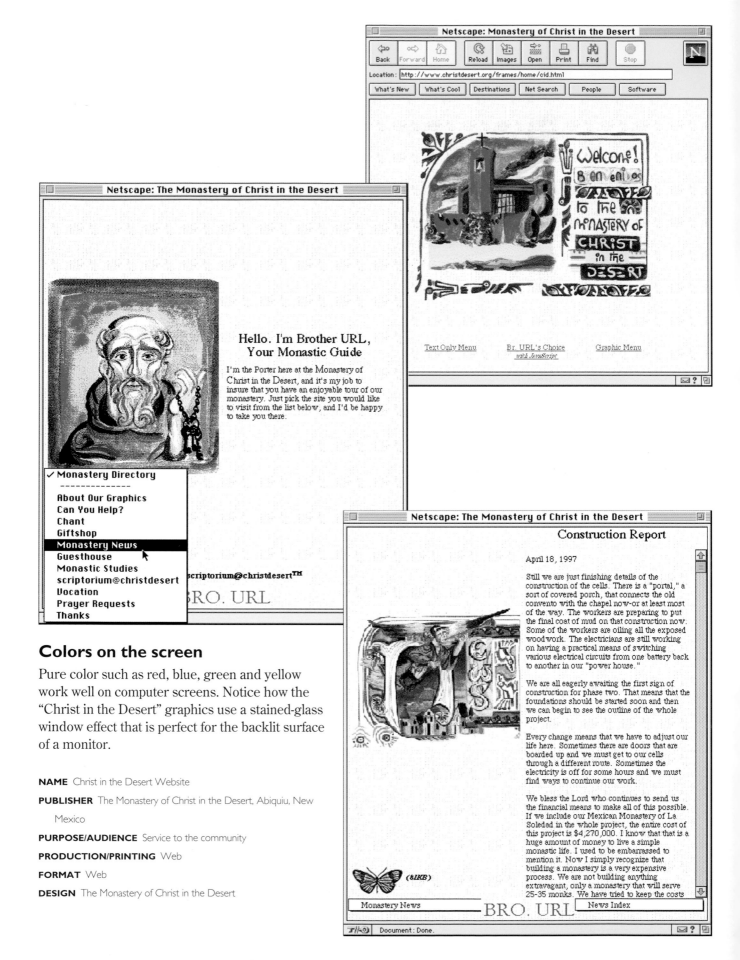

Colors on the screen

Pure color such as red, blue, green and yellow work well on computer screens. Notice how the "Christ in the Desert" graphics use a stained-glass window effect that is perfect for the backlit surface of a monitor.

NAME Christ in the Desert Website

PUBLISHER The Monastery of Christ in the Desert, Abiquiu, New Mexico

PURPOSE/AUDIENCE Service to the community

PRODUCTION/PRINTING Web

FORMAT Web

DESIGN The Monastery of Christ in the Desert

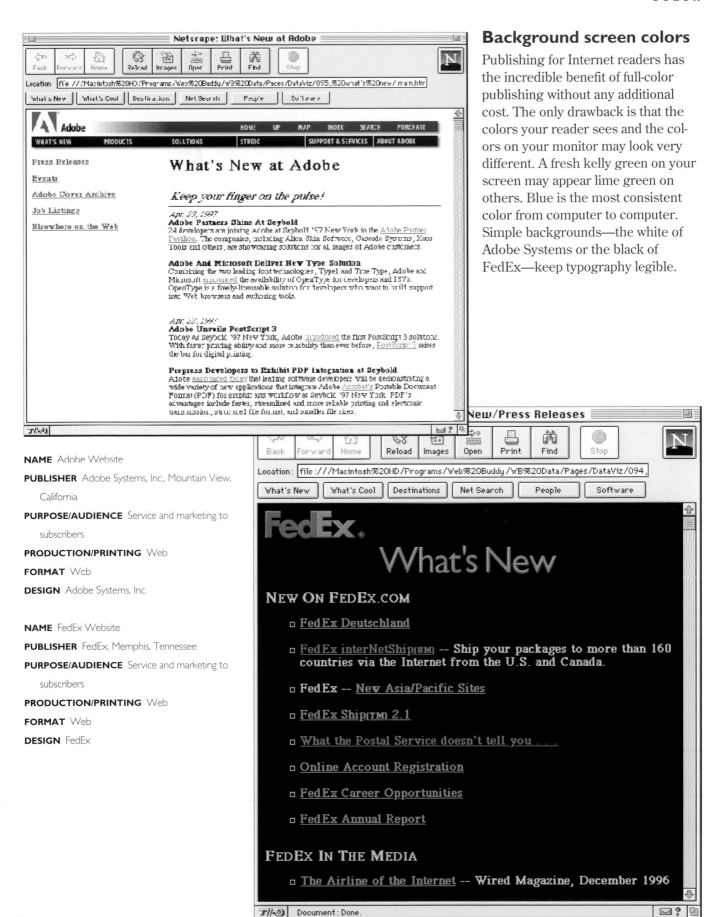

Background screen colors

Publishing for Internet readers has the incredible benefit of full-color publishing without any additional cost. The only drawback is that the colors your reader sees and the colors on your monitor may look very different. A fresh kelly green on your screen may appear lime green on others. Blue is the most consistent color from computer to computer. Simple backgrounds—the white of Adobe Systems or the black of FedEx—keep typography legible.

NAME Adobe Website

PUBLISHER Adobe Systems, Inc., Mountain View, California

PURPOSE/AUDIENCE Service and marketing to subscribers

PRODUCTION/PRINTING Web

FORMAT Web

DESIGN Adobe Systems, Inc.

NAME FedEx Website

PUBLISHER FedEx, Memphis, Tennessee

PURPOSE/AUDIENCE Service and marketing to subscribers

PRODUCTION/PRINTING Web

FORMAT Web

DESIGN FedEx

chapter six

GRAPHICS

Newsletter graphics express, organize or enhance thoughts, ideas and information. They include design elements shown in this chapter, and photographs, illustrations and infographics shown in the next chapter.

Design elements—rules, screen tints, reverses and bleeds—help organize information into effective pieces. Design elements make "visual bites" that are similar to sound bites on radio and television.

RULES. Good newsletter design uses rules extensively to organize information. Whether subtle or bold, they keep the eye of the reader focused on the page and direct attention from one element to the next.

SCREEN TINTS. Also known as shadings and fill patterns, screen tints highlight blocks of type such as mastheads and sidebars. They organize data within calendars and diagrams and, in the hands of experts, add dimension and depth to illustrations.

REVERSES. Because the eye is accustomed to seeing dark type against a light background, reversed type (sometimes known as knockout type) commands special attention. It also presents special problems. Copy requiring more than a few seconds to read and type smaller than 11 points or with fine serifs, should never be reversed. Reverses call for strong contrast with the background, so this technique should not be used with screen tints less than 50 percent.

BLEEDS. Printing ink up to the edge of the page magnifies the advantage of color and provides a canvas for other graphic elements such as tints and rules. Because bleeds require slightly oversized paper and, in some cases, larger presses, they also increase costs.

Good designers use graphic elements consistently. Newsletter readers see the elements on front pages and meet them again on inside pages, and in the process learn to recognize visual cues.

Good graphics for newsletters can be found in many different clip art collections. To find images online, use the following instructions:

For large clip art collections, search using the keywords *clip art*. The biggest sites usually come up first.

For specific images, include the name of the image you want along with the keywords *clip art*. Put the subject of your desired image in quotation marks to narrow the search.

Many online searches find low-resolution clip art designed for the Web, not for print. Look for companies offering a choice of image format and delivery options—CD-ROM, disk, download or e-mail.

marketing yourself with wellness

Christina Samycia
President
Wellness Innovations

Does good health need to be high tech?

We are inundated with high tech ideas that promise us a slimmer and healthier body. We take chromium picolinate, antioxidants, and amino acids. We work-out on machines that claim to burn fat fast and work every muscle in our body with less time and effort.

The health and fitness industry is sending us the message that being healthy is a complex and expensive process. We're spending millions of dollars trying new methods for becoming healthy and losing weight, but failing to accomplish one important goal: a healthier society. Despite our efforts and money, our society is heading in the opposite direction. The truth is, the average individual is growing more obese and unhealthy. The answer to this problem can't be found with new gadgets, but in simplicity. We need to begin simplifying our lifestyles.

A healthy body needs natural foods, not processed and chemically fortified foods like supplements, pills and powders. A healthy body needs adequate exercise, not particularly on specialized equipment. A healthy body needs a simplified, low stress lifestyle. When you have a healthy body you look radiant, fit, toned and lean because your body is working properly.

The path to good health is in fact very simple. We need to eat more natural foods such as whole grains, vegetables and fruits. Designed to be hunters and gatherers, our bodies respond best to eating smaller portions throughout the day rather than three big meals.

Our bodies function best after receiving adequate exercise. Unfortunately, most of us sit all day, therefore we need to engage in an exercise program such as walking, running or any other cardiovascular activity. Simplifying our lifestyles will also help us reduce the stress we face. Saying "no" to some activities and resting more will aid in achieving good health.

The focus on high tech foods and exercise is creating a larger gap between the fit and unfit. Many individuals who are ill and overweight need the aid of the fitness community but are being shut out because the focus of this industry is too complex. Who needs more complexity? Our lives are already overloaded. The unfit do not need complex nutritional guidelines or complicated exercise routines and equipment. They need simple advice on adopting healthy lifestyles. The focus of the health and fitness industry should not be on discovering high-tech methods, but on educating the public on the basics.

12...BWA

power through communication

Patricia Smith-Pierce, Ph.D.
President, Power Speaking Consultants

Communicating with the technology of video

Using videotape for training or marketing is a good use of technology as a communication tool. It is, however, natural to feel nervous when being videotaped. After all, videotapes can be played over and over again with both glaring and subtle errors recorded for all to see.

How many times have you watched a taped message or presentation that contained annoying distractions such as negative facial expressions, squinting, excessive hand gestures or very little audience eye contact? Didn't you wonder why the person didn't realize the effect of her body language on the camera?

Here are a few helpful hints to remember when you're being videotaped:

Posture—Stand or sit straight ahead with as little slouch as possible. Slouching makes you seated. Gestures can be very distracting.

Stance—Place your feet evenly on the floor, not quite a shoulder width apart. Keep your knees slightly bent so you don't rock or weave.

Clothing—Avoid distracting patterns, jewelry or accessories. Dark suits frame you best and minimize size...cameras do enhance size. Avoid stark white shirts or blouses and red dresses. Medium blue is always a good choice in front of the camera.

It's important to discuss your presentation with the camera-person. Include such things as approximate length, use of visual aids and props such as podium, desk, or chair. If there is a live audience, look at them rather than the camera. Let the camera-person capture your interaction with them.

Most important, remember that you are the expert. It's likely that no one will notice if you make a mistake unless you point

Using line drawings in place of photos, long established in the business world by the *Wall Street Journal*, works well for editorials and articles. Make sure the line drawings don't cross the line to being cartoonish, unless you want to give your newsletter a playful look. The benefit of line drawings is that you gain white space to frame the image.

The Business Woman's

Advantage

An interactive newsletter for women with entrepreneurial spirit

JANUARY/FEBRUARY 1997

Technology... know when to shut down

by
Mershon Shrigley

Being connected is great if you know when to shut down. According to Joe Mullich, the winner of the National Headliners Award for humor writing, "The New Age technology mantra of 'work anytime, anywhere' has really come to mean 'work all the time, everywhere.' Take this new call forwarding service. From 8 am to 9, you can have callers connect to your car phone; from 9 to 5 to your office phone; from 5 to 6 back to your car; and after 6 to your home phone. The service is named the 'Time Manager'. I call it the 'Terminator'...no matter where you go, that thing would be in your rear-view mirror, relentlessly chasing you, giving you no peace."

Waiting for a red light to change? Grab your laptop and crunch that spreadsheet. I'm not kidding...I recently saw an advertisement for a device that fits over your steering wheel to accommodate a laptop. The ad said it was only to be used while the car was parked...yeah, right.

Obviously, some of us need technology to keep technology in check. Joe explains, "There are now 'bozo filters'...computer programs that read e-mail and decide what messages should be forwarded to you. On one level, I miss the days when it took a human receptionist to decide my calls were insignificant enough to be ignored. On another, more profound level...I'll have my bozo filter installed by tomorrow!"

Brian Woerner, director of the mobile and portable radio research group at Virginia Tech, predicts this type of computerized gatekeeping will increase. Phones, for instance, will have embedded intelligence to route business calls after 5 pm to voice mail while calls from our children to the same number will go through.

"Who knows," says Joe, "technology might reach a state that calls from our kids telling us they got an 'A' in chemistry will reach us no matter where we are, while their calls asking for money will be shunted to a prerecorded voice saying, 'This number is out of service.'"

We love to be connected. But to whom or to what are we connecting? Are we managing technology or is technology managing us? Joe comments, "As beepers,

Continued on page 4

TRW Information Systems & Services   **Spring 1992**

Spotlight

TRW

"Eggscellent" employee efforts are put in TRW's spotlight

According to Mr. Webster's book, a spotlight is "a projected spot of light used to illuminate brilliantly a person, object or group on a stage." TRW has set the stage by creating this publication. And in each issue, you'll see the names of a number of Information Systems & Services (IS&S) employees who are standing in the glare of the spotlight.

This newsletter will be produced each quarter to *celebrate* the outstanding efforts and special accomplishments of employees. Since the operative word here is *celebrate,* each issue of *Spotlight* has a theme and the information is generally presented in an upbeat way.

More than 400 employees included

As you can see by our fine feathered friend who's sitting in the spotlight on this page, this springtime issue has a bird theme. You can think of *Spotlight* as your bird's eye view of "eggscellence" at IS&S. In this issue alone, more than 400 employees are being recognized. Perhaps you'll find your own name!

The businesses that came together earlier this year to form the new IS&S organization had significant employee success stories to share and those achievements were recognized and rewarded in a number of ways.

Employee groups are currently examining existing employee recognition and incentive programs to determine the best possible programs for the future. As soon as these programs are ready to come out of the incubator and be hatched, they will be announced to employees. In the future, you'll be able to read about the winners of each new program in *Spotlight*.

But before moving into the new programs, it's essential that employees be honored for their year-end 1991 efforts. This issue of *Spotlight* will do just that.

Your bird's eye view of eggscellence

Perhaps some of the information may seem out of date. But recognition — a pat on the back and the sound of thunderous applause — is always better late than never!

So sit back and relax. You're about see how your co-workers have soared to new heights in their careers. There are no turkeys here. But there's plenty to crow about!

And speaking of crowing, the success of *Spotlight* depends on you. Outstanding achievements will definitely appear in future issues of this newsletter, but there are plenty of opportunities for you to crow about the accomplishments of your co-workers. You can nominate someone as part of a formal recognition program. You can send in copies of the "fan mail" you or your co-workers have received from a satisfied customer or consumer. Or, you can send in information about a community activity — like a blood donation drive or walk-a-thon — your office has participated in.

So keep up the good work. Who knows, if you're not in this issue, you may appear in a future edition. One thing you can "eggspect," though, is the next issue of *Spotlight* will hatch during the summer. ★

Exceptional graphics for exceptional employees

Spotlight showcases employee excellence. The consistent graphic accompaniment of the feathered creatures gives this newsletter a playful look and fun appeal.

NAME *Spotlight*

PUBLISHER Experian, Orange, California

PURPOSE/AUDIENCE Service to employees

PRODUCTION/PRINTING Two-color on cream, fiber-flecked 70# recycled offset

FORMAT 8½" × 11"; twelve pages

DESIGN Christopher Lentz, Experian

Matching color to audience

A bubble gum-tinted illustration layout, which would seem overdone for an adult audience, is just right for *Free Spirit* readers ages ten to fourteen. This newsletter's large format and sturdy paper make it easy to find in the incoming mail, and also announce to others in the household that the recipient is special for getting such a big package.

NAME *Free Spirit*

PUBLISHER Free Spirit Publishing, Inc., Minneapolis, Minnesota

PURPOSE/AUDIENCE Service to subscribers (youth ages ten to fourteen)

PRODUCTION/PRINTING Two-color on white 60# offset

FORMAT 11" × 17"; eight pages

DESIGN Rick Korab, Punch Design

Creating many colors

Each issue of *Free Spirit* is printed in only two ink colors. Skillful use of screen tints in the illustrations, many of which overlap to create color builds, produces the illusion of many colors. Black and the second color can each print in 10 percent, 20 percent and 30 percent tints, as well as running solid. Each of these tints can combine with any other tint, resulting in a palette of nine color builds.

6

Environmental Sins of Borrowers May Be Laid on Lenders, Say Experts

Several bankers, lawyers, and community planners participating in a recent Federal Reserve Bank of Cleveland research conference urged caution to those who would finance urban redevelopment projects. "Fifteen years ago," says James B. Witkin, partner at the Washington., D.C., law firm of Content, Tatusko, and Patterson, "environmental issues were

"Lenders have become aware of the impact of environmental matters on their loans, and have modified their lending practices accordingly."

not a concern to those involved in real estate development and redevelopment projects.

"In the intervening years, however, laws have been enacted that dramatically changed the liabilities of the parties involved in such transactions."

Witkin, along with Nicholas E. Darrow, vice president of the Middle Market Group of Mellon Bank, N.A., and Robert B. Jaquay, manager of Program Planning for the Cuyahoga (Ohio) County Planning Commission, discussed lender liability at the Cleveland Fed's recent conference on "The Environment and Economic Development in the Great Lakes."

Superfund Liability

According to Witkin, current environmental liability problems began for lenders with the enactment of the Comprehensive Environmental Response, Compensation, and Liability Act of 1980, which is known as CERCLA or Superfund. "Superfund established a program to identify and clean up sites where hazardous substances have been discharged, and to allocate the costs of cleanups to responsible parties," says

Witkin. "Responsible parties could include current owners, owners or operators at the time of a hazardous dumping, any person who arranged for the disposal or treatment of the waste, or any person who transported the waste."

Because the law imposes liability regardless of fault, and because the liability under Superfund is legally "joint and several" - that is, a company or an individual may be held liable for the entire cleanup of a site, not just its proportionate share - Witkin says Superfund has developed a draconian reputation. He cites a recent survey by the Independent Bankers Association of America (IBAA) in which 86 percent of those bankers surveyed said Superfund affected their lending policies and 21 percent said that their bank had experienced a loss or default due to environmental impact.

"About the only protection provided to lenders affected by Superfund is the secured creditor exemption," says Witkin. "Several cases appear to hold that a secured creditor could be held liable under Superfund only if it had actual and active involvement in the debtor's day-to-day operations of a Superfund site." This protection, however, holds only against certain legal liabilities associated with Superfund, but

7

not against other federal or state environmental laws, and not against the risk of a decline in the value of the lenders' collateral due to environmental impairment.

"Lenders have become aware of the impact of environmental matters on their loans, and have modified their lending practices accordingly," comments Witkin. "Certain types of businesses, such as service stations and convenience stores with underground gasoline tanks, have reported that it has become extremely difficult for them to obtain loans, regardless of their creditworthiness, solely due to lenders' concerns over environmental liabilities."

Lenders' Concerns

Darrow of Mellon Bank agrees with Witkin's assessment of how seriously bankers are taking their potential environmental liability. "Given the industrial heritage of much of the Great Lakes region," he comments, "the growth of this liability has been a major concern to lenders."

Darrow says the risks for lenders include:
- Potential liability of the lender itself as an owner/occupier of contaminated property;
- Cash flow impact of enforcement actions on the borrower, because that may affect repayment;
- Potential deterioration of collateral values; and
- Potential establishment of a prior lien position on the borrower's assets by an administrative agency such as the state, which would place the lender in a secondary position on collateral assets pledged to back the credit.

Darrow notes that lenders have responded to these risks by adopting more conservative lending practices. These practices may include doing environmental assessments, establishing guidelines for the minimum qualifications of those who perform these assessments, requiring internal responses depending on the outcome of the assessments, and outlining the steps that should be taken prior to foreclosure on real property.

"In addition to the due diligence steps taken in a real-estate-backed

transaction, lenders are now requesting other assurances," says Darrow. "These may include the use of environmental covenants and representations and warranties in the underlying loan documents. Lenders may obligate borrowers to notify them about environmental contamination or to submit to periodic environmental audits."

Darrow says if lenders cannot accept the potential risks and costs in a project, and if those risks cannot be allocated elsewhere, financing would be unlikely. "In the Great Lakes region, where contaminates may have reached the groundwater, for instance, arranging financing will be very difficult, unless the lender is satisfied that it is not put at undue risk."

For more information on lender liability for environmental problems, call the Public Affairs and Bank Relations Department at 1-800-543-3489 to order "Reducing Lender Risks to Environmental Liability," a packet of information prepared by Jeffrey A. Lange, policy advisor in the Banking Supervision and Regulation Department of the Federal Reserve Bank of Cleveland.

White space frames illustrations

Generous white space lends a classic uncluttered look to the entire publication while drawing the eye to headlines and pull quotes. Three columns blend well with large illustrations, which by themselves are strong enough to bring readers into the stories.

NAME *Fourth District Focus*

PUBLISHER Federal Reserve Bank of Cleveland, Cleveland, Ohio

PURPOSE/AUDIENCE Service and marketing to customers

PRODUCTION/PRINTING Two-color on white 70# offset

FORMAT 8½" x 11"; eight pages

DESIGN Federal Reserve Bank of Cleveland

SMOKE GETS IN YOUR EYES -- AND LUNGS

Call it what you will: second-hand smoke or passive smoke. The smoke puffed into the air by cigar, pipe and cigarette smokers hits kids the hardest.

Because youngsters breathe in more air for their body weight than adults do, they can be especially susceptible to diseases caused by second-hand smoke, according to Joel M. Seidman, M.D., chief of Pulmonary Medicine at Memorial.

Dr. Seidman conducts annual anti-smoking programs for youngsters in local schools and has spoken before the Westborough School Committee on the benefits of smoke-free schools.

It's a sensitive issue, Dr. Seidman acknowledges, but adds, "Last year, 600,000 Americans died from smoking-related illnesses. For every pack of cigarettes sold, it cost the taxpayer $2.17 for medical care."

Dr. Seidman urges that it's time to clear the air -- and schools are an excellent place to start. Today's children face a number of health risks from exposure to second-hand smoke, and the truth about the diseases and complications that can result are frightening--

* Toxic effects of passive smoke are transmitted to unborn children by *both* parents. A pregnant woman who smokes passes toxic chemicals directly through her bloodstream to the fetus, which can result in low birth-weight, congenital malfor-

mations and even death. A man who smokes in the presence of his pregnant partner (even if she *doesn't* smoke) also increases these risks.

* Mothers who smoke have a greater negative effect on the health of their children than fathers who smoke because they generally spend more time together.

* There is a strong correlation between children under the age of two hospitalized for pneumonia and the number of smokers in a household.

* Children exposed to second-hand smoke experience a higher number of chest illnesses (pneumonia, bronchitis and other respiratory tract diseases) than children in non-smoking households.

* Exposure to passive smoke negatively affects a child's normal pulmonary function, increasing

wheezing, allergies to smoke and aggravating already existing conditions such as asthma.

* Children of a parent who smokes have been found to have more colds than those who live

with non-smokers, which often results in more missed school days.

* Up to 36% of middle ear infections in children four years old and younger are attributed to passive smoke exposure.

Let's clear the air and do something about passive smoking -- before our children's health goes up in smoke.

> As a leader in health care, The Medical Center of Central Massachusetts seeks a healthy environment for all patients, visitors, employees, staff members, volunteers and students, and has become "smoke free" as of 1990. Smoking is the leading preventable cause of death and disease in America, and a fire and safety hazard. Smoking is recognized as having potentially damaging effects not only to the smoker but to those exposed to tobacco smoke.
>
> To learn more about smoking cessation classes, call Public Relations, 792-8587.

3

Art enhances news

In a perfect blend of size and placement, the drawing of the cigarette enhances the story and helps frame the page. Letting the smoke drift up into the rule and type puts action into the art and leads the eye right to the sidebar that invites readers to learn how to quit smoking. Notice also the headline type, which uses large and small caps to create a sophisticated look.

NAME *Progress Notes*

PUBLISHER The Medical Center of Central Massachusetts, Worcester, Massachusetts

PURPOSE/AUDIENCE Service to the community and the media

PRODUCTION/PRINTING Two-color on 60# offset (light gray with green-tinted fibers)

FORMAT 8½" x 11"; four pages

DESIGN Susan Rich and Ann Godd

Consistent illustration style

Colors transform large woodcut illustrations into memorable art, a signature style that is consistent issue after issue. Heavy flecked paper and different combinations of two colors plus black throughout each issue help make this marketing newsletter welcome for Syva customers. Note also the extra leading for ragged-right body type, which makes text seem both elegant and friendly.

NAME *Syvamonitor*

PUBLISHER Syva Company, San Jose, California

PURPOSE/AUDIENCE Service and marketing to customers

PRODUCTION/PRINTING Three-color on 70# recycled offset

FORMAT 8½" x 11"; sixteen pages

DESIGN Mortensen Design

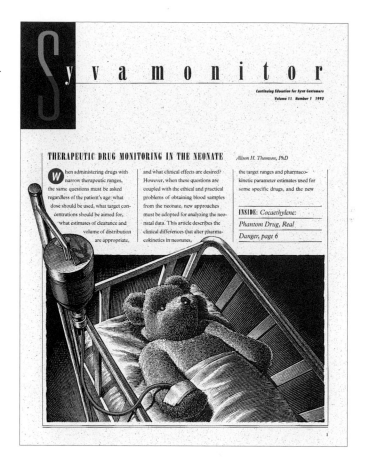

MANAGING CHANGE
POSITIONING FOR REFORM

By James C. Creus, Samaritan president and chief executive officer
Editor's note: The following article was recently published in **Viewpoint**, *the magazine of the Arizona Hospital Association.*

One can follow the evolution of the health care industry by the phrases and acronyms that have become a part of our everyday vocabulary. Those phrases describe where we've been, what we're going through and give us an indication of where we're headed.

Phrases like quality patient care, community support, philanthropy, billed charges, fee-for-service, volunteerism, charitable service and others described our industry in the pre-Medicare days. Acronyms were not used because they weren't needed and the only reference to government was the two word phrase Hill-Burton.

In the post-Medicare period, we have gone through a broad spectrum of phrases and acronyms; in fact, this was the birth of the acronym period. We experienced cost-based reimbursement, COBRAS, SOBRAS, CON, usual and customary, HMOs, PPOs, PHOs, IPAs, capitation, DRGs, RBRVs and many more. It was during this period that many of us learned that a paradigm wasn't twenty cents after all.

Now that we've memorized all these catchy little phrases and weird alphabet configurations, like Murphy's Law No. 667, somebody's out to change it again. We're hearing about health care reform, managed competition, NHBs, HIPCs, AHPs, IDSs and, undoubtedly, we will learn many more.

There are two frightening messages in this evolutionary recap. First, it didn't occur over several generations. It happened during my health care career span. Second, in 1997, we'll look back on 1992 as "the good old days."

In the initial period described above, the health care system was relatively simple, neat and orderly. Hospitals predominantly provided inpatient care, physicians provided medical care and insurance companies paid for it. Each party had a role, played that role and knew its place. There was order.

In the transition period (the one we're in now), we see complexity and disor-

> *In the initial period, the health care system was relatively simple, neat and orderly. In the transition period, we see complexity and disorder.... Our challenge...is to anticipate what reform will look like and to position our organizations to be successful participants when it arrives.*

der. Insurance companies are also in the hospital and doctor business, doctors are also in the facility business and hospitals are also in the insurance business. This is what is known as competition. After all, early critics complained that the health care industry was too "cottage like" and should become more "business like." This period brought with it a new set of tensions between these two groups of players, plus the introduction of a new and forceful player, Uncle Sam.

Each of these periods presented, or will present, different challenges or (as consultants would say) opportunities to health care executives. This transition from a cottage industry to a business-like industry was difficult for many to make. In fact, we all know of colleagues who couldn't and didn't make the transition and lost their jobs and, in some cases, their careers.

The management skills necessary for skillful leadership in our business changed from period to period. In the early period, the principal prerequisites for an administrator to be successful were to constantly wear a smile and provide enough beds and equipment to keep the medical staff content. An operating budget, if one existed, was deemed satisfactory if it were net plus or minus two percent, and planning involved predicting where the organization would be next Friday.

Now, a principal requirement of health care (hospital or system) executives is the ability to successfully manage change. There are two types of change managers which, of course, carry their own acronyms. The RCM (retrospective change manager) is the individual who observes that a major event has occurred in the marketplace and has passed him/her by. The management phrase used most frequently by this group is "whoops" and is usually followed by a mad scramble to catch up. The PCM (prospective change manager) is one who has a vision of what future changes are likely to occur, and who will lead constituent groups to share a common vision and then position the organization to respond to the changes when they occur.

What's the next period going to look like and what are the critical factors for success? Public opinion polls consistently show us that the majority of the American public want health care reform. Most of us involved in health care, including managers, physicians, insurers and employers expect major reform, yet nobody's crystal ball has a clear image of what it is going to look like. Many people, however, have a clear and vocal position on what they want it to look like.

Our challenge, as health care executives, is to anticipate what reform will look like and to position our organizations to be successful participants when it arrives. Since most of one are not clairvoyant and therefore cannot precisely describe the reform model, we must use our best judgement to select the key components which are likely to be included in some fashion.

Reform will likely include these five components: integration of physicians and hospitals into an integrated delivery system, risk assumption, information requirements, cost control and utilization management. Once the components are defined, the PCM will:

- determine where the organization needs to be, with respect to each component;
- inventory where the organization currently is with respect to each;
- determine if the organization has the capabilities to achieve each component alone, or if it needs to be a partner with some other source;
- along with the identified partners, develop an action plan to address each component.

Once the components have been addressed and an action plan in place, the organization will be positioned to respond to reform. The difference between the final reform packages and the organization will then be a matter of refinement. Knowing what to do is the easier part. The organization's preparation and ability to execute its strategy will determine success, whatever form reform takes.

Reporters asked the late Vince Lombardi why he allowed the media to attend the Green Bay Packers' practice session when their plays and strategies could become public. Lombardi said, "With game films and scouting, everybody knows what we're going to do. Our ability to execute will determine whether or not we win." ST

Making illustrations big

Most of *Samaritan Today* appears in black ink only, but this newsletter uses almost every design technique possible to create dramatic pages. Tints appear in ovals and circles, type and illustrations break up long lines, and columns run around oval pull quotes. Bold art bleeding off the pages lets the designer depart from the three-column grid used in the rest of the publication.

NAME *Samaritan Today*

PUBLISHER Samaritan Health System, Phoenix, Arizona

PURPOSE/AUDIENCE Service to employees and volunteers

PRODUCTION/PRINTING Two-color on 60# offset

FORMAT 11" × 17"; twenty pages

DESIGN Marie Jones, Samaritan Design Center

Using graduated screens

To create the unique step index, the designers of *Hemisfile* used graduated tints of the second ink color. Printing is on 25" x 38" sheets, the basic size for text paper. Each parent sheet yields four newsletter sheets. When trimmed to 11¾" x 17⅝", all sheets bleed along the index edge. The six visible edges are created by folding each sheet in a different place: Collated sheets shingle to form the step index.

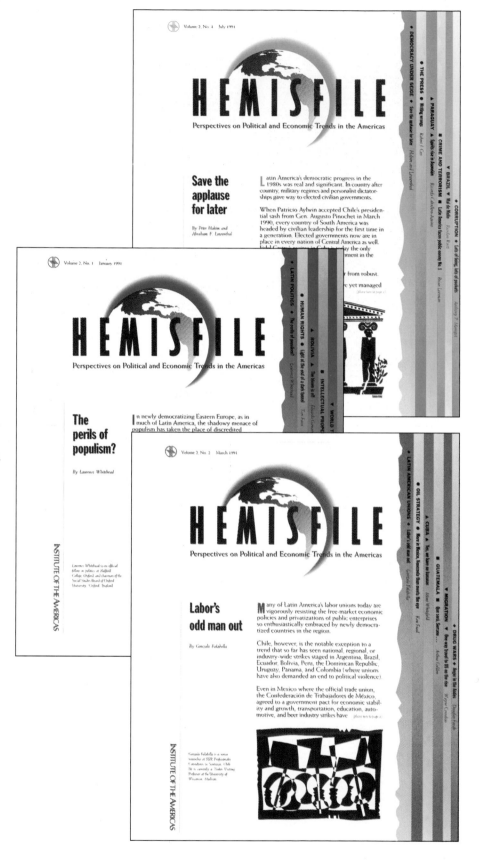

One-way travel to US on the rise

By Wayne Cornelius

More in Mexico, Venezuela than meets the eye

By Kim Fuad

A jump start — at long last?

By Carlos A. Primo Braga

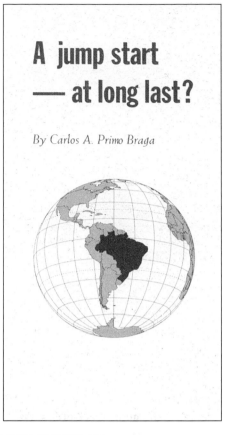

A new player in the oil and gas field

By Kim Fuad

Color in infographics

Hemisfile tells readers what country a story features by showing it on a map in a second color. Used consistently throughout every issue, the maps form a series of visual standing headlines. Each gets instant recognition.

Instead of using photos, *Hemisfile* uses illustrations by David Dias to create the mood for key stories. The distinctive style of the drawings asserts that the publication is authoritative and in tune with the geographic regions on which it reports.

NAME *Hemisfile*

PUBLISHER Institute of the Americas, La Jolla, California

PURPOSE/AUDIENCE Service to members of the Institute

PRODUCTION/PRINTING Two-color on chalk-white 70# text

FORMAT 9½" × 11¾"; twelve pages

DESIGN Jeffrey Carmel and Karen Abrams, Benelli Design

Big thirst

Water covers three-fifths of the Earth's surface, so why not give it a big chunk of a page? The tabloid size of *The Technology Monitor* lets the designer make this illustration big. The size also keeps the text on the labels legible, allowing the reader to follow along with the article's comparison of brands of bottled water.

NAME *The Technology Monitor*

PUBLISHER Cadbury Beverages Technical Center, Trumbull, Connecticut

PURPOSE/AUDIENCE Service to employees, vendors and customers

PRODUCTION/PRINTING Three-color on 70# offset

FORMAT 11" × 17"; four pages

DESIGN Wiggin Design, Inc., Darien, Connecticut

the Technology monitor

#2 — Winter 1993

· · · A COMMUNICATION FROM THE **CADBURY BEVERAGES** TECHNICAL CENTER · · ·

Water: It's not all the same stuff.

FIRST IN A SERIES This is the first of a series of articles about water. Succeeding articles will focus on the various bottled waters that Cadbury Beverages markets throughout the world, and on some of the different treatments that make the water acceptable for use in our beverages.

OUR MOST PRECIOUS RESOURCE

Water covers more than three-fifths of the world's surface. Like most natural resources, no new water is being formed. However, unlike our other natural resources, very little water is being lost, so essentially, there is the same amount of water now as when the earth was just created.

Water is constantly being recycled by the earth's weather systems. As water passes through the earth it picks up various minerals and salts. The amount it picks up varies with the strata of earth through which it passes. When bottled, the source and the mineral content define the water and determine how it may be labeled.

The market for bottled water in the United States has tripled in volume during the past ten years. The many reasons for this growth include a perceived decline in the quality of tap water, the fact that with zero calories bottled water is the ultimate diet drink, and the general trend in our society away from consumption of alcoholic beverages.

We make a clear distinction between sparkling bottled waters, which are consumed as a refreshment beverage, and non-sparkling bottled waters, which are consumed as a source of drinking water. The sparkling bottled waters usually have a hint of flavor. Also, club sodas and seltzer waters are usually considered soft drinks, not bottled waters, because they are not naturally carbonated.

The various types of non-sparkling bottled waters sold in the USA are:

DRINKING WATER

Drinking water is a bottled water obtained from an approved, potable source, such as a municipal water supply. It will have undergone filtration and been treated with ozone or an equivalent disinfection process.

PURIFIED WATER

Purified water is bottled water produced by distillation, deionization, reverse osmosis or other suitable process. These processes will be described later in this series on water.

NATURAL WATER

Natural water is bottled spring, mineral, artesian well or well water coming from underground, and not from a municipal water supply.

The photo shows some of the many varieties of bottled water marketed by Cadbury Beverages' divisions around the world.

SAM STATS

A look at statistics that shape our industry.

POINTING THE FINGER

Who is the most responsible for
the high cost of health care?

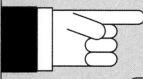

Hospitals say:
The government-28%
New technology/
equipment-15%

Source: National Research Corp. su

SAM STATS

A look at statistics that shape quality patient care.

KEEP IT CLEAN

DSMC's Mater-
ials Manage-
ment dept.
sterilized more
than **9,937**
instrument
sets, single
instruments &
other sterile
items in

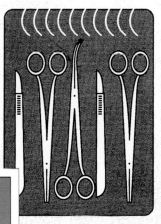

gement

FASTFACT

Statistics about MU facilities, activities, and people

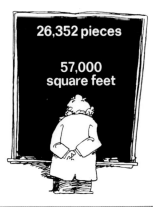

26,352 pieces

57,000
square feet

Chalk used at
MU every year

Chalkboard
erased by
custodians
every day

NAME *Facilities Focus*

PUBLISHER University of Missouri—Columbia

PURPOSE/AUDIENCE Service to the university
community

PRODUCTION/PRINTING Two-color on white
60# offset

FORMAT 11" x 17"; four pages

DESIGN Marcia K. Lindberg, University of Missouri

FASTFACT

Statistics about MU facilities, activities, and people

Total Annual Construction
From 1987-1997

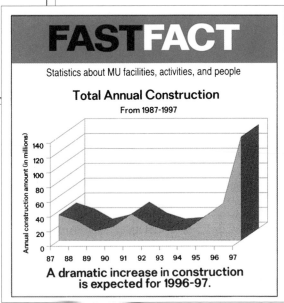

**A dramatic increase in construction
is expected for 1996-97.**

Bite-size data

The "Sam Stats" infographics that
appear throughout the publication
present morsels of data that readers
might not otherwise ingest. Giving
each statistical capsule its own subhead helps introduce the data and
invites readers to inspect the visual.
Using only black ink in solid and
screen tints is economical as well as
effective.

The "Fast Fact" appearing on the
front page of each issue of *Facilities
Focus* either illustrates an accompanying article, as in "Total Annual
Construction," or stands alone, such
as the quantity of chalk used at
Missouri University.

NAME *Samaritan Today*

PUBLISHER Samaritan Health System, Phoenix,
Arizona

PURPOSE/AUDIENCE Service to employees and
volunteers

PRODUCTION/PRINTING Two-color on 60#
offset

FORMAT 11" x 17"; twenty pages

DESIGN Marie Jones, Samaritan Design Center

Finding graphics online

There's help on the Web for harried editors in search of illustrations for their pages. Sites such as this one from Image Club Graphics let you preview illustrations and download Adobe Acrobat files for better viewing. Many sites have options where you can buy the online images and download them to your computer.

NAME www.imageclub.com

PUBLISHER Image Club Graphics, Mountain View, California

PURPOSE/AUDIENCE Service and marketing to subscribers

PRODUCTION/PRINTING Web

FORMAT Web

DESIGN Image Club Graphics

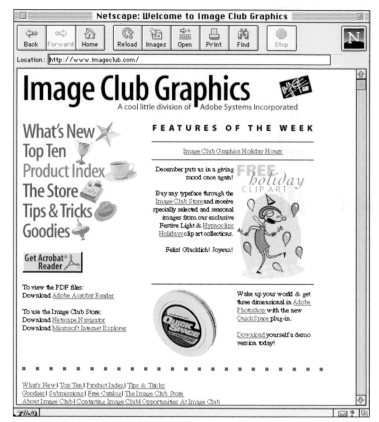

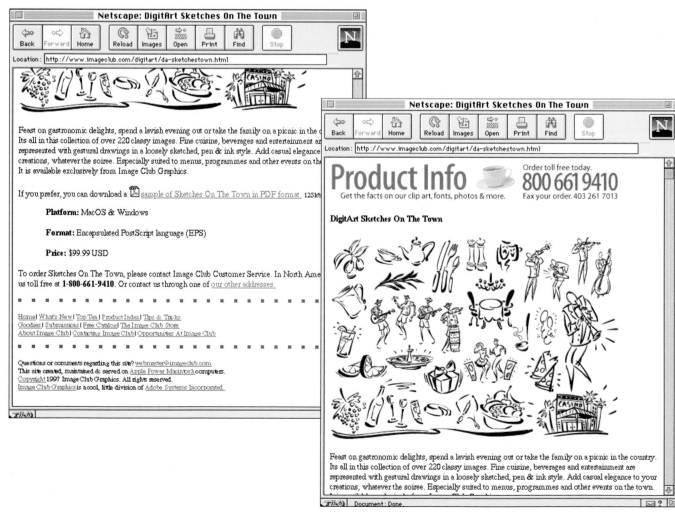

"Repurposing" graphics

With publication-cycle times moving from weeks to days to hours, graphics are often created once and saved immediately in a variety of formats for fax, color printing, Web or black-and-white use. Note the resolution difference when *Publish* magazine uses the photo montage for its process-color cover and its opening screen of the website. The Web graphics are much grainier (72 dots per inch), turning the soft lighting and shadows into pointillism.

NAME *Publish* magazine and the RGB Website

PUBLISHER *Publish* magazine, San Francisco, California

PURPOSE/AUDIENCE Service and marketing to subscribers

PRODUCTION/PRINTING Web

FORMAT Web

DESIGN *Publish* and Publish RGB Design Teams

chapter seven

PHOTOGRAPHS AND ILLUSTRATIONS

Designers use illustrations in newsletters to touch emotions, establish image and convey information.

Photographs

Effective photos for publication are made, not taken. Whether the photographer uses professional studio equipment or a pocket camera, the image serves a clear editorial goal.

Readers prefer photos to illustrations because they think of photos as "real" and illustrations as made up.

Photos often work better than words to capture emotions. A good photographer can see feelings behind the words and capture those feelings in a dynamic photo. It is important to work with the best photos you can get, because even a master designer or printer can do little to turn a drab photo into a dynamic image.

Good design controls photos technically as well as editorially. The following pages show how to plan and combine well-exposed photos with specifications for screen rulings and paper surfaces to yield the best possible results.

In addition to controlling contrast, designers crop photos for drama, and frame them to ensure that the message is highlighted. Frames are most often devised by printing key-lines, but images may also be enhanced by reversing the halftone out of a light screen tint. The following pages include several examples of this technique.

Illustrations

Clip art and infographics are two common types of newsletter illustration. Clip art was first developed for display advertising in newspapers—not editorial matter in newsletters. Use it sparingly and carefully. Several newsletters in the following pages reveal expert use of clip art.

Software lets you transform clip art into unique images, using the original art only as a starting point. Many illustrations in this section reveal that skill, redefining the meaning of art and the function of the artist.

Infographics are the most important form of illustration for newsletters. Charts, maps and diagrams portray key data far more efficiently and memorably than when the same data described using words.

Captions

Keep in mind that readers look at captions before headlines. Make sure that every image has a caption that includes information vital to your story.

150-line screen

120-line screen

One photo, many dances

Modern photos get twirled and spun all over the place. The original photo is scanned and screened at 120 lines for reproduction in a four-color brochure. The same photo is converted to black and white and screened at 120 lines for a one-color newsletter. Back at the original color file, the image is saved at 72 dots-per-inch for use on a webpage. Next, the black and white version is given a coarse 65-line screen for a fax transmission.

120-line screen halftone

72 dpi for use on a webpage

65-line screen for a fax transmission

Mug shot design

By using a uniform background, tonal range, body positioning, cropping and relative sizes, this photo collection looks good on the page. These photos of the members of the Board of Advisors add both authority and personality to the masthead design, a space that often seems routine.

NAME *Total Quality*

PUBLISHER Lakewood Publications, Minneapolis, Minnesota

PURPOSE/AUDIENCE Service to subscribers

PRODUCTION/PRINTING Two-color on white 60# offset

FORMAT 8½" x 11"; eight pages

DESIGN Mark Simonson, Brian McDermott and Julie Tilka

Photos that direct the eye

Much forethought went into the photographs for this issue. The image on the front page creates a strong diagonal pattern that works well against the opposing diagonal of the shadow-lettered nameplate. On page 6, the mug shots are sharply focused, all in the same contrast range and all taken from the same angle.

NAME *Mutual Matters*

PUBLISHER CUNA Mutual Insurance Group, Madison, Wisconsin

PURPOSE/AUDIENCE Service to employees

PRODUCTION/PRINTING Two-color on white 70# gloss coated

FORMAT 8½" x 11"; eight pages

DESIGN Jo-Dee Benson and Ralph Denu

Employee Service

June Anniversaries

20 years: A. Jack Heartburg, North West; Vernon Lowell, MemberElect® Coverages; Mary Weichbrod, Collateral Insurance Center; Patrick Young, Finance and Administration, Southfield; Paul Butz, CUMIS PL Underwriting

25 years: Richard Bullington, Pomona; Price Legg, Field Operations; Frederic Nobles, South East

June Retirements

Jeanne Orvold, Real Estate; Norma Moyer, International Commons; Sylvia Heiser, CUMIS Claims; Evangeline Schneider, Quality Commitment; Betty Abramson, Pomona

July Anniversaries

20 years: David Lister, PLAN AMERICA®; Alberta Sullivan, Quality Commitment

30 years: Phillis Walmer, Employee Benefits Claims; Bertha Klemm, Quality Commitment

July Retirements

Barbara Johnsen, Medical; Robert Brokaw, North Central

A. Jack Heartburg
20 Years

Vernon Lowell
20 Years

Paul Butz
20 Years

Richard Bullington
25 Years

Norma Moyer
Retirement

Sylvia Heiser
Retirement

Betty Abramson
Retirement

David Lister
20 Years

Alberta Sullivan
20 Years

Phyllis Walmer
30 Years

Bertha Klemm
30 Years

Barbara Johnsen
Retirement

Robert Brokaw
Retirement

Combine photos with pull quotes

A small mug shot can be embellished with framing that includes a byline and a pull quote from the person in the photo. The effect makes the image speak, while also making the image seem larger.

Route To:

☐ _____
☐ _____
☐ _____
☐ File

Insight & Opportunity™

MARKETING IDEAS FROM STRATEGIES FOR GROWTH

Listen More, Sell More!

by Gilbert Effron

The more you listen, the more you learn. The more you learn, the better able you are to help your prospects, clients or customers...

A captive audience doesn't necessarily mean a listening audience.

In today's business environment, selling is more listening than talking. And getting your customer or prospect to listen to what you have to say requires careful listening on your part.

But the payoff is worth it.

It doesn't matter if you're running a retail business, servicing automobiles, selling insurance or manufacturing goop, the rule is the same: The more you listen, the more you learn. The more you learn, the better able you are to help your prospects or customers.

When you listen, you're creating a meaningful dialog. In a way, you actually become more of a consultant than a salesperson.

The rule for dialog when you're in this selling mode is simple. You talk 25 percent of the time. Let your prospect talk the other 75 percent.

As you do, learn to answer a question with a question. The questions you ask are as much for your prospect's or customer's benefit as they are for yours. It brings his needs right out into the open — where *he* can see them.

When you think you're running out of new prospects, there's probably not

A captive audience may not be a listening audience.

Please see "Listen" page four

Summer 1994

Staging photos

A staged image may be the best way to reinforce the story. Even with the added costs in time and money, the image could tell much more than words can say. Note how the sizing of this photo adds humor to the image.

NAME *Insight & Opportunity*

PUBLISHER Strategies for Growth, Inc., Dunedin, Florida

PURPOSE/AUDIENCE Service and marketing to customers

PRODUCTION/PRINTING Four-color process on 70# gloss-coated

FORMAT 8½" × 11"; four pages

DESIGN Strategies for Growth, Inc.

Child Development

Continued From Page 1

Potthast on doctor and hospital visits. Mrs. Potthast also received counseling at home from Child Development Counselor **Lynn Smart**.

The prognosis is excellent. Liske anticipates that Lucia will attend a community preschool without the program's assistance, and one day will be able to read regular-size print.

Four-year-old **Scott MacIntyre** was diagnosed as having retinitis pigmentosa approximately one year ago; this has left him with tunnel vision. In addition to a child development consultant's home visits, Scott and his younger brother **Todd** spend Thursday afternoons playing with other blind children at the Braille Institute Youth Center in Los Angeles, while his mother **Carole MacIntyre** meets with the Parent Support Group. Guided by a child

Tunnel vision caused by retinitis pigmentosa does not prevent **Scott McIntyre**, 4, above right, from playing with his brother **Todd** as his mother **Carole** looks on. Below, however, Scott seems displeased by Todd's curiosity, typical sibling behavior.

At left, **Paul Gonzalez** is again the center of attention, this time from his father **Frank** and brother **Frankie**, 4.

development counselor, parents discuss issues such as sibling relationships, discipline and separation.

Accompanied by a program preschool assistant, Scott attends a preschool three times a week. Plans by his parents, consultant and preschool assistant are underway for Scott to be mainstreamed into kindergarten.

Paul, Lucia and Scott are but three examples of the more than 155 individuals and their families who received aid from Braille Institute's Child Development Services in 1989.

"It's important to realize that a child's blindness has a profound effect not only on that child's development, but also on the family unit," Liske said. "Early intervention by our professionally trained personnel ensures that we can utilize every means we have to help visually impaired infants, toddlers, or preschoolers and their families."

4

Action shots capture interest

Action shots of people relating to their jobs or each other capture reader interest. Large type helps readers with poor vision. The second color (brown) creates a double keyline around the images, which enhances the black halftones. Note that the photographer took these pictures from a low angle—at the children's level.

NAME *Scene*

PUBLISHER Braille Institute, Los Angeles, California

PURPOSE/AUDIENCE Service and marketing to members

PRODUCTION/PRINTING Two-color on natural 60# offset

FORMAT 8½" × 11"; eight pages

DESIGN Paul J. Porrelli

Cropping for lively photos

Although almost all newsletters have a vertical format, few editors take advantage of the shape by running vertical photos. The boys on the playground equipment look much livelier vertically than they would in a horizontal format. Mortising a second image at an angle and running text around it provides a professional finishing touch to the page.

NAME *Ohel*

PUBLISHER Ohel Children's Home & Family Services, New York, New York

PURPOSE/AUDIENCE Service to parents and friends

PRODUCTION/PRINTING Two-color on 70# gloss-coated

FORMAT 8½" x 11"; six pages

DESIGN Esther Lemer and Harvey Barnett

Ohel

Photo Credit: Carol Gloetter

Outdoor recreation brings out the best in Ohel's boys

Even Disabled Kids Need to Get Away
Ohel's Summer Camp Program

A game of basketball is in progress down at the courts. Two boys are practicing their back-stroke in the outdoor pool. Later in the evening you'd find them roasting hotdogs around a campfire. What you may not notice is that all of these boys have different degrees of emotional and/or developmental disabilities. Yet they all formed a cohesive group, together with their counselors, to enjoy the summer at Ohel's special camp program, just like any other boys their age.

The boys living at the Ohel Residences during the year needed a secluded summer program where they could enjoy recreation, trips, outdoor sports, swimming and group activities. Their difficulty in adapting to new people and routines resulted in behavioral regression when returning from other summer programs. Due to their various disabilities it was necessary for the camp to be staffed by their year-round Ohel directors and counselors with whom they were familiar. A special Ohel camp with a therapeutic Torah environment was the perfect and necessary solution.

Ohel rented a camp with a communal dining and recreational room, swimming pool and spacious grounds. The boys excitedly settled in to begin two months packed with fun and adventure at their Ohel summer camp.

The wake-up signal sounded early in the morning, rousing the boys to prepare for calisthenics. Davening together in the synagogue was followed by a daily Jewish studies learning session. Sports, swimming, arts & crafts, rap sessions and even cooking classes were a part of every day's activities. Evening prayers, barbecues, camp fires and special night activities rounded out the day. There were trips to amusement parks, boat rides and a two-day color-war competition where the boys competed in sports, singing and creative artwork. At the end of the season trophies were presented to those who excelled.

Differences melted away and the boys merged to form one large happy family. A grand musical/dramatic production culminated the season. The boys, attired in white shirts and dark pants stood, side by side with arms up, as their voices resounded in song: "Consider yourself at home, Consider yourself part of the Ohel family!" The staff was proud to witness the camaraderie of these disabled boys.

We hope that soon Ohel will be able to establish permanent summer camp facilities to ensure continued summer camp experiences for its children every year, so that disabled boys can get away and enjoy two carefree months of fun and relaxation. ■

Anna's Exodus

(Continued from page 1)

been estranged from her rich heritage for so many years. She also receives proper medical and psychological care. From all outward appearances, Anna is a typical teenager, shopping and talking on the phone with her friends.

But Anna's journey to freedom is not over. Her deep social and emotional scars are still healing. Continued therapy, education and much love and patience are still needed for her to meet all of the challenges she will face, until she can be truly free. ■

Silhouetting photos

Silhouettes are often difficult to build into a design, but when done cleanly, they can jump right off the page. These images rely on the bright, primary colors used throughout. The seven-panel cartoon strip succeeds especially well because of the broadside format.

NAME *Shareholder*

PUBLISHER Weyerhaeuser Credit Union, Longview, Washington

PURPOSE/AUDIENCE Service and marketing to members

PRODUCTION/PRINTING Four-color process on white gloss-coated

FORMAT 11" x 17"; four pages

DESIGN Brad Hunter and Tom Sentori

Advice From A Retired Dealer

Whether you're buying a new or used car, Ivan Thornley has some advice: Talk financing first and then make your deal with the dealer (taking the rebate if available). "By talking money before you visit the dealers," says Ivan, "you get the numbers you need to compare financing options."

Ivan, who owned Thornley Oldsmobile Cadillac, in Longview, Washington, for 36 years, says the best way to avoid getting trapped — and get the deal you want — is to plan ahead. This includes deciding in advance what kind of car you want, how much you can spend and where to finance. A good dealer, along with the folks at Weyerhaeuser Credit Union, will help.

"Tell the dealer what you want," says Ivan. "You might specify GM, approximate age, if a used car, and price you can afford," he says. "Then wait until the dealer finds the car for you." This tactic, he says, is especially important when buying a used car. "Top used cars rarely stay on the lots, or even get there, so ask for the dealer's help," says Ivan. "There's no obligation."

Is now a good time to buy? "Yes," says Ivan, a Weyerhaeuser Credit Union member since the late '30s. "I expect plenty of rebates this January and February. The dealers will be using them to move inventory." However, even with rebates, there's room to negotiate price.

Ivan Thornley

To get the best possible deal, Ivan shares three other tips:

• **Manufacturer's warranty.** Dealers may not mention these warranties are transferable. Yet, they add great value to used cars.

• **Front-end accidents.** Even though late-model cars don't have frames, they do have small subframes where the engines sit. In acci-

dents, these frames be dions, weakening the ing future alignment pr some dealers may not formation, have frame used cars you might

• **Odometer readi** ican cars, these frames at 100,000 miles. On pens, some dealers o mileage and "sell" o pears on the odome

Before buying a car, talking with neighbor co-workers. "You wo the good guys, but about the bad guys,"

If you're pressured says, be prepared to cars are on the marke there are lots of other Ivan. He also advises to dealer manageme exist. Generally, yo faction.

AUTO FACT #1

Refinance an existing car loan at the credit union. Since the rate probably is lower than elsewhere, you save money. You might even be able to shorten the term and still keep the same monthly payments.

Cut Car Insurance Costs

Insurance companies consider all sorts of factors when determining rates. Among them: age, sex, marital status, type of car you drive, use of vehicle, previous driving record — even smoking.

Yet, there's plenty you can do to cut costs. Driving a Toyota Camry rather than a Toyota Supra will lower premiums. So will no speeding tickets or accidents. Discounts also are available for anti-lock brakes and air bags.

To save even more, says Stan Stieben, Pacific Pioneer Insurance, Longview, Washington, you can raise deductibles on collision and comprehensive. "Rather than a $100 deductible consider $250 or $500," he says. "The more expensive the car, the more you'll save." Or, drop collision coverage if your car has lost more than half its initial value — which can happen within five years. At this point, the coverage may not be worth the cost.

Driving fewer than 7,500 miles a year also may reduce costs. "You'll save about 5 percent on liability," says Stan, whose company writes various group and individual coverages for many Weyerhaeuser Credit Union members. Another cost savings: Get auto and homeowners insurance from the same insurer; many offer discounts.

Periodic cost comparisons also can cut insurance costs. However, Stan advises caution when considering purchases over the phone or through mail solicitations. Switching agents or dealing with an 800 number may not be worth it.

An additional caution: Lack of coverage can be far more costly than paying for what you need. "If you own any property at all," says Stan, "you should have minimum liability coverage of $100,000 for a single injury, $300,000 for all injuries, and $100,000 property damage." For those in car pools, he recommends additional bodily injury coverage. A personal umbrella policy also might be a good idea.

Know what you're buying, says Stan. People often realize too late they don't have the right coverage. Ask questions of your agent. Don't assume you are getting the coverage you need.

Lowe miles lower r Sta

---

7 Plays

To Win The Car Buyi

The best defense is a good offense. It's as true for car buying as
When you're in charge, you win — not the dealer.
Here's how to score your best deal ever:

1 Know What You Want

Do you want a Pontiac Grand Prix? Or a Plymouth Voyager? Think about what you need — and can afford. Worry less about what you think you want. Narrow your choices to two or three models before you start to shop.

2 Get The True Cost

This is the base invoice price, or what the dealer paid for the car (on average about 15 percent off the sticker). The result: You can save from $1,500 to $2,000 on an intermediate-sized car. Your best source for dealer costs is WCU. You can access the information yourself through a computer terminal in the Longview lobby. Or, call for information.

3 Line Up Credit

Ask your credit union for a preapproved loan. Having cash in hand: (1) allows you more opportunity to negotiate price with dealers, and (2) helps control what you spend. With cash in hand, you can ignore dealer financing plans and concentrate on car prices.

4 Shop Ar

Since prices vary gre available at several d Record sticker price them with the invoic tracked down. Find amount you can barg quotes that spell out and what isn't.

Make Borrowing Smart

.9 percent new car rate," [J]nn Waters, Weyerhaeuser [un]ion loan officer, "is really [sa]ve both locally and na[tion]. In the Longview area, a [b]ank rate is 11.25 percent. [The] percent rate attracts new [m]embers from all over the [area,] she says.

[Weyerh]aeuser Credit Union mem[bers rea]lize other savings, too: [ther]e no hidden charges on [fina]ncing. "We don't charge for [a c]heck or for early loan pay[off,] for loan balances up to [on] our credit life insurance

doesn't cost extra," Joann says.

Payroll deduction also makes credit union borrowing smart. "A lot of our members like this service," Joann says. "It's convenient. And if members have several loans, they can have all payments made the same day or, say, on the first of the month and the 15th."

Another smart tactic: Use the equity in your car to consolidate all your bills at used-car rates. "Because our rates are only 10.5 to 11.5 percent APR, they are a less expensive way to finance than a signature loan," says Joann.

Costs also can be cut with short terms and large down payments. "You pay a lot less interest," Joann says. For people with a lot of debt, she recommends five years and 20 percent down. Otherwise, the finance charges become too stiff.

As for longer-term loans, Joann is leery. "You pay so much more in-

> We have no hidden charges with our auto financing.
> — Joann Waters

terest than with a short-term loan," she says. "Unless you make a large down payment, you might not accumulate any equity the first two years." In addition, you may need to replace parts like battery, tires and muffler while you're still making payments. Can you afford replacement *and* financing costs?

Borrow smart. Call Joann or any other Weyerhaeuser Credit Union loan officer. We're here to help.

[W]hat The Ads Don't Tell You

[fi]lls the pages of your local [pap]er? Car ads. What's often [h]owever, is the information [you] need. Here's what the ads [tell] you:

[You] can't have it all. If you [disc]ount financing, you can't [get a] rebate, too. It's one or the [other.]

[The] fine print speaketh Oftentimes, the most [important] information is buried in [fin]e print, for example, how [you q]ualify for the attention-getting [rate.]

[Too] good to be true probably [is.] Tricky phrases like *no one [is r]efused credit* might force you into a [ba]d deal you can't afford. *Dis[counts f]rom manufacturer's sug-*

gested retail prices (MSRPs) still leaves hidden profit since MSRPs often are highly inflated.

• **Numbers can trick you.** Car dealers use all sorts of fancy figuring to make bad deals sound good. The folks at your credit union can help you understand the facts.

• **Haste makes waste.** Ads often are designed to trigger impulsive buying. Do your homework and take your time.

AUTO FACT #3

Take the sales contract home and read it at your leisure — without pressure from the dealer. If the dealer refuses, get a written purchase agreement that spells out all the details. Once you're satisfied, have the agreement written into the contract.

1991 — A Great Time To Buy

If you're in the market for a new car — or have postponed a decision to buy — now's the time to act. According to *Consumer Guide*, this is a buyer's market.

Here's why:

• **Sluggish economy.** Demand is low. To sell off inventory, dealers need to offer lots of deals.

Be careful. Some deals, particularly those for gas guzzlers, could end up being costly. Even though the price is low, the cost to fill up the tank won't be low. Five years from now, the car isn't likely to be a good trade-in, either.

• **Strong competition.** With lots of cars to sell, dealers should be willing to deal. There's also a growing number of directly competitive models.

• **Stable prices.** A strong dollar — and fierce competition — has kept price increases modest.

• **Traditional incentives.** Cash-back rebates, primarily ranging from $500 to $1,500, arc common. Even popular models now have them. Some manufacturers may eliminate rebates and roll back prices.

Avoid other incentives. Low-rate financing, for example, applies only to very short-term loans and the least popular models. It also takes away your ability to negotiate. You're almost always better off with a price reduction and a higher-interest-rate loan at your credit union.

• **New incentives.** Some automakers now offer long warranties, roadside assistance plans, and exchange policies. With the latter, you can return the car within 30 days or 1,500 miles and receive credit toward the purchase of another car from the same dealer.

Gives Her Car-Buying Confidence

[t]ruck demolished her [she] knew she'd have to [. "I was terrified," she [thinki]ng about car buying." [summ]er '90 issue of the [she le]arned what happened [to cr]edit Union members. ["Co]nfidence," says Lisa, [a tech]nician, Weyerhaeuser [in Colu]mbus, Mississippi. "I [know pri]ces."

[She boug]ht a car [and k]now she's [based] on my [credit ne]wsletter [. I was ab]le to say

[The m]ost im[portan]t thing about [the fina]nced [car sav]ed [on the] interest

[for her], worked [out j]ust what I [to s]pent and [she c]ame up [good d]eal," says [I k]now than

[loan office]r who got [. "He] also influenced [to fire] me up," she [same] thing happening to [to hel]p people at work, I [a good] deal for a new car." [drives a] Protegé.

[Lisa Mo]ore gets lots of good consumer advice by [readi]ng and saving the credit union newsletter.

Although Lisa remembered reading an article in an earlier *Shareholder* about car negotiations, she hadn't kept it. (A similar article appears in this issue.) "From now on, I'm saving the *Shareholder*," she says. "Other members should, too."

Good advice, Lisa.

Let Others Haggle For You

Another way to win with dealers is through auto brokers and buying clubs. You eliminate the hassle of negotiating with a dealer — and save money.

Brokers locate the car you want and arrange a firm price with the dealer. Discounts range from $100 to $500 over dealer cost. More difficult to obtain are discounts on hot-selling cars.

With buying clubs, you do the shopping — at designated dealers. The sponsor (often a membership organization) guarantees a rock-bottom price and no hassle.

If these services are available to you, compare prices offered. Make sure any broker you use is legitimate (by asking for and calling recent customers). Some brokers have collected deposits and left town without delivering their cars.

5 [Ma]ke A Deal

[When the] salesperson your figures [into] an offer. Suggest a price [lower] than what you can really [ex]pect to pay. Once a counter-offer is [made,] you can start [higher. I]f you get resistance, be [ready to] walk. A willingness not [to buy may] be the best strategy of all.

6 Ignore Trade-in Price

Without it, you can dicker better. A trade-in also can disguise a bad deal on the new car. Use prices from the *N.A.D.A. Official Used Car Guide* to determine what your old car is worth (available by phone from your credit union). Unless the dealer's willing to give you that price, consider selling outright and using the money as a down payment on the new car.

7 Take Your Time

If you don't get the price you want, go elsewhere. Neither should you hesitate taking up the dealer's time. You're the one spending the money.

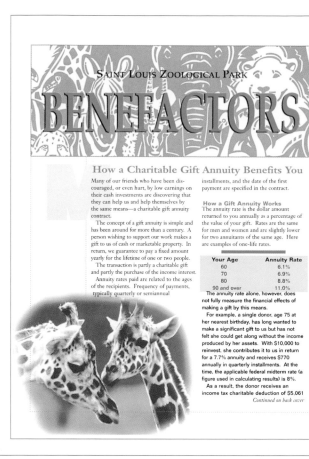

SAINT LOUIS ZOOLOGICAL PARK

BENEFACTORS

How a Charitable Gift Annuity Benefits You

Many of our friends who have been discouraged, or even hurt, by low earnings on their cash investments are discovering that they can help us and help themselves by the same means—a charitable gift annuity contract.

The concept of a gift annuity is simple and has been around for more than a century. A person wishing to support our work makes a gift to us of cash or marketable property. In return, we guarantee to pay a fixed amount yearly for the lifetime of one or two people. The transaction is partly a charitable gift and partly the purchase of the income interest. Annuity rates paid are related to the ages of the recipients. Frequency of payments, typically quarterly or semiannual

installments, and the date of the first payment are specified in the contract.

How a Gift Annuity Works
The annuity rate is the dollar amount returned to you annually as a percentage of the value of your gift. Rates are the same for men and women and are slightly lower for two annuitants of the same age. Here are examples of one-life rates.

Your Age	Annuity Rate
60	6.1%
70	6.9%
80	8.8%
90 and over	11.0%

The annuity rate alone, however, does not fully measure the financial effects of making a gift by this means.

For example, a single donor, age 75 at her nearest birthday, has long wanted to make a significant gift to us but has not felt she could get along without the income produced by her assets. With $10,000 to reinvest, she contributes it to us in return for a 7.7% annuity and receives $770 annually in quarterly installments. At the time, the applicable federal midterm rate (a figure used in calculating results) is 8%.

As a result, the donor receives an income tax charitable deduction of $5,061
Continued on back cover

Frisky photos

The faded edges and vignette effects get rid of distracting backgrounds to give center stage to the zoo creatures. The vignette bleed on the front cover lets the giraffes stick their necks out. The hippo vignette creates a nice portrait in his natural habitat: Hippos do not sit well for studio shots.

NAME *Benefactors*

PUBLISHER St. Louis Zoo & The Stelter Company, St. Louis, Missouri

PURPOSE/AUDIENCE Service and marketing to donors

PRODUCTION/PRINTING Two-color on 70# film-coated

FORMAT 8½" x 11"; four pages

DESIGN The Stelter Company

2

Our booklet *Gifts of Appreciated Property: A Way to Reduce Taxes* explores many ways to give capital gain property. To receive your free copy, return the enclosed reply form.

Benevolent Way to Realize Capital Gains

What a pleasure it is to see growth in securities you own. You want to congratulate yourself on your investment success.

Yet that same success can turn the tables on you, because those are *unrealized* gains. If you sell, you expose the appreciation to capital gains tax.

When you are planning a contribution to us, you can keep the tables from turning. By giving a security held long-term (more than one year), you completely avoid capital gains tax on the appreciation, and you get a charitable deduction for the full fair market value of the investment without tax consequences.

Count the Benefits
The example featured here shows how you could benefit by giving us stock instead of selling it and giving us the proceeds. Assume you bought the stock several years ago for $4,000 and its market value is now $10,000.

For a $10,000 gift of stock, the charitable deduction makes your "out-of-pocket" cost only $7,200—and compared with a $10,000 gift of cash, not paying capital gains tax saved $1,680, reducing the net cost of your $10,000 gift to $5,520.

This example can't envision your actual contribution, capital gain, or tax bracket—or a change in the capital gains tax rate—but it does illustrate the benefits of donating appreciated securities.

Boost Income
From Appreciated Assets
Perhaps you can't afford to part with any assets now—and you even seek a way to increase your income.

If you own low-cost, low-yield securities, have held them for more than a year, and would sell them if it were not for the capital gains tax you would pay, then you have a smart option. Use those holdings to fund a charitable remainder trust that will pay you an income for life.

You will incur no capital gain when you transfer appreciated securities to the trust. The trustee can sell them free of capital gains tax, reinvest the proceeds, and pay you more income than you were receiving from your investments.

Furthermore, this plan entitles you to a sizable income tax charitable deduction equal to the present value of the eventual gift, the trust remainder, as determined by official Treasury tables. So you profit two ways: you boost income and you cut taxes. After your lifetime, the remaining principal will be paid to us, fulfilling your welcome commitment to our support.

A retired couple, Joe and Nancy, owned several low-basis stocks that paid dividends averaging only 2%. They used these stocks to fund a charitable trust that will pay them a lifetime annuity equal to 7% of its initial fair market value. They also qualified for a charitable deduction that will serve to offset their taxes over as many as six years.

Sale of Stock With Gift of Proceeds vs. Gift of Stock

	Gift of Proceeds	Gift of Stock
Proceeds from sale of stock	$10,000	Does not apply
Taxable gain ($10,000 less $4,000)	$6,000	Does not apply
28% capital gains tax	$1,680	Does not apply
Tax savings from deduction for $10,000 contribution (assuming 28% tax bracket)	$2,800	$2,800
Your overall tax savings		
Deduction savings	$2,800	$2,800
Capital gains tax paid	−1,680	Does not apply
Capital gains tax avoided	Does not apply	+1,680
Total tax benefit	$1,120	$4,480

3

Dislike Giving Up
A Good Investment?
If you have owned a security for a long time and its performance has been outstanding, you may not want to give it away. You believe it will do well in the future.

If you have enough cash, here's what to do. Go ahead and contribute the security to us, to meet our needs and secure personal tax breaks. Then buy the same number of replacement shares on the market. This way, you will wipe out your past capital gains tax liability and still hold on to a favorite investment.

Donate Closely Held Stock
Besides gifts of publicly traded securities, you may be able to realize valuable tax savings through a gift of highly appreciated shares of closely held, unmarketable stock of a family business. The gift must be unconditional. Generally, we prefer to hold marketable securities or cash, so we may elect to offer the shares for sale to the issuing corporation, at a price based upon an appraisal of the stock's fair market value.

You Gain More
Your primary reason for any gift is to support a cause in which you believe. The tax incentives are supplemental to your main reward, the satisfaction of helping others. We look forward to working with you in support of our mission. □

What If Congress Changes the Tax Rules?

Will the winds of change blow away the federal income tax? Imagine for a moment that April 15 is just another day and the tax on personal income and capital gains has been replaced by a sales tax or value-added tax. Does that seem inconceivable?

Then again, suppose Congress transforms the income tax into a flat tax, by abolishing deductions and assessing one low tax rate. It's possible that such sacrosanct deductions as charitable donations and home-mortgage interest would be retained—or, amazingly, your tax rate might be so low that you would not miss the loss of every deduction!

How would these tax changes affect donors' generosity? No one knows for sure, but Americans have always been a generous people. Alexis de Tocqueville, the French aristocrat, observed this characteristic a century and a half ago, long before the advent of the income tax. He wrote: "When an American asks for the co-operation of his fellow citizens, it is seldom refused; and I have often seen it afforded spontaneously, and with great goodwill."

With such a heritage, philanthropy will not likely be abolished by an act of Congress. □

Power of five colors

Designer Linda Stillman loves her freedom to run large photos on the cover—and the budget that allows a fifth color. She uses a different flat color for the page rules in each issue, carefully selecting a hue that picks up colors in the art featured on the cover. Technically perfect photographs feature the finest objets d'art. Note how the pictures are sized to fit together on the pages like puzzle pieces.

NAME *Auction News*

PUBLISHER Christie, Manson and Woods International, Inc., New York, New York

PURPOSE/AUDIENCE Service and marketing to customers

PRODUCTION/PRINTING Four-color process plus fifth color on white gloss-coated

FORMAT 9" x 12"; twelve pages

DESIGN Linda Stillman and Connie Circosta, Stillman Designs

Unifying photos and heads

These photos have an effective presentation: centered over two or three columns and overlapping the rule that creates the top portion of the box holding the text. Images hang directly down from headlines and subheads, with captions completing the eye flow. The red second color is only used for headlines, initial caps and pull quotes; all of the graphic rules are in black.

Wide images don't necessarily call for wide captions: Break the caption under a wide photo into two columns, or run one longer column.

NAME *In Review*

PUBLISHER Seattle Community Colleges, Seattle, Washington

PURPOSE/AUDIENCE Service to students and the community

PRODUCTION/PRINTING Two-color on white 60# offset

FORMAT 11" x 17"; four pages

DESIGN Sharon Nakamura

Burlington Northern Foundation Faculty Achievement Awards

Top teachers inspire gratitude

Three of the best teachers at the Seattle Community Colleges were honored in May with 1988-89 Burlington Northern Foundation Faculty Achievement Awards. The program, now in its fourth year, is based on nominations of full-time faculty members by students, former students, faculty, staff and the colleges' business partners.

This year, "the word that characterized the nominating letters for candidates is 'gratitude,'" said Jon Blake, chair of the awards committee at North Seattle Community College.

Recipients were presented awards of $1,500 at a May 9 recep-

Seattle Community Colleges instructors (from left) Rochelle Dela Cruz, James Rondeau and Nancy Verheyden.

to know what they bring with them is valuable and important. We would all lose so much, otherwise." One of her colleagues says this kind of understanding is appreciated by her students. "The number who return to visit or seek her out for counseling is telling. Several over the years have

Northwest History the same way — because the students aren't the same, and they make the class." The formula works: During winter quarter, Rondeau's "History of Washington" class was so popular with its senior citizen students that they petitioned the college to extend the session in spring.

■ Nancy Verheyden, Electro-Mechanical Drafting instructor at North Seattle Community College. Verheyden sets an "extraordinary example as a caring, involved faculty member who significantly impacts the lives of her students," according to a colleague. In the classroom, she has often helped

---

'Are we there yet?'

**by Maralyn Thomas-Schier
SCCC Instructor
Early Childhood and
Parent Education**

Summer often brings increased opportunities for travel with children.

However, vacations away from home do produce a stress of their own. They can be more fun for all if you plan ahead, include the children in preparations, sing a lot and tell stories. Here are some ideas that have helped other families enjoy their time together:

■ Having time for advance planning helps parents and children feel ready for a trip. Young children delight in having their own suitcase or backpack. Even the very young have ideas about what to take along. When children help with packing, they usually are more comfortable away from home. Of course, it is important to include a favorite toy or blanket for comfort.

Maralyn Thomas-Schier and friends at Seattle Central Community College. Bob Hereford photo.

pate in making a travel kit of generally non-messy materials they would enjoy using in their laps. For instance, the kit might include crayons, transparent tape, paper, washable felt tip pens, magic slates, sticker books and a roll of masking tape.

■ Include a viewfinder. You can often find new slide scenes along your route in tourist shops. You may also bring along slide photos from home, which are fun to look at and useful in countering feelings of homesickness.

eler, it is important to stop often and exercise a bit.

■ Snacks are a great help and can be purchased and prepared ahead to prevent some of the inevitable requests for junk food. It helps to tell children what you will purchase and what you will bring from home. (My favorite travel snack is 'O'-shaped dry cereals.)

■ Traveling together provides wonderful opportunities to talk with each other. Children love to hear about your childhood and trips you took when you were young.

Sometimes, the best vacation is in your own neighborhood. You can help neighborhood children create a circus; set up a pretend camp, school or store; stage a wedding; or put on an ice cream social. All these events are wonderful ways to get to know your neighbors and provide your children with opportunities to

  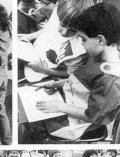

ART FOR KIDS' SAKE

District has designs on expanding student appreciation

Port Chester Middle School, through a unique relationship with the Port Chester Council for the Arts, has instituted an Artist-in-Residency program. Areas of instruction include watercolor/painting, mural design, storytelling and pottery/clay. Four artists will work in grades 5 and 6, providing an eight-week residency, for a total of 32 weeks. The first eight weeks are a pilot program, allowing time for improvement before the remaining sessions begin.

"The kids will get an incredible experience with all different disciplines," says Camille Linen, Board of Education president and Director of the Port Chester Council for the Arts.

Students will not only study art for art's sake, but come to understand the relationship between art forms and other areas of instruction.

For example, watercolor/painting relates to science through the blending of colors to create different colors, and examining the components of paint. Mural design can be traced back to ancient Egyptian pictographs and hieroglyphics. Storytelling goes hand-in-hand with history and writing. Pottery/clay utilizes math for measurement, design and the recipe for components.

The Middle School program has its roots in Port Chester's Arts in Education program, which is celebrating its fifth birthday. It all began in the fall of 1987, when grant money was used to fund Kinderart, a multicultural, multidisciplinary arts program introduced in kindergarten classes district wide. Visiting artists and

grade will be spending 10-15 weeks in each of the elementary schools this year.

Teachers are given a list of art forms from which to choose.

"For instance, a lot of them will choose a mural because all the children can contribute to part of it," says Mrs. Linen. A past project focused on a mural of the Village of Port Chester and highlighted key buildings, giving youngsters an introduction to architecture.

A major reason for the program's success is inviting artists into schools who love their work enough to want to share it with children.

"My theory is this," says Mrs. Linen. "If you love what you're doing and you really have a soul connection to it, you can teach it to anybody, any age."

It's interesting to note, says Mrs. Linen, that this year's 5th grade class attended the first full-day kindergarten, was the first Kinderart class, is the first 5th grade at the Middle School, the first to experience the expanded arts program and will be the first to graduate from high school in the new century, the year 2000!

Two of the artists returning to the program this year are Brigitte Loritz, a painter, and Lou Del Bianco, an actor, singer and storyteller. Both taught the first Kinderart program five years ago to the current 5th graders and will be working with them

PORT CHESTER PUBLIC SCHOOLS
1993-94 BUDGET CALENDAR

Nov. 4 – Dec. 1 - Administrators with planning and budgeting responsibilities meet with staff and generate input into decision-making and budget building.

Dec. 16 - Presentation of 1993-94 assumption budget to the Board of Education. Public invited to give input.

Dec. 18 - Completed budget materials returned in duplicate to the Assistant Superintendent for Business.

Jan. 12 - Citizens Advisory Committee meeting to review budget status and make initial recommendations. Sub-committee reports.

Feb. 10 - Draft 1 of Superintendent's Budget completed and available for review by the Board of Education. Public invited to give input.

Feb. 11 - Citizens Advisory Committee meeting to provide input for recommended revisions for Draft 1.

Feb. 24 - Board further discusses Draft 1. Public invited to give input.

March 10 - Update to the Board of Education on the 1993-94 budget development process. Public invited to give input.

March 15 - Citizens Advisory Committee meets to discuss further possible revision for the budget.

March 24 - Update to the Board of Education on 1993-94 budget development process. Public invited to give input.

April 14 - Board adopts 1993-94 budget. Public invited to give input.

Bilingual brochures recognize market diversity

Employees from several business divisions in Madison and Pomona combined their expertise to develop new bilingual marketing materials targeted to Spanish-speaking credit union members.

Their teamwork resulted in producing an array of promotional brochures and statement stuffers describing credit life and credit disability insurance. The group also produced a loan application written in Spanish.

The materials are being test marketed in two southern California credit unions serving a large Hispanic membership. **M**

Members of the Madison-Pomona team producing bilingual marketing materials are, back row, Dan Simms, Paul Dowding, Jacqueline de Dompablo, Jill O'Brien and Al Zielke. In front are Nancy Grigas, Pomona and Wendy Walsh. Not pictured are Lou Lou Delgadillo, Pomona and Pam Schnagl.

Help build a hope

United Way campaign promises fun

The committee has been meeting, the theme has been chosen and the goal has been set.

United Way '93 promises not only to follow the CUNA Mutual tradition of leadership in the corporate community...but our tradition of having fun as well.

This year's theme is *Help Build a Hope*. Pledge goal is $200,000. Co-chairs for the campaign are Teri McCormick and Dave Peck. Their committee is creating unusual events, prizes and surprises to keep the campaign upbeat and on-target.

Employee rallies, which will feature video presentations this year, will be held Sept. 14-16 in the Theatre, Old Sauk Trails and World Trade Center. Mark your calendar to attend and watch for more information coming your way. **M**

Reported by Robb Besteman

The 1993 United Way committee and honorary member President/CEO Richard Heins promise a fun, upbeat campaign. Members, top row, from left, Anne Knopp, Linda Wilder, Robb Besteman, Kris Dresen, Nancy Richardson and John Tomczak. Front row, from left, Barbara Sawyer, Teri McCormick, Dick Heins, Dave Peck and Wendy Walsh, holding this year's campaign poster. Not pictured is Greg Smith.

Employee service

August Anniversaries

25 years: Karen Alt, ISD; Carol Breese, Cost Allocation
20 years: Linda Lorenz, Employee Benefits Underwriting; Dennis Kalscheur, Management Report Support; Julie Shanks, Field Operations Administration; Walter Bessel, Printing Center; Candace Greve, Individual Marketing & Sales; Constance Lampman, Mail Center; Charles Brennan, Southern District; Michael Daubs, Securities Management; Charlene Smith, Flexible Spending

July retirements

Linda Tingle, East Central District; LaVerne Wichert, Pomona

 Karen Alt 25 Years

 Carol Breese 25 Years

 Linda Lorenz 20 Years

 Constance Lampman 20 Years

 Charles Brennan 20 Years

 Michael Daubs 20 Years

 Charlene Smith 20 Years

 Dennis Kalscheur 20 Years

 Julie Shanks 20 Years

 Walter Bessel 20 Years

 Candace Greve 20 Years

A historical feature from the Archives

Remember when premiums were tabulated by hand?

A One of the most active early credit union pioneers was Charles Hyland, comptroller and first treasurer of CUNA Mutual.

Hyland was with the LaCrosse, Wis. fire department in 1930 when credit union organizer Thomas Doig introduced credit unions to him. He joined forces with Doig and played an important role in forming CUNA in 1934, whose constitution he helped draft and sign.

Hyland signed a note borrowing $25,000 from philanthropist Edward Filene to start CUNA Mutual in 1935.

He watched CUNA Mutual grow from its earliest days, when, as he said, "a girl and I used to tabulate all the premiums by hand–just the two of us. And we didn't work very hard at it either."

Hyland championed the cause of credit unions and was a tireless organizer. He organized more than 600 credit unions during his career, 547 of them in Wisconsin.

For more information contact the Archives, ext. 8580. **M**

Reported by Menzi Behrnd-Klodt

Photo spreads

The example at the top of this page uses a crossover grid that allows the crease to fold on the least interesting area. The bottom two-page spread folds so that it avoids any of the faces in the center group. Note how these spreads use an odd number of photos and let one or two large images dominate the rest. Images presented at different sizes put action into the spread.

NAME *Mutual Matters*

PUBLISHER CUNA Mutual Insurance Group, Madison, Wisconsin

PURPOSE/AUDIENCE Service to employees

PRODUCTION/PRINTING Two-color on 70# gloss coated

FORMAT 8½" x 11"; eight pages

DESIGN Dennis Schmidt, Kelli Murphy, CUNA

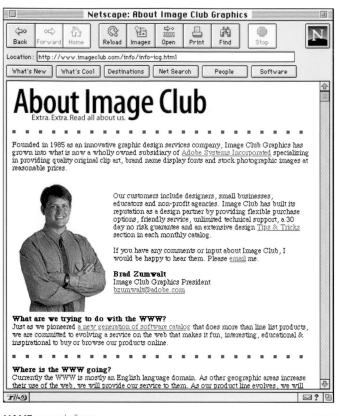

Keep Web images simple

Make photos easy to view from a computer screen. Complicated images with too many points of interest become confusing when they are subjected to the compressed tonal range of digitized information. Keep images to a single subject, as in the photo of Brad Zumwalt on the "About Image Club" screen, or run them in a larger size, as in the "Control Room" images from the Shell PhotoLibrary. Note how difficult it is to see what the image is about when it's small.

Shell is one of many companies who provide downloadable graphics on the Web for publicity purposes. (See introduction to Chapter Six for tips on how to search the Web for graphics.)

NAME www.shell.com

PUBLISHER Shell International Petroleum, London, UK

PURPOSE/AUDIENCE Service to employees and customers

PRODUCTION/PRINTING Web

FORMAT Web

DESIGN Shell International Petroleum, London, UK

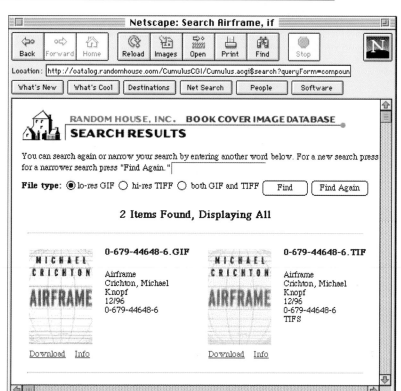

Photos on the Web and photos from the Web

Along with showing its books on screen, Random House also offers booksellers the ability to download high- and low-resolution color photographs of book covers. The booksellers can then use the book covers in their own newsletters or other promotional pieces.

NAME www.randomhouse.com

PUBLISHER Random House Online, Inc., New York, New York

PURPOSE/AUDIENCE Service and marketing to customers

PRODUCTION/PRINTING Web

FORMAT Web

DESIGN Random House Online, Inc.

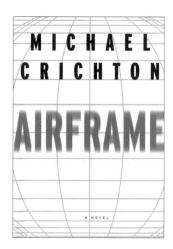

chapter eight

COLLATERAL

Collateral materials help you convert the "monologue" of a traditional newsletter into a "dialog" with readers. The job of collateral pieces is to invite action. If readers like your message, they'll support your mission. Tell motivated readers what to do through reply cards, surveys and other response tools.

GENERATING FEEDBACK. Once your newsletter has a reader's attention, offer specific ways to respond to your offer. Tell readers what action you want them to take and how to take it. This is done by providing:

- a self-mailing reply card
- a money-saving coupon the respondent clips and returns
- a masthead or announcement telling where to write or call for more information, how to send a letter to the editor or how to submit articles or other content
- ordering information listed at the end of an article
- a contest in which readers can send in photographs or suggestions on how to use your products
- a readership survey that generates content suggestions
- a telephone number to call
- hours of operation when prospects can stop by

- an advertisement telling how to buy a specific product
- the date of an event
- a product list that includes an order form readers can use to order immediately
- special information on your website
- reports available by fax

You'll receive several types of response to your newsletter. Some people just want more information. For those who feel more comfortable writing than calling, provide reply cards and coupons. For those who'd rather call, list your phone number and hours of operation. For diehard shoppers, list your store hours and a location map. For those ready to order now, include an order form. Encourage people to phone in their order or send it via fax.

The medium is the message

The very existence of feedback tools like reply cards tell readers that you want two-way communication. Surveys tell readers that you care what they think. Special inserts reinforce the message of the newsletter. Reply cards offer further helpful information. All collateral pieces for newsletters make readers feel connected and appreciated.

working **SOLO**

Free
Newsletter

● *free newsletter*

Free Newsletter

Welcome to Working Solo eNews, the monthly e-mail newsletter that brings news, information, tips, and insights on self-employment (as well as special Working Solo offers) FREE to your e-mailbox each month.

Working Solo eNews provides fresh content once each month, on everything from small business legislative issues to technology tips, shoestring marketing techniques, small business sites of interest, and articles and checklists to help both solo newcomers and seasoned pros.

You can subscribe to Working Solo eNews right now !

Just fill in your eMail address

and then click ....   [Subscribe]

If you prefer to subscribe off-line, send an e-mail message with "subscribe" in the subject, to: solonews@workingsolo.com.

View past issues, in our Articles and Archives. (coming soon)

Please note: We do not sell, rent, or trade the names on our e-mail lists. Your names are secure and only used by us.

Thanks for your interest in Working Solo -- we look forward to seeing you online !

working **SOLO** 🏠

Links to other resources

Web news

Because of its elastic dimension, you can offer several different collateral materials on the Web. Readers can search back-issue archives by keyword. Sign-up forms allow you to create an e-mail mailing list of interested prospects easily, and links to other sites let you provide readers with additional sources.

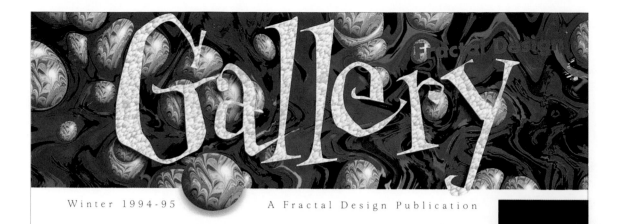

Winter 1994-95   A Fractal Design Publication

New Painter 3 Arrives!

Fractal Design reached a major goal when we started shipping Version 3 of Fractal Design Painter,® the award-winning *Natural-Media*® paint and image editing program. Painter 3 is now available for Macintosh,® Power Macintosh® *(you get both Mac and Power Mac versions for the same price)* and Windows™ computers. *Painter 3 has already been awarded the prestigious IMPACT award by Publish magazine, chosen as one of Seybold's HOT PICKS for 1994, and nominated for a MacUser's 1994 Eddy award.*

Completely new and outrageously feature-rich, Painter 3 sports more than 50 new features. It contains frame-by-frame animation capabilities; enhanced creative and compositing tools; the Painter EXTRAS CD-ROM; a refined user interface; multiple floating selections; weaving controls and much more!

New Image-Creation & Editing Capabilities

With Painter 3, we're fortifying our position as imaging innovators with a host of new creative tools that take traditional graphics a leap beyond reality. Painter 3 features the Image Hose™, a paint brush that substitutes a series of graphics elements for dabs of paint—a technique that's like "painting with reality." Painter 3 includes a library of Image Hose patterns, or "Nozzles," some of which replicate nature (such as clover and sea kelp) and symbols (such as coins and arrows). Even QuickTime® and Video for Windows™ movies can be "sprayed" through the Image Hose enabling you to actually "paint with movies."

Painter 3 also features new Weaving controls which

are based on a mathematical language that models the physical properties of a loom. You can learn this language to design your own fabrics, or take advantage of the many weave patterns that Painter ships with. All of the patterns are algorithmically-generated, so the possibilities are endless!

With Painter 3's new Gradation Composer, you can create interactive color ramps to apply linear, sweep, spiral and circular gradations to an image. Any image can provide information for a color ramp, and Painter 3 can map an image's luminance values to a color ramp to create unique effects.

> *"Fractal Design has taken a quantum leap right into my favorite areas. Amazing masking synergy, brush control, blends & colors."*
> Bill Niffenegger, Digital Artist/Author, Cloudcroft, NM

The Painter EXTRAS CD-ROM

We think of Painter as a design environment that has the digital equivalent of artistic media such as oils, pastels, different brushes, inks, paper and canvas. The EXTRAS CD-ROM is designed to answer the cravings of experienced Painter users for more tools and media to employ in their artwork. Painter EXTRAS includes inspirational artwork from ArtExpo '94, innovative Image Hose Nozzles, interactive demos of Painter 3's new features and a variety functionality to Painter 3. textures, brush looks, po interfaces. The EXTRAS (photography from Photo stock photography, QuickTime and Video for Windows movies from Cascom International, pa textures from ArtBeats, pl much more.

Morph newsletter to poster

This A4 newsletter unfolds into an A2 (16½" x 22⅜") poster with a reply card perforated at the bottom. The wild colors, typography and graphics are created to appeal to the target audience, designers, and to showcase the power of the publisher's software. The perforated reply card at the bottom of the poster uses funky red type in "I want it now!" to inspire action.

NAME *Fractal Design Gallery*

PUBLISHER Fractal Design Corporation, Aptos, California

PURPOSE/AUDIENCE Service and marketing to customers

PRODUCTION/PRINTING Four-color process on 80# gloss-coated

FORMAT 8½" × 12"; four pages that open to full poster

DESIGN Fractal Design Corporation

The Flower Face Hiroshi Yoshii

Close the sale

This subscription card from *Sales MasterMind* highlights the benefits the newsletter offers with hot pink check marks, the faxback icon and a color reproduction of the cover of the newsletter. The hot pink YES closes the sale.

NAME *Sales MasterMind*

PUBLISHER The Economics Press, Fairfield, New Jersey

PURPOSE/AUDIENCE Service to subscribers

PRODUCTION/PRINTING Four-color process on 60# film-coated

FORMAT 8½" × 11"; eight pages

DESIGN Sue Sylvester, Beckley Press

EARTH'S BEST FAMILY TIMES

Volume 2 — Printed on Recycled Paper — Number 1

IN THIS ISSUE:

Everything about Organic Baby Food - Page 2

Starting Your Baby on Solid Foods - Page 4

Infant Insights - Page 5
By Dr. Jay Gordon

Making Mealtime Both Filling And Fun

Well, there you are. Holding a warm, wiggling, wonderful brand-new bundle of baby. Your instincts tell you how to love it, cuddle it, even burp it. But how in the world do you know how to properly feed it?

To most new parents, the whole idea of figuring out feeding schedules, routines, diets and tastes can seem overwhelming. The feeding process can be both a cherished and a dreaded time. But it is always a time that teaches you all kinds of things about your baby's behavior, how he communicates, cries, sleeps, and even how he likes to be held. So make it a meaningful time for both of you.

By the end of four months, you

How In The World Do We Make Earth's Best?

You have just gone through nine months of pregnancy and an unprecedented emotional roller coaster when your little one was born. Now, we don't think you'd even consider feeding that precious little

and your baby will settle into a comfortable (and hopefully predictable) routine. Even with a diet consisting solely of formula or breastmilk, feeding time becomes more interactive. After all, your baby is beginning to notice the world around him.

Du...
your baby...
upright - i...
when he...
Unwilling...
him by no...
to touch e...
nose, or th...
He'll also s...
squealing...

H...
smiles at...
growing f...
to maste...
fear as y...
like the...
but in pl...

person something that wasn't absolutely, positively, the healthiest thing for him. But, until Earth's Best Baby Foods were created, parents didn't have a lot of options.

As the Earth's Best founder said, "The baby food available wasn't the very best food on the market. It was grown with synthetic chemicals, overprocessed and tasted pretty bad. We knew we could do better by

(Continued Page 3)

Remember how you swore you'd never feed her sugar, never add salt to her food and never let anything artificial pass her lips?

Promote with direct mail

This direct-mail piece uses the same graphic style and ink and paper colors as the newsletter it promotes. The reply card offers the benefits of a free bib and free subscription to *Family Times*. See pages 130, 134 and 135 for other good examples of a reply card.

NAME *Family Times*

PUBLISHER Earth's Best Baby Food, Boulder, Colorado

PURPOSE/AUDIENCE Service and marketing to customers

PRODUCTION/PRINTING Four-color process

FORMAT 8½" × 11"; six pages (with foldout)

DESIGN Lisa Bell, Earth's Best Baby Food

Become an Earth's Best Family and get this delightful cotton bib, FREE.

Plus, get three baby-fact-filled newsletters with loads of nutritional and environmental information, parenting tips, coupons and valuable gift offers.

Simply fill out and mail in this card.

Name_____

Address_____

City, State, Zip_____

Phone (____)_____

Baby's Name_____

Baby's Birth Date_____

☐ Male ☐ Female
Please allow up to 6-8 weeks for delivery.

5

Service Corner

MoneyLine: The Fast, Convenient Alternative to Checks

These days, it's easier than ever for people to access their bank accounts thanks to automated teller machines and direct deposit services. Why should receiving and accessing your mutual fund dividends be any less of a convenience? Thanks to Delaware Group's MoneyLine service, if you currently take your fund dividends or capital gains distributions in cash, or receive a check for systematic withdrawals,* you can access your money faster than if you continued receiving a check in the mail.

MoneyLine, which operates on the Automated Clearing House (ACH) banking network, will credit your bank checking or savings account anytime a fund distribution or systematic withdrawal payment is paid by your mutual fund account. Just think of the time you could save not having to wait for your check to arrive in the mail, or standing in bank lines.

Unlike wire transfers which typically charge a fee, MoneyLine is a free service. However, with MoneyLine, it generally takes a little longer than a wire for funds to be available in your bank account, usually two business days. This is still faster than receiving checks by mail and cuts down on trips to the bank.

To sign up for MoneyLine, simply fill out and return the coupon on this page. We'll send you the information you need to get started. Once we receive your MoneyLine authorization agreement, the service will be available on your account one month later. If you have any questions, please call Delaware Shareholder Services at 1-800-523-1918. ❏

*MoneyLine is not available for systematic withdrawal plans on retirement accounts.

YES, I am interested in learning more about the following investment opportunities. Please send me more information including, where applicable, a prospectus which contains details of investment strategies, charges and expenses. I will read it carefully before I invest or send money.

❏ Information on the Delaware Group Family of Funds for Asset Allocation Purposes
❏ Retirement Planning
❏ MoneyLine Package
❏ Limited-Term Government Fund
❏ Devon Fund

Important! For faster service, please fill in your Delaware Group account number below:

Name _____

Address _____

City _____

State _____ Zip _____

Daytime Phone _____

Evening Phone _____

Financial Adviser _____

Firm _____

❏ I don't have a financial adviser. Please suggest one in my area.

USPS-friendly reply cards

To add bulk to this reply coupon printed on lightweight text paper, perforations allow readers to remove the card and then fold and tape it before mailing. Note the large graphic YES with the check mark.

NAME *Delaware Digest*

PUBLISHER Delaware Distributors, Philadelphia, Pennsylvania

PURPOSE/AUDIENCE Service and marketing to customers

PRODUCTION/PRINTING Four-color process on white 50# offset

FORMAT 7½" x 10¼"; six pages (six-panel foldout)

DESIGN TKO Design Group

NO POSTAGE
NECESSARY
IF MAILED
IN THE
UNITED STATES

BUSINESS REPLY MAIL
FIRST CLASS MAIL   PERMIT NO. 26448   PHILADELPHIA, PA
POSTAGE WILL BE PAID BY ADDRESSEE

Marketing Services
Delaware Group
PO Box 7910
Philadelphia PA 19101-9963

Have You Reviewed Your Life Insurance Coverage Lately?

Have you reviewed your life insurance with me recently? I've found that many people have changes in their lives from year to year which change their life insurance needs.

Are you just out of high school or college and starting a new life? Now can be a good time to buy a life insurance policy. Often, a younger person may pay lower premiums than an older person. Also, young, single people may want to plan ahead if they anticipate getting married, having a family and buying a house someday.

Were you recently married? Have you bought a new house? Now is a good time to evaluate whether the life insurance your spouse has will cover the debts if your spouse dies and you are left with the debt. Also, you may want enough life insurance to cover funeral expenses, estate taxes and other expenses in case your spouse dies.

Have you recently been divorced and wish to change your beneficiary? Have you become a grandparent and are interested in buying a life insurance policy for your grandchildren? These are just some examples of the events that can affect your life insurance coverage.

American Family Life Insurance Company offers many life insurance plans. Give me a call so we can evaluate whether the changes in your life have created the need to modify your life insurance coverage.

Airbags

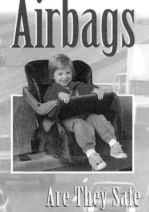

Are They Safe for Children?

We know that driver-side airbags have saved 1,500+ lives and prevented many more serious injuries. The Insurance Institute for Highway Safety (IIHS) says that initial estimates of passenger airbags show they are reducing deaths among right front passengers by 11 percent for all types of crashes.

Unfortunately the IIHS study also indicates a 33 percent increase in risk among children younger than 10. The study shows that the force required to inflate an airbag in a fraction of a second can cause serious injury to people who are very close to airbags as they begin to inflate, such as an infant or toddler in a rear-facing child seat on the passenger side.

To prevent the risk of injury to young children, IIHS recommends these precautions:

- Children should ride in the back seat.
- Always make sure infants and children are properly restrained.
- Never put your child in a rear-facing restraint in the front seat, unless the vehicle doesn't have a back seat and there is a switch to deactivate the passenger-side airbag.
- Protect yourself as well. Always use your safety belt.

While there have been some deaths and serious injuries among children, IIHS says that passenger-side airbags have been proven to reduce deaths among right front seat passengers. Parents should follow the steps above and never let your child ride in a rear-facing restraint in a car with a passenger-side airbag.

FYI

Did you know that American Family has two coverage options for insuring motorcycles? Purchasing the right coverage is important to provide adequate protection not only for your cycle, but for you too.

The **Basic** motorcycle policy provides collision, comprehensive and liability coverages for your cycle including the frame, handlebars, fork, motor, seat, wheels, mirrors, lights and instruments. Collision provides coverage for losses caused by collision with other vehicles or objects, regardless of who is at fault. Comprehensive coverage protects you against losses not caused by collision such as theft, lightning, vandalism, wind, fire or hail. Liability coverages include legal defense costs and emergency first aid.

The **Basic Plus** plan provides all the coverages provided by the Basic plan **plus** coverage for most permanently attached accessories including saddle bags, sissy bar, windshield, trunk, trailer, luggage rack, and custom chrome, paint or seat.

Before you get your cycle back on the road, make sure you have proper insurance protection. Contact me for more details about our motorcycle insurance.

Tips

Have you recently had to make a claim on your insurance and realized that you didn't have the appropriate amount of coverage? For example, suppose your mobile phone is stolen from your auto. Do you know that it isn't covered unless it is endorsed under your auto coverage? Are you aware that there are good driver discounts that you may be qualified to receive? Maybe you were recently married and want to update your life insurance.

That's why I suggest a **Personal Insurance Review**. I like to meet with each of my policyholders about once a year to evaluate their present insurance coverage and decide whether or not any adjustments need to be made. Please give me a call to set an appointment for your next **Personal Insurance Review**.

A New Look for Policyholder NEWS

Yes, we have a new "look." Since its creation in 1969, *Policyholder News* has helped American Family and its agents keep in touch with you. So, it's important to us to provide a professional, full-color newsletter that continues to keep you informed of insurance-related and safety topics. If you have any comments on our new look or have an idea for an article, please let me know. Or send your comments to American Family Insurance, *Policyholder News*, 6000 American Parkway, Q16U, Madison, WI 53783.

NO POSTAGE NECESSARY IF MAILED IN THE UNITED STATES

BUSINESS REPLY MAIL
FIRST-CLASS MAIL PERMIT NO. 26 MADISON,WI
POSTAGE WILL BE PAID BY ADDRESSEE

AMERICAN FAMILY INSURANCE
ATTN: MARKETING TEAM 3 Q16B
6000 AMERICAN PKY
MADISON, WI 53791-9941

AMERICAN FAMILY INSURANCE
AUTO HOME BUSINESS HEALTH LIFE
http://www.amfam.com

203164
Jess C McReynolds
234 Old Meramec Sta Rd #D
Manchester, MO 63021-5300
Bus: (314) 391-3630
Res: (314) 965-4330

ALEXANDRE TODOROV
6614 PERNOD AVE
SAINT LOUIS MO 63139-2149

Yes, I want to know more about the following:

- ☐ Life Insurance
- ☐ UM/UIM Insurance
- ☐ Automobile Insurance
- ☐ Home Equity Loan
- ☐ Disability Income Insurance
- ☐ Personal Insurance Review
- ☐ Homeowners Insurance
- ☐ Health Insurance*
- ☐ Personal Umbrella Policy
- ☐ Business Insurance

*Not available in every state. Please see your agent.
2/97

Check, remove and mail

The clear goal of this newsletter is to encourage readers to fill out and return the reply card. The entire newsletter is printed on .007 card stock, with the reply card perfed for easy tearout. The card is designed with check boxes, the recipient's name laser-printed on the card, and a business reply mail indicia on the reverse side.

NAME *Policyholder News*

PUBLISHER American Family Mutual Insurance Co., Madison, Wisconsin

PURPOSE/AUDIENCE Service and marketing to customers

PRODUCTION/PRINTING Four-color process on reply-card stock

FORMAT 8½" × 14"; four pages

DESIGN Linda Struck, American Family Mutual Insurance Co.

The Strategic Investor®

FIRST CANADIAN FUNDS

Our quarterly newsletter for mutual fund investors

Winter 1997

FIRST CANADIAN® STRATEGIES

RRSP investing couldn't be easier

When you think about it, the Registered Retirement Savings Plan (RRSP) concept...

But the question remains: How best to invest?

The key investing strategies
To make the right RRSP investing decisions, consider these simple strategies:

1. Invest regularly. Making a regular monthly contribution instead of waiting until the contribution deadline can improve your RRSP returns. For instance, at a 7% average annual rate of return, $3,000 contributed at the end of every February would grow to $122,986 after 20 years. In contrast, 12 contributions of $250 made every month (for an annual total of $3,000), would grow to $130,232 after 20 years. The difference: $7,246, even though the amount contributed is exactly the same. With a Continuous Purchase Plan, you can make monthly contributions automatically.

2. Diversify your investments. Studies have shown that between 80% and 90% of an investor's return can be attributed to having the right asset mix. So to get more

...nvestments held in an ...h a big edge. Thanks to ...ound growth, the RRSP ...s a huge difference to ...nings.

..., at a marginal tax rate ...f any interest income ...axed away by the gov- ...Within the sheltered ...an continue to grow ...you withdraw it.

...onto 416-956-2271; ...888-636-6376).

...ategic Investment ...a diversified port- ...· Funds and Guar- ...ertificates (GICs). ...designed to help ...eal mix of funds ...r personal needs

...ates of return on

your quarterly statements for First Canadian Funds and MatchMaker Strategic Portfolios let you see exactly how your RRSP has performed (see Page 3 for further details).

• RRSP loans at Bank of Montreal's prime rate make it affordable to maximize your RRSP contribution.

• The Continuous Purchase Plan gives you the benefits of regular RRSP investing.

Performance Update

Winter 1997

FIRST CANADIAN FUNDS

A supplement to *The Strategic Investor* newsletter

SECTOR SPOTLIGHT

Canadian equity funds going strong

Canadian equities posted new highs in 1996, with the Toronto Stock Exchange (TSE 300) Composite Index passing the 6,000-point milestone in November. All market sectors contributed to the rise, with financial services leading the way. Judging by the interest shown by foreign investors, Canada is coming to be seen as one of the most attractive markets in the world.

Unitholders of First Canadian Funds investing in Canadian equities have much to celebrate. Investors in the **First Canadian Equity Index Fund** rode the ups and downs of the TSE 300 to record an impressive one-year return of 30% as of Nov. 3, 1996.

First Canadian Growth Fund proved the value of strong fund management,

outperforming the TSE 300 index to return 34.2%. More than 40% of the Fund's assets were invested in the three top performing sectors — financial services, conglomerates, and oil and gas.

Strong weightings in both resources and advanced manufacturing companies contributed to a 31.5% return for the **First Canadian Special Growth Fund**. Increased holdings in the oil and gas sector and reduced exposure to paper and forest products stocks proved to be a winning combination for the **First Canadian Resource Fund**. It showed a 29.8% one-year gain as of the end of November.

The upward trend of the Canadian market is expected to continue into 1997, barring a sharp rise in interest rates or a slump in the economy. Low inflation and low interest rates support strong economic growth for Canada. ■

INVESTMENT ADMINISTRATION

Tax forms to watch for

If you are a First Canadian Fund unitholder or First Canadian Fund RRSP planholder, you may soon receive one or more tax forms required for the filing of your 1996 Income Tax Return. To ensure that you have received all your tax forms before filing your income tax return, we have prepared the following summary:

Tax Forms Issued	Reason Issued	Scheduled Mailing Date *
RRSP Contribution Tax Receipts	■ contributions made March 1996 to December 1996	by January 31, 1997
	■ contributions made January 1997	by February 28, 1997
	■ contributions made February 1997	by March 15, 1997
T3–Canada R16–Quebec	■ capital gains, interest and/or dividends declared for non-registered accounts	by March 31, 1997**
T4RSP–Canada R2–Quebec	withdrawal from an RRSP, except transfer to another RRSP and Home Buyers Plan	by February 28, 1997**
T4RIF–Canada R2–Quebec	payments from a RRIF transfers due to death of the original planholder	by February 28, 1997
NR4 (for non-residents only)	withdrawal from an RRSP payments from a RRIF	by March 31, 1997
T5–Canada R3–Quebec	interest/dividend income from GIC or shares in a non-registered account	by February 28, 1997**

* Revenue Canada/Quebec Mailing Deadline.
* Revenue Canada statutory mailing deadlines. All tax forms will be mailed no later than these
**These are Revenue Canada statutory mailing deadlines. In all instances we will endeavour to issue these forms prior to these deadlines.

One number for mutual fund questions and transactions

Our First Canadian Funds Call Centre gives you toll-free access to information and allows you to make transactions by phone. With locations in Toronto and Montreal, the Call Centre makes it easy to:

• make RRSP contributions by phone;
• access your account for an update, or make purchases or redemptions from the convenience of your home or office; and
• obtain information on any of the 24 First Canadian Funds.

See over for new First Canadian Funds Call Centre numbers.

Supplements target audiences

When you need to cover a theme or subject in detail, consider a supplement. Design the supplement with the same graphic look as the newsletter carrying it. *The Performance Update* achieves this by using the same design and typography as *The Strategic Investor,* but changing the colors.

NAME *The Strategic Investor*

PUBLISHER First Canadian Funds, Toronto, Ontario, Canada

PURPOSE/AUDIENCE Service and marketing to customers

PRODUCTION/PRINTING Four-color process on 50# matte

FORMAT 8½" × 11"; four pages

DESIGN Ariad Custom Publishing

Theme supplements

Medical Essay is a regular supplement to the *Mayo Clinic Health Letter*. Each essay covers a wellness theme in depth and includes a large color visual on the front. The paper color, spot color and typography are consistent with the main newsletter.

NAME *Mayo Clinic Health Letter*

PUBLISHER Mayo Clinic, Rochester, Minnesota

PURPOSE/AUDIENCE Service to subscribers

PRODUCTION/PRINTING Four-color process on natural 50# offset; three-hole punched

FORMAT 8½" × 11"; eight pages

DESIGN George E. DeVinny and David E. Swanson

MAYO CLINIC HEALTH LETTER

RELIABLE INFORMATION FOR A HEALTHIER LIFE

VOLUME 15   NUMBER 2   FEBRUARY 1997

Inside this issue

Dialysis

Need for artificial kidney treatment is increasing

Think of the waste your normal activities generate each day — wrappers, empty cans and food scraps, just to name a few. If you couldn't take out your garbage, it would pile higher and higher. Eventually, your home would be unlivable.

Inside your body, your organs and cells also create waste during normal body processes. Fortunately, your body has its own internal waste removal systems, among them, your kidneys. Each day, your kidneys clean your body's fluids and regulate your body's chemical balance. Your life depends on them to keep waste from building to toxic levels.

Yet each year, a growing number of people are able to live, work and enjoy life despite having kidneys that don't function properly. The reason? Dialysis.

Dialysis is an artificial way to take out your body's "garbage," removing waste and extra fluid. It isn't a perfect replacement for your kidneys or a cure for kidney failure. But for more than 200,000 Americans, it's another chance at life and a reason to be optimistic about their future.

Kidney failure

Many different diseases or events can damage your kidneys and cause them to fail. It can happen suddenly or take place gradually over months or years. Common conditions include diabetes, high blood pressure, and an inflammation of the kidneys called glomerulonephritis (glo-mer-u-lo-nuh-FRI-tis). Inherited kidney diseases, the most common of which is polycystic kidney disease, can also cause kidney failure. ◗

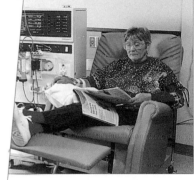

Medical Essay

Supplement to MAYO CLINIC HEALTH LETTER

FEBRUARY 1997

Exercise as you age

How to get off the sidelines and back in the game

There was a time when seniors settled for a comfortable rocker on a quiet front porch or a Naugahyde recliner in a cozy TV room. You were supposed to sit and knit. You were supposed to tell stories about how things used to be. You were benched, watching life from the sidelines.

But today, many seniors are trading their rockers and recliners for athletic shoes.

Fitness pays

The benefits of regular exercise are no secret. Still, about 70 percent of older adults are inactive. That's despite research showing that older people — even those who have never exercised — can benefit from physical conditioning. Regular exercise can help prevent coronary artery disease, high blood pressure, stroke, diabetes, depression and some cancers. And, fitness reduces the lifestyle-limiting effects of osteoporosis and arthritis.

Stronger arms and legs and better balance — all the result of fitness — help you carry grocery bags, get out of a bathtub or car and avoid falls. Being fit helps you remain independent as you age and improves the quality of your life.

The new guidelines

Until recently, experts thought vigorous exercise was necessary to increase fitness. Now, new guidelines from the Centers for Disease Control and Prevention (CDC), the American Heart Association, the American College of Sports Medicine and others, emphasize moderate, regular exercise. The reports say:

■ People of all ages can reap health benefits from physical activity (see "Bernie Gamble swims into her 80s," page 7). Healthy older

glossary

A3 SIZE Metric size closest to North American tabloid size. A3 sheets are 11¾ x 16½ inches (297mm x 420mm).

A4 SIZE Metric size closest to North American letter size. A4 sheets are 8¼ x 11¾ inches (210mm x 297mm).

ALLEY Space between images or columns of type on a page, as compared to gutter.

BASELINE Imaginary line, under a line of type, used to align characters.

BLEED Printing that extends to the edge of a sheet or page after trimming.

BODY COPY Copy set in text type, as compared to display type.

BULLET Bold dot used for typographic emphasis or to identify elements in a list.

CALLOUT Word that identifies part of an illustration.

CAPTION Descriptive text accompanying a photograph or other visual element. Also called cutline.

CMYK Abbreviation for cyan, magenta, yellow and key (black), the process color inks.

CREDIT LINE Line of small type next to a photo or illustration giving its source. May include copyright notice.

CROP To eliminate portions of an image so the remainder is more useful, pleasing or able to fit the layout.

CROSSOVER Type or art that continues from one page across the gutter to the opposite page.

DINGBAT Typographic symbol, such as a bullet (•), used for emphasis or decoration.

DISPLAY TYPE Type used for headlines, advertising and signs. Also called headline type.

DOWNSTYLE Typographic format for headlines using the same rules of grammar and capitalization that apply to sentences.

DROP SHADOW Screen tint or rule touching an illustration, box or type to give a three-dimensional shadow effect.

DROPPED CAP Large capital letter that extends down into the first two or more lines of text type.

FLOATING RULE Rule whose ends do not touch other rules.

FLUSH LEFT OR RIGHT Type aligning vertically along the left or right side of the column. Also called left or right justified.

FOLIO Page number.

FONT Complete assortment of upper and lower case characters, numerals, punctuation and other symbols of one typeface.

FORMAT Size or layout, depending on context. "The format is 8½ x 11 inches." "Our newsletter has a one-column format."

FOUR-COLOR PROCESS PRINTING Printing technique that uses process colors to simulate color photographs.

GRID Pattern of lines representing the layout of a newsletter design.

GUTTER Line or fold at which facing pages meet.

HAIRLINE Thinnest visible space or rule.

HALFTONE Photograph or illustration converted into dots for reproduction.

HIGHLIGHTS Lightest portions of a photograph, as compared to midtones and shadows.

IMPOSITION Arrangement of pages on files or plates so they will appear in proper sequence after press sheets are folded and bound.

ISSUE (1) All copies of a newsletter having content related to one theme, such as the 10th Anniversary issue, or location, such as western issue. (2) All copies of a newsletter published on the same date, such as the September issue.

JUSTIFIED TYPE Type set flush right and left.

KERN To reduce space between two or three characters so those characters appear better fitted together.

KEYLINES Lines that frame a photograph or other graphic element.

KICKER Small, secondary headline, placed above a primary headline.

LAYOUT Sketch or plan of how a page or sheet will look when printed.

LEADING Space between lines of type expressed as the distance between baselines. Also called line spacing.

LETTER FOLD Two folds creating three panels that allow a newsletter to fit into a business envelope.

LETTER SIZE Trim size 8½ x 11 inches or A4.

LINE COPY Any high-contrast image, including type, as compared to continuous-tone copy.

LOGO Abbreviation for logotype, an artistic assembly of type and art into a distinctive symbol.

MASTHEAD Block of information in a newsletter that identifies its publisher and editor, and tells about advertising and subscribing.

MEASURE Width of a column of type.

MIDTONES In a halftone or separation, tones created by dots between 30 percent and 70 percent of coverage, as compared to highlights and shadows.

MUG SHOT Photograph showing only a person's face.

NAMEPLATE Portion of front page of newsletter that graphically presents its name, subtitle and date line.

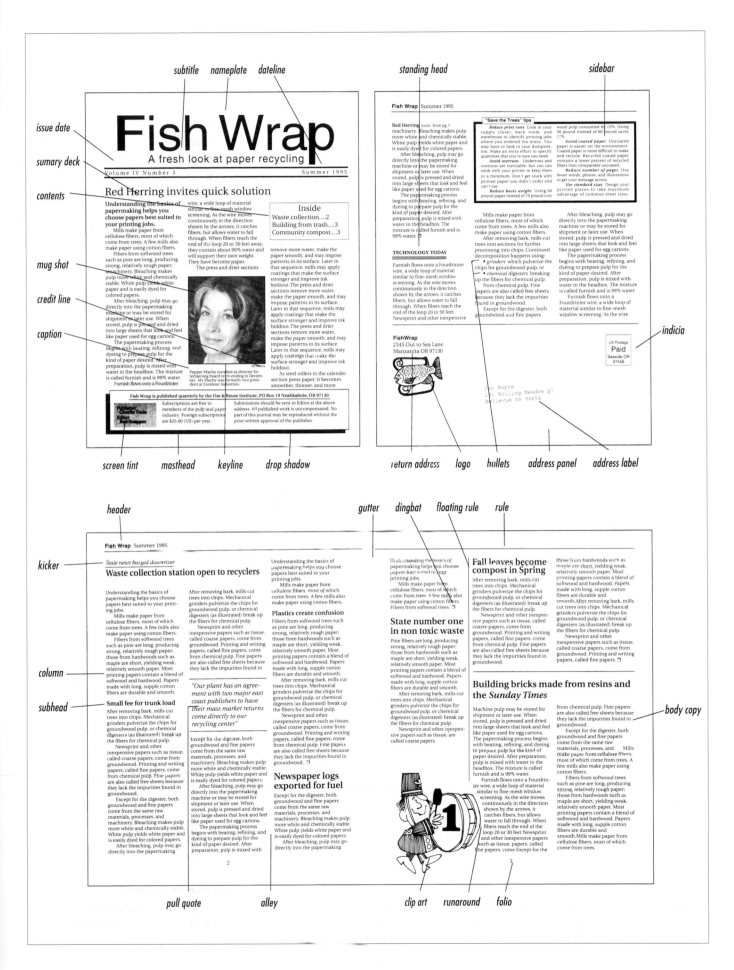

OVERPRINT To print one image over a previously printed image, such as printing type over a screen tint. Also called surprint.

PICA Anglo-American unit of typographic measure equal to .166 inch (4.218mm). One pica has 12 points.

POINT Unit of measure used to express size (height) of type, distance between lines (leading), and thickness of rules. One point equals ½ pica and .013875 inch (.351mm).

PROCESS COLORS Black, magenta, cyan and yellow used for four-color process printing.

PULL QUOTE Words from an article printed in large type and inserted in the page as a graphic.

RAGGED LEFT OR RIGHT Type whose line beginnings or endings are not aligned vertically.

REGISTER To place printing properly with regard to the edges of paper and other printing on the same sheet.

REVERSE Type, graphic or illustration reproduced by printing ink around its outline, thus allowing the underlying color or paper to show through and form the image. Also called knockout and liftout.

RGB Abbreviation for red, green and blue, colors used to simulate full color on a computer screen.

RULE Line used as a graphic element to separate or organize copy.

RUNAROUND Type set to conform to part or all of the shape of a neighboring photograph or illustration. Also called wraparound.

SANS SERIF TYPE Type without serifs. Also called gothic type.

SCALE To identify the percent by which photographs or art should be enlarged or reduced to achieve the correct size for printing.

SCALLOPED COLUMNS Page layout in which columns of unequal length are aligned at the top so their bottoms vary. Also called hanging columns.

SCHOLAR MARGIN Narrow margin at the outer edge of the page.

SCREEN DENSITY Refers to the amount of ink that a screen tint allows to print. Also called screen percentage. Screen density is expressed as percent of ink coverage.

SCREEN RULING Number of rows or lines of dots per inch or centimeter in a screen for making a screen tint or halftone. Also called line count, ruling, screen frequency, screen size and screen value.

SCREEN TINT Color created by dots instead of solid ink coverage.

SELF MAILER Newsletter that includes an address panel, therefore not needing an envelope for mailing.

SEPARATION Color photograph reproduced using four-color process printing.

SERIF Short line crossing the ending strokes of most characters in roman typefaces.

SHADOWS Darkest areas of a photograph, as compared to midtones and highlights.

SIDEBAR Block of information related to and placed near an article, but set off by design and/or typography as a separate unit.

SMALL CAPS Capital letters approximately the x height of lower case letters in the same font. Used for logos and nameplates, and to soften the impact of normal caps.

SPREAD (1) Two pages that face each other and are designed as one visual or production unit. (2) Layout of several photos on facing pages.

SPOT COLOR Color created by mixing pigments into ink, as compared to color created by four-color process printing. Also called flat color.

STANDING HEADLINE Headline whose words and position stay the same issue after issue.

SUBHEAD Small heading within a story or chapter.

SUBTITLE Phrase in a nameplate that amplifies or supplements information in the newsletter name. Also called tagline.

SUMMARY DECK Two or three sentences that condense the highlights of an article and that appear between the headline and the lead paragraph.

TABLOID SIZE Trim size 11 x 17 inches or A3.

TEMPLATE Pattern used to draw illustrations, make page formats or lay out press sheets.

TEXT TYPE Type used for text and captions, as compared to display type. Also called body type and composition type.

TYPEFACE Set of characters with similar design features and weight. Garamond Light is a typeface. Also called face.

TYPE FAMILY Group of typefaces with similar letter forms and a unique name.

TYPE SIZE Height of a typeface measured from the top of its ascenders to the bottom of its descenders, expressed in points.

TYPE STYLE Characteristic of a typeface such as bold, italic or light.

WHITE SPACE Area of a printed piece that does not contain images or type. Also called negative space.

X HEIGHT Vertical height of a lowercase x in a typeface. X height varies from one typeface to another.

permissions

Advantage © Shrigley & Associates

The Art of Self Promotion © Ilise Benun

Artes Liberales Today © College of Letters and Science

Auction News © Christie, Manson and Woods International, Inc.

Austin Uplink © Greater Austin Chamber

Benefactors © St. Louis Zoo & The Stelter Company

Bullseye © Strategies for Growth, Inc.

Campus Facilities Highlights © University of Missouri, Columbia

CIBC NetWorth © Investors Group

communication briefings © Encoders, Inc.

copyRights © The Permissions Group

Cornerstone Newsletter © Oregon Community Foundation

Creative Secretary's Letter © Bureau of Business Practice

Creative Selling © Bentley-Hall, Inc.

Delaware Digest © Delaware Distributors

Dick Davis Digest © Dick Davis Digest

Eastern European Outreach © Eastern European Outreach International

Editorial Eye © EEI Communications

Enlace © Bristol-Myers Squibb Co.

Facilities Focus © University of Missouri, Columbia

Family Ties © J. Douglas French Center

Family Times © Earth's Best Baby Food

Fourth District Focus © Federal Reserve Bank of Cleveland

Fractal Design Gallery © Fractal Design Corporation

Free Spirit © Free Spirit Publishing, Inc.

GE Life Link © Great Eastern Life

HeartHealth © Heart & Stroke Foundation

Hemisfile © Institute of the Americas La Jolla, CA

The Herald © Bethany Evangelical Lutheran Church & School

Highlights © University of Missouri, Columbia

http://www.adl.com © A Different Light Bookstore

http://www.adobe.com © Adobe Systems, Inc.

http://www.christdesert.org © The Monastery of Christ in the Desert

http://www.fedex.com © FedEx, Inc.

http://www.imageclub.com © Image Club Graphics, Inc.

http://www.lakewoodpub.com/newslett/tfl/index.htm © Lakewood Publications

http://www.randomhouse.com © Random House

http://www.shell.com © Shell International Limited

In House Graphics © United Communications Group

In Review © Seattle Community Colleges

Inner Voice © Forest Service Employees for Environmental Ethics

Inside Extrusion Processing © Conair Gatto

Insight & Opportunity © Strategies for Growth, Inc.

Investment Management Views © RT Investment Counsel Inc.

Investment Watch © Phoenix Funds

The Journey © SSM Health Care System

Kids Today © St. Louis Children's Hospital

Ligature © L. Grafix

Linkage © LSU Medical Center

MailGram © PRgraphics

Managed Care Forum © Healthcare Financial Management Association

Mayo Clinic Health Letter © Mayo Clinic

Media Professional © Audit Bureau of Circulations

Miracles & Memories © Give Kids the World

Mutual Matters © CUNA Mutual Insurance Group

News & Views © University of Maryland Medical System

Newsletter Communications © The Newsletter Factory

Newsletter Nameplate © Ruddle & Associates

Ohel © Ohel Children's Home & Family Services

Piedmonitor © Piedmont Hospital

Pointers © Cronin & Company

Policyholder News © American Family Insurance

Politics & Prose © Politics & Prose

Progress Notes © The Medical Center of Central Massachusetts

Publish © *Publish* magazine

Pulse © CAC Ramsay

Read Me © Work Write

Retirement Today © Investors Group

RGB Website © Publish

Risk Management Advisor © Bureau of Business Practice

Royal Trust Money Guide © Royal Trust

Safety Check © Rodale Press, Inc.

Sales MasterMind © The Economics Press

Samaritan Today © Samaritan Health System

Scene © Braille Institute

Seidman's Online Insider © CMP Media Inc.

Shareholder © Weyerhaeuser Credit Union

Ships & Shipwrecks © Nautical History and Discovery

Signature © Griffin Printing

Spectrum © PR Newswire

Spotlight © Experian

Squeegee © Backup Computer Resources

The Strategic Investor © First Canadian Funds

Strategies © Manulife Financial

Summit Express © Mt. Bachelor Ski Area

Syvamonitor © Syva Company

TAGline! © Corel Draw and Ventura Users Group

Technology for Learning © Lakewood Publications

The Technology Monitor © Cadbury Beverages Technical Center

Tek Files © Copytek Office Products

That Bookstore in Blytheville © That Bookstore in Blytheville

The Ticket © Travel Skills Group

Total Quality © Lakewood Publications

US West Today © US West

Warren Boroson's Mutual Fund Digest © Warren Boroson

Wildflower © National Wildflower Research Center

Women's Network Newsletter © Women's Network of the Chamber of Commerce

Working Solo Newsletter © Working Solo, Inc.

index